W9-BTC-540

LOST IN SPACE

Probing

Feminist

Science

Fiction

and

Beyond

LOST IN

MIDDLEBURY COLLEGE LIBRARY

The
University
of North
Carolina
Press
Chapel Hill
& London

MARLEEN S. BARR

SPACE

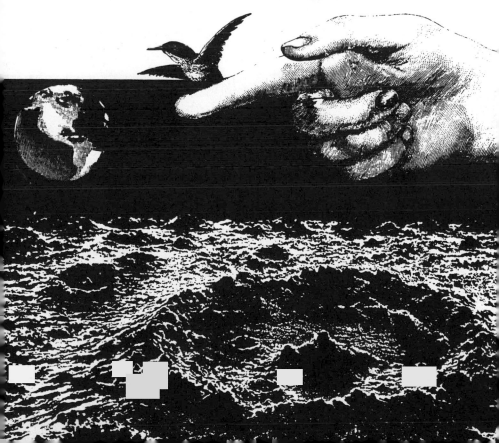

© 1993 The University of North Carolina Press

All rights reserved

Manufactured in the United States of America

The paper in this book meets the guidelines for permanence and durability of the Committee on Production Guidelines for Book Longevity of the Council on Library Resources.

Library of Congress Cataloging-in-Publication Data

Barr, Marleen S.

Lost in space : probing feminist science fiction and beyond / by Marleen S. Barr.

p.   cm.

ISBN 0-8078-2108-X (alk. paper). — ISBN 0-8078-4421-7 (pbk. : alk. paper)

1. Science fiction, American—Women authors—History and criticism. 2. Science fiction, English—Women authors—History and criticism. 3. Feminism and literature.   4. Sex role in literature.   5. Women and literature.   I. Title.

PS374.S35B33   1993

813′.08762099287—dc20

93-12466

CIP

Permission to reproduce previously published material can be found on pages 223–24 of this volume.

97 96 95 94 93   5 4 3 2 1

For **Norman N. Holland,**

who told me to write in my own voice

and **Jane Kelley Holland,**

who always encourages me

CONTENTS

FOREWORD

Marleen Barr is in one of her incarnations the re-
discovered and refurbished girl child of her critical essays, in
which she pursues the image of the girl not yet crippled by sex
roles and punishments, willful and self-determined. This girl
child Marleen stands outside the elaborate imitation Gothic edi-
fices of academic criticism and says, But Why and How Come and
Why Not and Who Says So and Phooey. She keeps asking, but how
come you leave out all the fun and really inventive stuff?

She has a sharp, inquiring, and mischievous mind. All cultural
artifacts—from art deemed high and awarded Nobel Prizes to television re-runs that secretly form our inner world of common images
—are the matter of her discourse.

She writes wickedly too and she will surely be punished for it
by being taken less seriously than if she had taken the trouble to
write badly. She invents jargon, as all critics must, but keeps it to
a minimum. Whether or not you can accept some of her wilder interpretations and more heterogeneous yokings of disparate writers,
you will always follow her argument, because she has taken great
care to lay it out clearly for you. But her readings of the various
texts she discusses are always illuminating and fascinating, and
will undoubtedly send many readers to those texts for the first time
as well as calling us back to a new reading of something we had
thought we had understood or that we had dismissed unfairly.

Now cultural critics are exilers or shepherds. Exilers erect standards which they take great pains to prove nobody meets but one or
two heroes of the mind. They are always wanting to lop off the head
of that one's novel or the tail of this one or tear out the faithless
heart of that other. Think of Helen Vendler confronting yet another
poet who is not Robert Lowell.

Shepherds pursue through rocks and thorn bushes the lambs
that have been labeled as straying, and they are to be brought back
into the fold and properly explained and renamed. They did not
mean to go off into that arroyo into lostness. They were all of the

time beating a new path to the true path. It just requires a different perspective.

Barr is one of those includers. She finds feminist creation and recreation of our somewhat common culture in the expected places, but she also finds it in the work of men most women would not anticipate finding enlisted under the banner of women's self-determination and the reconstruction of literature under the force of the female imagination.

One of Barr's intentions is to rescue women's science fiction from the ghetto of intellectual neglect where it has been in exile. If you doubt the fear of that label, when my novel *He, She and It* won the Arthur C. Clarke award for the best work of science fiction published in the United Kingdom, my American publisher would not sticker the books for fear winning this prize would actually hurt sales. You don't want it shelved among science fiction, she said. Indeed, of all my novels, this one—one of the most ambitious and complex—received the fewest reviews in the feminist press, because of its genre.

The way to get the wildebeest into the tent is to build a bigger and differently shaped tent, which is what Barr is doing wittily and inventively. The name of the new tent is "feminist fabulation." She wants to rescue works of science fiction from critical neglect and intellectual dismissal. She redefines the postmodernist critical canon to include feminist fabulation—works of science fiction, utopias, fantasy—which share with certain works in what has been called the mainstream—a direct or indirect restructuring of patriarchal imperatives and mythologies.

Such works of feminist fabulation deconstruct the dominant myths of our culture from within or refract them through altered realities; or simply create realities in which such assumptions as we daily make about up and down, good and bad, deserving and reprobate, are turned about ninety or one hundred eighty degrees or simply ignored and replaced by something quite, quite different.

When first-rate work is exiled from the canon because of how it is labeled and thus perceived and then dismissed from intelligent attention, a mission of rescue is desperately required. Marleen Barr teaches us how to view a whole set of writings by and about women by renaming the set which they compose and by then re-positioning these works inside the redrawn map of postmodernist narrative. This is a highly readable and lively argument which I fervently hope will provide a framework for that reevaluation of the texts she discusses and others neglected and spurned because they are considered neither mainstream nor absurdist nor experimental, but "something else." Barr has redefined a mainstream "feminist fabulation" that includes griffins and minotaurs with the Persians and poodles, chickens and wolves.

—Marge Piercy

ACKNOWLEDGMENTS

I direct special thanks to Peter Bauland, Carol Braham, Terry Brown, Tony Distler, Monica Elbert, Minrose Gwin, Cheryl Herr, Edward James, Eric S. Rabkin, Ruth Salvaggio, Robert Shelton, Darko Suvin, and Beth Tipperman.

Sandra Eisdorfer is the most wonderful editor any author could ever hope to encounter. Our work on *Lost in Space* launched a new friendship as well as a new book. I am especially grateful for the help I received from my copyeditor, Stephanie Wenzel. I thank Brooks Landon and Ursula K. Le Guin for their attention to my work.

Norris Compton Barr and I appreciate the generosity of my parents, Roslyn and George Barr.

It is a special pleasure to dedicate this volume to Norman N. Holland and Jane Kelley Holland. Thanks Norm and Jane—from the variations on my identity theme that benefited from your encouragement and advice.

LOST IN SPACE

INTRODUCTION

Anyway, no woman wants her bedroom to be a garage, and least of all for a boring car.
—*Saul Bellow,* A Theft

The "proper use" to which Jameson refers[1] is presumably the socially sanctioned use, just as stop/ready/go is the "proper use" or interpretation of the red/orange/green traffic light system. For feminists to intervene in these social contracts, to de/re/construct them, revealing their ideological significances, means a fundamental intervention in the relationship between reader and text, a disruption of the reader's conventionalized understanding of the contract, the literary institution of the particular genre. To intervene without causing a traffic jam or a major crash is an extremely delicate procedure—and maybe there are times when the crash makes sense.
—*Anne Cranny-Francis,* Feminist Fiction
Feminist Uses of Generic Fiction

I want to explain why I chose to be a feminist critic who focuses on feminist science fiction. Why would I, a person who cares about professional success, embrace a twice marginalized field, a double whammy in relation to career advancement? Two decisions figure in my answer: I took Norman N. Holland's advice about writing in my own voice, and I damned the torpedoes and went full speed ahead regarding reading women's imagined alternatives to patriarchal structures.

This was not an easy choice to make. Despite the acceptance feminism and cultural studies now enjoy in many professional circles, most members of these circles have yet to come to terms with science fiction. Gary Westfahl, in "A New Campaign for Science Fiction," describes a 1990 Science Fiction Research Association conference panel about the future of science fiction in the academy. He reports that the panelists advised young science fiction scholars to develop a "cover story" about commitment to another literary area, to "smuggle in" science fiction texts, and to immerse themselves in an altogether different field (Westfahl, 6–7). Westfahl's reaction to this panel: "To say that a science fiction critic needs a 'cover story' implies that an interest in science fiction is somehow dishonorable, even criminal, and must be suppressed and hidden at all cost" (Westfahl, 7).

Westfahl advises science fiction scholars to look in a mirror daily while saying, "I will never conceal, compromise, or apologize for my interest in this field" (Westfahl, 10). When I look in a mirror, I am proud to see someone who (beginning with the 1981 publication of *Future Females*, the first critical anthology about women and science fiction), adheres to this advice. For me, such adherence is especially fraught with difficulty. If writing garden-variety science fiction criticism is still viewed as resembling a criminal act, I am at a loss for words to describe how, during the last decade, writing *feminist* science fiction criticism was perceived. Suffice it to say that I positioned myself in professional space located beyond the pale. The pledge never to conceal, compromise, or apologize for my interest in feminist science fiction[2] was (and still is) analogous to approaching my career according to the oath taken by Marion Zimmer Bradley's Free Amazons.[3]

Some aspects of the 1970s served as catalysts for my professional decisions. I started college in 1970, a year during which many women's studies programs were born. When I participated in my alma mater's first women and literature classes, I was impressed by what feminist professors had to say about women's lives. I decided to live according to the notes I took in those classes. I made this decision during human history's most opportune time for women's sexuality: the years sandwiched between the Pill and AIDS. When I encountered the many magazine articles that announced that women have the right to demand multiple orgasms, I read them in terms of what I had learned in women's studies classes. This reading strategy made me nervous. I wondered how I would feel if, at age seventy rather than at age seventeen, I first learned that women could and should have orgasms. I did not want to take my chronological luck for granted. Although I would not have stated it this way then, I wanted to investigate, before it was too late, how to deconstruct patriarchal myths.

I wanted to read, with an eye toward recognizing omissions and lies, patriarchy's stories about women. With Holland (he speaks of human identity according to a theme and variation model) and Stanislaw Lem (his protagonist Ijon Tichy encounters, in *The Star Diaries*, multiple versions of himself)[4] in mind, I will allow the present me to address past professional versions of myself: Marleens, y'all were engaged in recognizing the importance of a "feminist reading position" (Cranny-Francis's term).[5] When attempting to read to unmask patriarchal master narratives as mere fictions, I naturally turned to the literature I loved as a child, to science fiction. Chronology was again on my side. The golden age of feminist science fiction occurred during the 1970s.

While I watched the "women of wonder" (Pamela Sargent's term) emerge,[6] I wondered about patriarchal imperatives. My questions led me to feminist science fiction—literature that ranges beyond patriarchal reality and exaggerates "acceptable" sexism. Foot binding can be used to explain how feminist science fiction enables readers better to interpret patriarchy. Chinese women were made to think that foot binding was necessary. Contemporary women do not have to read feminist science fiction in order to understand the validity of countering this belief. Such insight, however, is not the typical reaction to present-day foot binding: high heels. Feminist science fiction writers would critique high heels by exaggerating the results of wearing them. A feminist dystopia, for example, might feature a planet whose octopuslike businesswomen, because of fashion, have some of their legs amputated and commute in many pairs of running shoes. Cranny-Francis makes a point that is applicable to these imagined alien octopuses:[7] "The convention of estrangement [Darko Suvin calls science fiction the literature of cognitive estrangement], for example, enables writers to displace the story setting to another time and/or place, immediately denaturalizing the society portrayed in the text and the events and characters set there. So readers and writers are freed from the restrictions of a realist reading which tends to restrict representation to an imitation of contemporary social practices" (Cranny-Francis, 193). The octopus scenario denaturalizes high heels.

Chinese women with bound feet would view contemporary societies, which do not require women to bind their feet, as feminist utopias. Like Kurt Vonnegut's "Harrison Bergeron," feminist science fiction focuses on artificial handicaps. Feminist science fiction, then, acts as a microscope in relation to patriarchal myths. In this volume, I read feminist science fiction as fiction that enlarges patriarchal myths in order to facilitate scrutinizing these myths. I also include examples of the criticism that results from linking feminist science fiction to the larger literary category I call feminist fabulation.

Vonnegut's fellow fabulator John Barth seems to speak to these efforts when he presents himself as a genie who announces, "The key to the treasure is the treasure" (Barth, 64). Feminist science fiction is a key for unlocking patriarchy's often hidden agendas; the treasure is a woman's ability to use feminist reading positions as a means to live as freely as possible. In other words, I value nullifying patriarchal myths about—for example—women, propriety, and orgasms. In still other words, I was lucky to become an adult at a time when many women rejected the patriarchal story about how their bedrooms should serve as garages for boring cars. To guard against still virulent patriarchal stories, I positioned feminist science fiction as a repair manual that can be used by women who wish to fix patriarchy. The manual instructed me about how not to live parked in sexist stereotypes.

The danger of unknowingly obeying patriarchal traffic signals— the stop signs, red lights, and yield and slow merge instructions that impede women—was more onerous to me than the risk of being denied tenure for choosing the "wrong" field of study. I gave myself the right of way before I had obtained a permanent license to teach in a university. Despite the chance of colliding with the patriarchal academy, I engaged in safe (according to my own needs) reading practices when I decided to value women's texts that address women. This choice was a violation, a reconstruction of the proper use of the assistant professor's role. (The "proper" way to approach this role involved supporting the opinion that "woman-to-woman writing is an oppositional mode and unacceptable" [Cranny-Francis, 23].) My violation resulted in a major crash. I, obviously, survived.

Although I saw the crash looming, I continued to write about the feminist space fiction the literary establishment placed in a marginal zone. I did not want my own voice and concerns to become lost in patriarchal space. It is, after all, logical to think about women's disempowerment while reading feminist power fantasies. This statement leads me to recall writing the swordswoman chapter ("Heroic Fantastic Femininity: Women Warriors") in *Alien to Femininity: Speculative Fiction and Feminist Theory*. At the time, when I encountered my extremely conservative male colleagues in the mail room (they made no secret of their belief that the department only had room for males), I grasped my pen, waved it back and forth, and smiled. These men never knew that I had become a female feminist Walter Mitty. I followed the examples my swordswoman chapter described; my pen became my sword. I imagined myself as an assistant professor/swordswoman dueling my way past those who wished to impede me.

My experiences resemble the moment when Eugene Debs Hartke, the protagonist of Vonnegut's *Hocus Pocus*, has *Black Garterbelt* delivered to his garage. The UPS "kid" who brings the magazine "was awed by the woman on the magazine cover. He might have been an astronaut on his first trip in space" (Vonnegut, *Hocus Pocus*, 187). Like the woman on the *Black Garterbelt* cover, most women depicted in feminist science fiction are not normal. When I first encountered these women, I, like the UPS kid, said, "Wow" (ibid.). I might have been an astronaut/critic encountering feminist space fiction and learning to define "normal" patriarchal female roles as obscene.

Hartke "stayed in the garage" (ibid., 188). He explains why and describes the doings of Tralfamadorians: "I didn't want to go into the house. I didn't want to go outdoors either. So I sat down on my footlocker and read 'The Protocols of the Elders of Tralfamadore' in *Black Garterbelt*. It was about intelligent threads of energy trillions of light-years long. They wanted mortal, self-reproducing life forms to spread out through the Universe. So several of them, the Elders in the title, held a meeting by intersecting near a planet called Tralfamadore" (ibid.). Hartke's behavior and reading material speak to my close encounters with feminist science fiction. Although I recognized that inside domestic spaces and outside professional spaces are constructed according to patriarchal stories, I did not want to be constrained by footlockers—metaphorical contemporary versions of bound feet. By focusing on feminist science fiction, I tried to thwart the footlockers, to ensure that my life design would not resemble a boring garage. My feminist reading position in relation to feminist science fiction helped me to deconstruct the protocols of patriarchal Elders.

Instead of using my intelligent threads of energy to reproduce patriarchal life forms, I devoted myself to feminist texts that rewrite Elders' stories. Knowing full well that the tenure committee Elders would not be impressed by attention to feminist versions of Tralfamadorians—despite the decision they would make at their meeting—I went ahead with my research. The result of my attention to new feminist myths does not mirror the experience of the female scholar *Black Garterbelt* describes. Elders take control of the brain of this woman who transcribes origin myths: "It so happened, according to this story that the legend of Adam and Eve was being written down for the first time. A woman was doing it. . . . The Elders let her write down most of the origin myth just the way she had heard it, the way everybody told it, until she got close to the end. Then they took control of her brain and had her write down something which had never been part of the myth before" (ibid., 189).

Lost in Space exists because the assistant professor version of my present self wrote about feminist science fiction's critique of male-centered myths. Instead of allowing patriarchal Elders to take control of my brain, I decided to embrace a dangerous professional double whammy, enabling me to counter the Elder male administrators' "lethal hocus pocus" (ibid., 148), the patriarchal discourse whose "ammunition was language instead of bullets" (ibid.). Male administrators' lethal linguistic hocus-pocus did not transform my written voice into acceptable proper use, the "blah blah blah" (ibid., 149) palatable to patriarchy.

Both Hartke and I derive important insights from reading "unacceptable" literature. Hartke describes his experience: "What sort of writer, after all, would submit a work of fiction for possible publication in *Black Garterbelt*? . . . I did not realize at the time how much that story affected me. But down deep the story was beginning to work like a buffered analgesic. What a relief it was, somehow, to have somebody else confirm what I had come to suspect. . . . That Humanity is going somewhere really nice was a myth for children under 6 years old, like the Tooth Fairy and the Easter Bunny and Santa Claus" (ibid., 194). What a relief it was to read feminist science fiction, to have somebody else confirm my views about patriarchy. Feminist science fiction let me know the answer to a specific question: what does patriarchy want? Patriarchy wants all women to wear black garter belts. Kathy Acker's Airplane, the protagonist of *In Memoriam to Identity*, articulates this point in the form of a question and an answer: "Question: Why do girls become whores? Answer: A lot of girls do for a while. The ones who don't just for a while, die" (Acker, 99). Patriarchy says women should derive self-worth from wearing black garter belts. I say I surmise that boring cars park in garages attached to whorehouses.

Feminist science fiction presents blueprints for social structures that allow women's words to counter patriarchal myths. Mary E. Wilkins Freeman's "The Revolt of 'Mother' " is a realistic precursor to these blueprints. Freeman's protagonist, Sarah Penn, seizes the power to redefine space according to woman-centered needs. She believes that a newly built barn would serve as a better domicile than her family's cramped house. When her husband, Adoniram, is away, she tells her children to move household goods into the barn and barn paraphernalia into the house. Sarah satisfies her family's need for space by taking control of space. Adoniram returns and notices that cooking odors emanate from the barn and "all four cows were domiciled in the house." He asks, "What on airth does this mean, mother?" (Freeman, 618).[8] When he inquires about his wife's new and viable definition of space, Adoniram, rather than insisting on the power of fathers' words, empowers women's words. Freeman answers those who think that patriarchy will not change until the cows come home.

Her pen overthrows patriarchal law in the Penn family. In the days before garages, Sarah asserts herself by parking cows in her house, by redefining usual rules. In regard to "airth's" patriarchal laws, feminist science fiction writers aspire to the same goal.

They want men to speak in Adoniram Penn's voice. Willa Cather's
Rosicky is one man who does so. He articulates a choice that forms
the next stage of Adoniram's utterance when he declares, "I guess
we'll do like she [his wife] says" (Cather, 1017).

Instead of denigrating feminist science fiction by separating it
from the female literary tradition, the literary establishment might
approach this literature in terms of Adoniram's and Rosicky's
statements. When encountering the feminist stories set away from
"airth," readers might try to follow these male protagonists' examples in relation to reconstructing patriarchal space and privilege. Cows can live in houses; women who agree with Marion
Zimmer Bradley's Free Amazons can inspire alternatives to present
domestic constructions. Feminist science fiction can inspire real-
world change.

Lisa Tuttle's "Husbands" conjectures about this change by commenting on men who share Adoniram's and Rosicky's familial role.
The story's second section, called "This Longing," is set in an all-
female society. In the manner of Joanna Russ's "When It Changed,"
men will return to this society. The female children who have "their
own language, their own rituals" (Tuttle, 114), are preparing for
the change. The adult narrator believes that these children are
"reinventing gender" (Tuttle, 114). She articulates a wish that is at
the heart of feminist science fiction: "Maybe they'll get it right this
time" (Tuttle, 114).

Michael Whelan seems to have created a portrait of one of
Tuttle's young female reconstructors. Whelan's painting *The Ultimate Sandbox* pictures his daughter attired in a pink spacesuit
(adorned with a Miss Piggy patch) seated on the moon with a pail
and shovel in hand. A large purple *A* appears on the girl's pack.
No scarlet letter to brand women improper, this *A* celebrates feminist alternatives the child might eventually build beyond "airth."
I imagine that while playing in the sand, she, like Tuttle's young
protagonists, thinks of new social constructions.

These new constructions might invalidate Russ's comment about
Mr. Piggy: "The authors are not subtle in their reasons for creating
separatist utopias: if men are kept out of these [feminist utopian]
societies, it is because men are dangerous. They also hog the good
things of this world" (Russ, "Recent Feminist Utopias," 77). In any
event, the girl who makes sand castles—constructs foundations

for new feminist fairy tales that might come true—is not building castles in the air. Whelan's painting does not represent the fantastic. It is possible for a little girl clad in a spacesuit to sit on the moon. She can build castles in a place that has no breathable air.

Reality unfortunately conforms to the negative as well as the positive visions of feminist science fiction. As I explain in chapter 7 when I discuss reproductive technology, feminist science fiction does not describe dystopian visions that are more egregious than true misogynistic scenarios. This statement applies to beauty myths as well as to reproductive technology myths. Marge Piercy's *He, She and It*, for example, describes employees surgically altering their bodies to fit corporate images. Naomi Wolf tells us that reality's counterparts to this imagined situation are more extreme. I argue that the literary establishment denigrates feminist science fiction; Wolf argues that patriarchy denigrates women by turning them into science fiction protagonists:

Women are comparing themselves and young men are comparing young women with a new breed that is hybrid nonwoman. . . . The specter of the future is not that women will be slaves, but that we will be robots. First, we will be subservient to ever more refined technology for self-surveillance. . . . Then, to more sophisticated alterations of images of the "ideal" in the media. . . . Then, to technologies that replace the faulty, mortal female body, piece by piece, with "perfect" artifice. This is not science fiction: the replacement of women has begun with reproductive technology. In Great Britain and the United States, research is well underway to develop an artificial placenta . . . and cosmetic surgery has given us little reason to doubt that when the technology exists for it, poor women will be pressed to sell actual body material. . . . If that seems grotesquely futuristic, cast yourself back just ten years and imagine being told that the invasive alteration on a mass scale of women's breasts and legs would come to pass so soon. . . . Adjustable breast implants are now a reality, allowing women to be adapted to each partner's preference. The Japanese have already perfected a lifelike geisha robot with artificial skin. . . . Whatever the future threatens, we can be fairly sure of this: Women in our "raw" or "material" state will continue to be shifted from category "woman" to category "ugly," and shamed into an assembly-line physical identity. . . . The machine is at the door. Is she the future? (Wolf, 267–68)[9]

Feminist critics use war metaphors to describe women's and men's competing stories.[10] A contemporary version of literary gender war positions feminist science fiction against the patriarchal myths that are just now beginning to transform real-world women into hybrid nonwomen. The academy judges critics' attention to feminist science fiction to be an improper use of interpretation; the larger patriarchal world deems it perfectly proper to re-create women as science fiction cyborgs and robots. Women cannot afford to loose battles in the literary gender war currently being waged in postmodern fields.

I have explained that my interest in feminist science fiction stems from the literature I enjoyed during my childhood. Well, when I first read Isaac Asimov's *I, Robot*, I never imagined that feminist discourse would rightly warn that this title threatens to describe a future version of myself. I never imagined that female flesh could become a mechanistic convenience—a contraption analogous to an automatic garage door opener. The patriarchal stories—the male fantasies—that currently present plans for this potential future reality are the true alien texts.

Feminist science fiction is at once a stop sign in relation to patriarchy and a go-ahead signal for women. As I proclaim in chapter 9, the green pencils are coming. The alien green pencils—not alien little green men—are coming to rewrite the patriarchal hocus-pocus that threatens to turn women into robots. I do not expect that the reentry vehicle James Rosenquist depicts (in *Space Dust*) propelling these green pencils—a symbol, as I explain in chapter 9, of feminist science fiction as alien writing—to crash land.

In regard to my professional road, which *Lost in Space* maps, I never deviated from believing that feminist space vehicles are more exciting to write about than boring cars. If I could locate a time machine and begin my career again, I would still damn the torpedoes and go full speed ahead.[11] I would still use the insights I derived from focusing on feminist science fiction to formulate my ideas about feminist fabulation.

Feminist fabulation, a new reading practice, critiques patriarchal master narratives. It is feminist metafiction: fiction about patriarchal fictions. In *Feminist Fabulation: Space/Postmodern Fiction*, I claim Robert Scholes's "fabulation" for feminist theory and feminist fiction. Scholes defines fabulation as "fiction that offers us a world clearly and radically discontinuous from the one we know, yet returns to confront that known world in some cognitive way" (Scholes, "Roots," 47). Feminist fabulation is feminist fiction that offers us a world clearly and radically discontinuous from the patriarchal one we know, yet returns to confront that known patriarchal world in some cognitive way. Feminist fabulation is a specifically feminist corollary to Scholes's "structural fabulation." Structural fabulation addresses man's place within the system of the universe; feminist fabulation addresses woman's place within the system of patriarchy. Feminist fabulation functions as a corrective to a situation in which many feminist writers (especially feminist science fiction writers) are shut out of postmodern literary canons. I want to reclaim canonical spaces for contemporary feminists by broadening postmodern fiction's definition to include the subject matter and structures characterizing contemporary feminist writing.

Lost in Space includes essays I wrote before and after I coined the term *feminist fabulation*. In the volume's first section I approach feminist science fiction in a manner independent from its connection to feminist fabulation. In this section I discuss feminist science fiction works that might be unfamiliar to many of my readers: dystopian visions (such as *Walk to the End of the World* by Suzy McKee Charnas, *Benefits* by Zoë Fairbairns, "The Women Men Don't See" by James Tiptree [also known as Alice Sheldon], and *Where Late the Sweet Birds Sang* by Kate Wilhelm), utopian visions (such as *Motherlines* by Charnas, *The Wanderground* by Sally Gearhart, and "Houston, Houston, Do You Read?" by Tiptree), woman warrior tales (such as *The Northern Girl* by Elizabeth A. Lynn and "The Prodigal Daughter" by Jessica Amanda Salmonson), and science fiction popular among general readers (such as *Dragonsong* by Anne McCaffrey).

Dragonsong serves to explain the rationale that informs this volume's first and second sections. In 1982, I argued that *Dragonsong* discusses efforts to subvert women artists and shares much in common with discourse generated by Hélène Cixous and Tillie Olsen. Now, after having written *Feminist Fabulation: Space/Postmodern Fiction*, I would add that *Dragonsong* is unfairly demeaned by its association with science fiction. *Dragonsong* critiques master narratives about female artists' inferiority. Hence, while I once stopped short at reading McCaffrey's feminist science fiction novel in terms of feminist theory, I now connect her work to other feminist fiction—to feminist fabulation. Part 1, then, probes the imaginative literature called feminist science fiction. Part 2 moves beyond this designation and exemplifies what criticism written in terms of feminist fabulation looks like. According to the new reading practice I call feminist fabulation, it is appropriate for this volume to include authors who do not write science fiction (Saul Bellow, for example).

I return to my definition of feminist fabulation to explain why this is so. Feminist fabulation is analogous to Eric S. Rabkin's view of the fantastic. Rabkin's fantastic is an umbrella term (or "super genre") that includes science fiction, fantasy, and utopian literature. According to Rabkin, fantasy, for example, is at once a subgenre and a part of the fantastic. I view feminist fabulation as an umbrella term that includes science fiction, fantasy, utopian literature, and mainstream literature (written by both women and men) that critiques patriarchal fictions. Feminist science fiction, then, is at once a separate entity and a part of the super genre I call feminist fabulation. Feminist fabulation challenges fixed definitions of literary hierarchies, the prestige accorded only to particular authors and types of writing. Hence, in this volume's sections, such diverse writers as Atwood, Bellow, Emecheta, Le Guin, Murakami, Rushdie, Russ, Theroux, and Wiggins are grouped together. They are all feminist fabulators.

Feminist fabulation, then, replaces exclusion that can be attributed to gender and genre with cooperation between feminist science fiction writers and the female and male mainstream writers engaged in the postmodern critique of patriarchal master narratives. In other words, as I explain in chapter 13, Atwood, Bellow, and Russ are all concerned with challenging the lack of importance attributed to the female child's story, and as I point out in chapter 10, Rushdie also calls for seeing women's stories. So much for literary gender war. Feminist fabulation arms feminist writers with a reason to be included in postmodern canons. I am glad I damned the torpedoes.

Peter Pan, which figures prominently in chapter 9, speaks to my insistence on devoting the early part of my career to feminist science fiction, to my version of torpedo damning. The struggle to move feminist science fiction from shadow to limelight—the struggle to think lovely feminist literary thoughts about flying from patriarchy—has had a great impact on my efforts to grow up. To paraphrase the adult Wendy's explanation to Peter, I am now ever so much older than twenty-five—my age when I first began to write essays about feminist science fiction. It is now time for a new generation to say "never" to patriarchy land. It is now time for a new generation to read feminist imaginative works that use stars to point toward woman-centered directions that are never positioned second to the conservative right and straight on to female mourning. Finding this direction coincides with eradicating the need to ask victims of patriarchal imperatives, "Girl, why are you crying?"

Lost in Space exists because when I was a young assistant professor confronted by institutional powers that attempted to silence me, I had the courage to clap my fingers against typewriter keys while insisting that I believe in the importance of feminist science fiction. It is now my pleasure to view the essays I include in *Lost in Space* as a new form of Tinkerbell's fairy dust—called feminist space dust—and to let this dust touch you. Read my essays while thinking lovely feminist thoughts. Tell me where you fly.

NOTES

1. Cranny-Francis points to Fredric Jameson's definition of genres. According to Jameson, "Genres are essentially literary *institutions*, or social contracts between a writer and a specific public, whose function is to specify the proper use of a particular social artifact" (Cranny-Francis, 18; Jameson, 106).

2. I argue that the term *feminist science fiction* should be a part of the term *feminist fabulation*. For clarity, in this volume I continue to refer to feminist science fiction.

3. Free Amazons pledge not to appeal to men for support, to renounce allegiance to family, to marry as a free mate, not to be known by the name of any man, to defend themselves by force if attacked, to bear children only by choice, and to regard other Free Amazons as mothers, sisters, and daughters. The oath states, "If I fail . . . let them slay me like an animal and consign my body unburied to corruption and my soul to the mercy of the Goddess" (Bradley, epigraph).

4. According to Holland, "We can be precise about individuality by conceiving of the individual as living out variations on an identity theme much as a musician might play out an infinity of variations on a single

melody. We discover that underlying theme by abstracting it from variations. . . . Identity is like a musical theme on which variations are played:
not the notes themselves but their structural relationship to one another
remains constant through a lifetime of transformations. . . . Identity defines what the individual brings from old experiences to new ones, and
it is the newness of experiences, both those from the world without and
those from the biological and emotional world within, by which the individual creates the variations which are his life lived in historical time"
(Holland, 814–15). Tichy explains, "When I regained consciousness, the
cabin was packed with people. There was barely elbowroom. As it turned
out, they were all of them me, from different days, weeks, months, and
one—so he said—was even from the following year. . . . The situation
was complicated by the fact that there now had appeared morning me's
and afternoon me's—I feared that if things went on like this, I would
soon be broken into minutes and seconds—and then too, the majority of
me's present were lying like mad, so that to this day I'm not altogether
sure whom I hit and who hit me when that whole business took place,
triangularly, between the Thursday, the Friday and the Wednesday me's,
all of whom I was in turn" (Lem, 15–16).

5. According to Cranny-Francis, a feminist reading position enables
readers to "re-evaluate and reconstruct their own position within the
present order and in so doing become part of the subversion and renego-
tiation of that order. . . . In adopting that [feminist] reading position
the reader is inevitably led to a very different perception of her/his
own society. . . . Feminist generic fiction constructs a reading position
which . . . deconstructs femininity revealing it is an ideological construct,
[and] . . . deconstructs the patriarchal narrative, showing it as a mechanism by which women are constructed in purely gender terms, and as
subject to men who are constructed in terms of gender, class and race"
(Cranny-Francis, 53, 63, 192).

6. See Pamela Sargent's three anthologies for an introduction to science
fiction written by women.

7. This is how Jean Bethke Elshtain addresses the point: "We are
trapped in our own representations. . . . I am searching for a language—
one that breaks us out of our engendered prisons—a language in and
through which we could all, men and women, see that dependence and
independence, powerlessness and power, are deeply related and that not
all forms of human vulnerability can or should be rationalized about our
theories and our ways of being in the world" (Elshtain, 128, 131).

8. Adoniram's comment is in contrast to Mrs. Darling's question to her
husband (discussed in chapter 9). Mrs. Darling asks, "George, what can it
[the presence of Peter Pan and his shadow] mean?" Unlike Mrs. Darling,
Sarah Penn constructs meaning herself.

9. The female machine is on NBC television. "Mann and Machine," the story of a male police officer and his perfect female cyborg partner premiered on 5 April 1992. Although the series placed women in positions of authority, it stressed that the coupling of a male human and a female machine is most advantageous.

10. Sandra Gilbert and Susan Gubar use this metaphor in *The War of the Words*, the first volume of *No Man's Land: The Place of the Woman Writer in the Twentieth Century*. Jane Tompkins, in *West of Everything*, discusses literary gender war when she argues that the cowboy novel is a masculinist answer to the nineteenth-century female sentimental novel.

11. Both critical and imaginative discourse advise that this decision is my only option: In terms of imaginative discourse, I believe in adhering to the *Star Trek* prime directive about not altering the past; in terms of Norman N. Holland's critical discourse, I cannot alter my identity theme.

WORKS CITED

Acker, Kathy. *In Memoriam to Identity*. New York: Grove Weidenfeld, 1990.

Asimov, Isaac. *I, Robot*. Garden City, N.Y.: Doubleday, 1950.

Barr, Marleen S. *Alien to Femininity: Speculative Fiction and Feminist Theory*. Westport, Conn.: Greenwood Press, 1987.

———. *Feminist Fabulation: Space/Postmodern Fiction*. Iowa City: University of Iowa Press, 1992.

———, ed. *Future Females: A Critical Anthology*. Bowling Green, Ohio: Bowling Green State University Popular Press, 1981.

Barrie, J. M. *Peter Pan*. 1911. Reprint. New York: Scribner's, 1980.

Barth, John. *Chimera*. New York: Fawcett Crest, 1972.

Bellow, Saul. *A Theft*. New York: Penguin, 1989.

Bradley, Marion Zimmer. *The Shattered Chain*. New York: DAW, 1976.

Cather, Willa. "Neighbour Rosicky." In *The Norton Anthology of American Literature*, edited by Nina Baym et al., 2:1011–31. New York: Norton, 1989.

Charnas, Suzy McKee. *Motherlines*. New York: Berkley, 1978.

———. *Walk to the End of the World*. New York: Ballantine, 1974.

Cranny-Francis, Anne. *Feminist Fiction Feminist Uses of Generic Fiction*. New York: St. Martin's Press, 1990.

Elshtain, Jean Bethke. "Cultural Conundrums and Gender: America's Present Past." In *Cultural Politics in Contemporary America*, edited by Ian Angus and Sut Jhally, 123–34. New York and London: Routledge, 1989.

Fairbairns, Zoë. *Benefits*. London: Virago Press, 1979.

Freeman, Mary E. Wilkins. "The Revolt of 'Mother.'" In *The Norton Anthology of American Literature*, edited by Nina Baym et al., 2:608–19. New York: Norton, 1989.

Gearhart, Sally M. *The Wanderground: Stories of the Hill Women*. Watertown, Mass.: Persephone Press, 1979.

Gilbert, Sandra M., and Susan Gubar. *No Man's Land: The Place of the Woman Writer in the Twentieth Century*. Vol. 1, *The War of the Words*. New Haven: Yale University Press, 1988.

Holland, Norman N. "UNITY, IDENTITY, TEXT, SELF." *PMLA* 90 (1975): 813–22.

Jameson, Fredric. *The Political Unconscious: Narrative as a Socially Symbolic Act*. London: Methuen, 1981.

Lem, Stanislaw. *The Star Diaries*. Translated by Michael Kandel. London: Secker and Warburg, 1976.

Lynn, Elizabeth A. *The Northern Girl*. New York: Berkley, 1980.

McCaffrey, Anne. *Dragonsong*. New York: Bantam, 1977.

"Mann and Machine." NBC. Created by Glenn Davis and William Laurin. Produced by Dick Wolf and Bob DeLaurentis. 1992.

Piercy, Marge. *He, She and It*. New York: Knopf, 1991.

Rabkin, Eric S. *The Fantastic in Literature*. Princeton: Princeton University Press, 1976.

Russ, Joanna. "Recent Feminist Utopias." In *Future Females: A Critical Anthology*, edited by Marleen S. Barr, 71–85. Bowling Green, Ohio: Bowling Green State University Popular Press, 1981.

———. "When It Changed." In *The Norton Anthology of Literature by Women*, edited by Sandra M. Gilbert and Susan Gubar, 2262–69. New York: Norton, 1985.

Salmonson, Jessica Amanda. "The Prodigal Daughter." In *Elsewhere*, edited by Terri Windling and Mark Allen Arnold, 119–50. New York: Ace, 1981.

Sargent, Pamela, ed. *More Women of Wonder: Science Fiction Novelettes by Women about Women*. New York: Vintage, 1976.

———. *The New Women of Wonder: Recent Science Fiction Stories by Women about Women*. New York: Vintage, 1977.

———. *Women of Wonder: Science Fiction Stories by Women about Women*. New York: Vintage, 1975.

Scholes, Robert. "The Roots of Science Fiction." In *Science-Fiction: A Collection of Critical Essays*, edited by Mark Rose, 46–56. Englewood Cliffs, N.J.: Prentice Hall, 1976.

———. *Structural Fabulation: An Essay on the Fiction of the Future*. Notre Dame and London: Notre Dame University Press, 1975.

Suvin, Darko. *Metamorphoses of Science Fiction: On the Poetics and History of a Literary Genre*. New Haven: Yale University Press, 1979.

Tiptree, James, Jr. "Houston, Houston, Do You Read?" In *Aurora: Beyond Equality*, edited by Vonda N. McIntyre and Susan Janice Anderson, 36–98. Greenwich, Conn.: Fawcett, 1976.

———. "The Women Men Don't See." In *Warm Worlds and Otherwise*, edited by Robert Silverberg, 131–64. New York: Ballantine, 1975.

Tompkins, Jane. *West of Everything: The Inner Life of Westerns.* New York: Oxford University Press, 1992.

Tuttle, Lisa. "Husbands." In *Alien Sex*, edited by Ellen Datlow, 105–17. New York: Dutton, 1990.

Vonnegut, Kurt. "Harrison Bergeron." In *Welcome to the Monkey House*, by Kurt Vonnegut, 7–13. New York: Dell, 1968.

———. *Hocus Pocus.* New York: Putnam, 1990.

Westfahl, Gary. "A New Campaign for Science Fiction." *Extrapolation* 33 (1992): 6–23.

Wilhelm, Kate. *Where Late the Sweet Birds Sang.* New York: Pocket Books, 1974.

Wolf, Naomi. *The Beauty Myth: How Images of Beauty Are Used against Women.* New York: William Morrow, 1991.

Feminist Science Fiction

BEFORE FEMINIST FABULATION

The Ultimate Sandbox by Michael Whelan
© 1984 by Michael Whelan

1

THELMA AND

LOUISE

*This road movie's brand of escapism offers
transcendence, not instruction—and it rises
above both the everyday and the limits of
its genre.* Thelma and Louise *is transcendent
in every way.*

—Janet Maslin, "Lay Off Thelma and Louise"

I went in search of astral America, not social
and cultural America, but the America of the
empty, absolute freedom of the freeways, not the
deep America of mores and mentalities, but the
America of desert speed, of motels and mineral
surfaces. . . . For the mental desert form expands
before your very eyes, and this is the purified
form of social desertification.

Disaffection finds its pure form in the
barrenness of speed. All that is cold and dead in
desertification or social enucleation rediscovers
its contemplative form here in the heat of the
desert. Here in the transversality of the desert and
the irony of geology, the transpolitical finds its*

*generic, mental space. The inhumanity of our
ulterior, asocial, superficial world immediately
finds its aesthetic form here, its ecstatic form.
For the desert is simply that: an ecstatic critique
of culture, an ecstatic form of disappearance.*

—*Jean Baudrillard,* America

Thelma and Louise share Baudrillard's search for astral America. Disaffected women who desert patriarchy, they embrace the America of desert speed, enjoy the freedom of the freeways, and contemplate themselves. Disappearing in the desert enables them to author an ecstatic critique of patriarchal culture. Their road trip is not, as they state, a journey to Mexico (a country, of course, offering no feminist haven) but rather a transcendent merger with the desert defined as transpolitical mental space. Submerged in the desert, which is "a sublime form that banishes all sociality, all sentimentality, all sexuality" (Baudrillard, 71), these escapees from dead-end female lives enter a terrain beyond patriarchal language—ultimately beyond all aspects of patriarchal reality. Ensconced in alternative space, they experience Baudrillard's question and answer: "Why are the deserts so fascinating? It is because you are delivered from all depth there—a brilliant, mobile, superficial neutrality, a challenge to meaning and profundity, a challenge to nature and culture, an outer hyperspace, with no origin, no reference-points" (Baudrillard, 123–24). I argue that their journey in outer hyperspace, their drive beyond patriarchal meaning systems, conforms to feminist science fiction tropes. *Thelma and Louise*, transcendent in every way, offers feminist escapism—the ability to rise above the patriarchal real.

British director Ridley Scott's *Thelma and Louise* has much in common with his science fiction films *Alien* and *Blade Runner* (the latter based on Philip K. Dick's *Do Androids Dream of Electric Sheep?*).[1] Ripley, the female protagonist of *Alien*, fights a monster on another planet. Thelma and Louise, who learn that females are treated as alien Others on planet Earth, battle the monstrous patriarchy. Further, while *Blade Runner* focuses on how Deckard, a police officer, hunts replicants (androids), *Thelma and Louise* portrays police chasing newly remodeled women who no longer replicate patriarchal imperatives. Thelma and Louise, hunted, re-created, alien women, soldiers poised to shoot anything resembling a patriarchal bug-eyed monster, try, when confronted with the end of their world, to create a women's world of their own. The note Thelma leaves in the microwave communicates finality. "The microwave, the waste disposal . . . this soft, resort-style civilization irresistibly evokes the end of the world" (Baudrillard, 31). The end of Thelma's and Louise's lives in the patriarchal world occurs when Thelma realizes that she inhabits a micro-world and Louise realizes that it is a waste to spend her life moving food from restaurant table to waste disposal. Their last resort is, in the manner of Ibsen's Nora, to slam the door on patriarchy.

Thelma and Louise allows viewers to look through the keyhole of Nora's slammed door, to see fugitive women fleeing patriarchy by driving a "get away car," a mobile room of one's own on the road in a desert space outside society. In the wide open space of the American West, in Baudrillard's fantastic, meta-representational desert hyperspace, Thelma and Louise are not corralled within spaces of female limitation. Thelma, no longer a Stepford wife (Ira Levin's term), and Louise, no longer a servile meal server, proclaim that women are not components of a mindless female herd that men shepherd, that women are not electric sheep who follow automatically whenever patriarchy plugs in sexist master narratives.

Their proclamation answers the question Janet Maslin poses in her defense against charges that the film exemplifies toxic feminism. Maslin asks, "But what is it that really rankles about *Thelma and Louise*? . . . Once again, what's so egregious about *Thelma and Louise*?" (Maslin, 11). What's so egregious is that the film, like feminist science fiction, utilizes Darko Suvin's cognitive estrangement to unmask and name constructed reality as toxic patriarchy. What's so egregious is that, in both the film and feminist science fiction, "the men . . . don't really matter[;] . . . they [men] are essentially powerless" (Maslin, 16). What's most egregious is that the film and feminist science fiction, power fantasies for women, portray women who are essentially powerful. (I would like to remind those who criticize Thelma and Louise for deriving power from theft that a precedent exists for tolerating fictitious thieves. We do not, for example, routinely chastise Robin Hood for stealing from the rich in a location outside society's mainstream. Although Thelma and Louise are expected to obey the law in the desert—and the black "boyz" are expected to obey the law " 'n the hood"—Robin Hood is exempt from this expectation in the forest.)

Women need power fantasies: feminist nonrealistic fiction provides women's only escape from a reality that brands them as Other. Yet the general public, and even some feminist critics, do not routinely emphasize this point. For instance, according to public opinion voiced in the form of a letter to the *New York Times* (in response to Maslin's article), "I don't remember that women were treated so badly by men in those buddy films, but the males really take it in *Thelma and Louise*. With one exception, every featured male character is either a sex freak (the truck driver), a dishonest lover preying on women (the hitchhiker), a hateful spouse (the husband), or a sniveling coward (the motorcycle cop)" (Cole, 4). With few exceptions, females living under patriarchy really take it from husbands, cops, and male characters of various sorts. The roles the letter writer describes exemplify the sorts of men women routinely confront. In other words, while I am not trying to cast all women as heroes and all men as villains, it is, for example, true that male truck drivers who harass women are more numerous than female truck drivers who harass men.

The truck driver's lewd comments and actions epitomize a socially sanctioned toxic masculinism that is so routine, even *The Guardian*'s female reviewer chastises Thelma and Louise—not the driver. The reviewer mentions "one of the movie's most objectionable scenes, when Thelma and Louise hold up the driver of a petrol tanker who has been making obscene gestures at them. First they shoot out his tyres, then—in a wanton piece of environmental pollution—they blow his lorry sky-high" (Smith, 17). Thelma and Louise merely express an exaggerated opposing response to patriarchy's dictum that women greet objectionable, dehumanizing male gestures in terms of the silence of the lambs. The obnoxious truck driver fares better than the male invaders who might deservedly face death in James Tiptree's "Houston, Houston, Do You Read?" The truck, the elongated silver phallus on wheels, the invading enemy vehicle piloted by a polluter of Thelma's and Louise's woman-controlled desert environment, should be shot. The sight of the exploding truck imparts a new, nonpatriarchal meaning to the term "truck stop."

Thelma and Louise is so egregious because it shows precisely how easy it is for women who no longer act as silent lambs and electric sheep to blow up a truck driven by a male chauvinist pig. The film shows precisely how easy it is for women to empower themselves, to command the male-centered environments truck stops epitomize, to pull the trigger, to kill the rapist—to explode patriarchy. What really rankles about *Thelma and Louise* is that it portrays a feminist version of the moment Joanna Russ calls "When It Changed." In Russ's science fiction story, the lives of a community of women change when men come to the feminist utopia called Whileaway; in *Thelma and Louise*, two women's lives change when they leave the utopia for elite men called America. Like Russ's story, the film is threatening and thus has been the target of much criticism. Patriarchy does not react well to women who change, to women who rewrite their lives in a feminist, postmodern act of defying patriarchal master narratives. Patriarchy does not react well to powerful, mobile women. The film challenges the notion that the American desert West was never meant to be a wide open space for women. The film reminds Saudi men exactly why they do not allow women to drive.

Thelma and Louise reach a point where they no longer want to engage with patriarchy. Louise turns down an offer of marriage. Perhaps, like the protagonist of Suniti Namjoshi's *The Conversations of Cow*, she comes "to the conclusion that men are aliens[,] . . . the Men from mars, the Unearthly Aliens" (Namjoshi, 90) and does "not want to be married to a Martian" (Namjoshi, 93). Thelma, the former Stepford wife, steps forward to offer her own ideas about survival skills: she shoots the state trooper's radio, obliterates the literal voice of patriarchal law. The trooper is imprisoned in his car; Thelma and Louise, liberated in their car, are free to interpret the desert as a vast natural space that does not necessarily adhere to patriarchal definitions. Inspired by the clear evidence that social and sexual intercourse with men yields trouble, like female feminist Huck Finns, Thelma and Louise light out from patriarchal civilization. This separatist action enables them to acquire a clear perspective about their lives. As Maslin explains,

One of the most invigorating things about this film is the way its heroines, during the course of a few brief but wildly eventful days, crystallize their thoughts and arrive at a philosophical clarity that would have been unavailable to them in their prior lives. By the end of the film, the director Ridley Scott and the screenwriter Callie Khouri are ready to allow Thelma and Louise the opportunity to take full charge of their lives and full responsibility for their mishaps too. (Maslin, 16)

In Baudrillard's terms, Thelma and Louise experience "an exalting vision of the desertification of signs and men" (Baudrillard, 63). Baudrillard comments further:

The natural deserts tell me what I need to know about the deserts of the sign. They teach me to read surface and movement and geology and immobility at the same time. They create a vision expurgated of all the rest: cities, relationships, events, media. . . . They form the mental frontier where the projects of civilization run into the ground. They are outside the sphere and circumference of desire. We should always appeal to the deserts against the excess of signification, of intention and pretention in culture. They are our mythic operator. (Baudrillard, 63–64)

The desert is Thelma's and Louise's transforming teacher, their Professor Henry Higgins who changes them from flowery feminine women to hardened freedom fighters who certainly are no ladies. The desert, like a feminist separatist planet, is their mythic operator, the place where they learn to reread patriarchal signs.

Thelma and Louise author their own version of Tiptree's "Houston, Houston, Do You Read?" When she shoots Thelma's attacker, Louise, who was raped in Texas, announces that Texas—and all America—must read (or understand) that she will no longer suffer abuse. After attempting to reinterpret Texas as an unreal location, Thelma and Louise remind themselves that it is impossible to travel from Oklahoma to Mexico without passing through Texas. When they leap beyond reality at the conclusion of the film, Texas's location no longer matters. Because they have become so adroit at rereading reality, because they know that for women "this country [America] is without hope" (Baudrillard, 123), Thelma and Louise can only perceive Texas—and patriarchy—as an absence.

Baudrillard's ideas apply to the point that Thelma and Louise can never return to a mainstream vision of the world; they can never emerge from the desert. With these observations in mind, I offer a positive view of the aforementioned letter writer's opinions about the film's conclusion. He asks, "Since when is not facing the music by suicide paying the price for crime?" (Cole, 4). I argue for interpreting according to a different tune: patriarchy is criminal—and it pays no price. Thelma and Louise are not suicides, not Kate Chopin's defeated Edna Pontellier. Because their awakening makes returning to patriarchal reality unacceptable, they, instead, forge ahead into a new fantastic reality. They are akin to Tiptree's Ruth and Althea Parsons, the protagonists of "The Women Men Don't See," who choose to leave Earth, join extraterrestrials, and embrace the cosmos. In contrast to Ruth and Althea, Thelma and Louise possess a spaceship of their own: their car.

The spaceship/car in Ridley Scott's *Thelma and Louise* evokes the spaceship/car in Jean-Luc Godard's *Alphaville*. Godard's Natasha Von Braun and Mr. Johnson/Mr. Caution, who are not "logical" according to this word's definition in Alphaville, enter another galactic zone when driving their Ford Galaxy through what the film's computer commentator calls "our splendid galactic thoroughfares." Thelma and Louise, who no longer assume "logical" female roles in patriarchal America, act in kind. Their behavior echoes Natasha's comment "I am no longer normal," and their fate can be understood in terms of a particular phrase Natasha quotes from a book: "dying or not dying." Thelma and Louise are not dying. They are, instead, Natasha's fellow female travelers on splendid galactic thoroughfares. And, unlike Natasha, they do not depend on a male savior/chauffeur.

When Thelma and Louise consult and decide to drive over the Grand Canyon's edge, they live Baudrillard's "crucial moment." According to Baudrillard, the "only question in this journey is: how far can we go in the extermination of meaning, how far can we go in the non-referential desert form without cracking up and, of course, still keep alive the esoteric charm of disappearance? . . . Aim for the point of no return. This is the key. And the crucial moment is that brutal instant which reveals that the journey has no end, that there is no longer any reason for it to come to an end" (Baudrillard, 10). Their key: the decision that their journey beyond patriarchy should have no end. Thelma and Louise choose to hurl themselves into a fantastic zone. As Baudrillard explains, the desert is replete with signs and the Grand Canyon is a magical, living, surrealistic presence: "Among this gigantic heap of signs—purely geological in essence—man will have had no significance. . . . For the desert only *appears* uncultivated. . . . The long plateau which leads to the Grand Canyon . . . [is] alive with a magical presence, which has nothing to do with nature (the secret of this whole stretch of country is perhaps that it was once an underwater relief and has retained the surrealist qualities of an ocean bed in the open air)" (Baudrillard, 3). Thelma and Louise plunge into a magical place of nonhuman signification; they enter an alternative text. By doing so, they themselves become fantastic, magical, surrealist. Their car does not adhere to the laws of gravity; instead of immediately falling, it flies. Thelma and Louise are no longer brought down by patriarchal law. Instead of allowing an army of men and machines to capture them, while ensconced within a vehicle that transcends the laws of nature, they enter a magical space—a place better than America/Alphaville. Never achieving the questionable goal of reaching Mexico, another patriarchal country, Thelma and Louise enjoy "an ecstatic form of disappearance" (Baudrillard, 5). These women who have been dehumanized transcend humanity and mortality.

After all, another letter writer observes that the "beauty of Callie Khouri and Ridley Scott's road movie is that Thelma and Louise are pitted in a no-win battle that man and woman alike fight daily—against a dehumanizing society" (Ellsworth, 4). *Thelma and Louise* underscores that in this battle men fare better than women, that patriarchy dehumanizes women. The presence of the Grand Canyon in the film pictures gender schism, the gouged gap between women and men. *Thelma and Louise* tells the story of a gulf war between women and men, depicts another operation desert storm. Thelma and Louise can win only by achieving the title of the last chapter in Baudrillard's *America*: "Desert For Ever" (Baudrillard, 121). They triumph because, like the inhabitants of feminist science fiction worlds, they desert patriarchal reality, leave it behind in the dust. These former electric sheep lead patriarchal law on a wild sheep chase. These former electric sheep look up.

NOTE

1. For my thoughts about *Blade Runner*, please see the companion piece to this article: Marleen Barr, "Metahuman 'Kipple' Or, Do Male Movie Makers Dream of Electric Women?: Speciesism and Sexism in *Blade Runner*," in *Retrofitting Blade Runner: Issues in Ridley Scott's*

"Blade Runner" and Philip K. Dick's "Do Androids Dream of Electric Sheep?," ed. Judith B. Kerman (Bowling Green, Ohio: Bowling Green State University Popular Press, 1991), 25–31.

WORKS CITED

Alien. Brandywine–Shusett/Fox. Produced by Gordon Carroll, David Giler, and Walter Hill. Written by Dan O'Bannon (based on a story by Dan O'Bannon and Ronald Shusett). Directed by Ridley Scott. 1979.

Alphaville, A Strange Case of Lemmy Caution. Athos/PATHE. Produced by André Michelin. Written by Jean-Luc Godard. Directed by Jean-Luc Godard. 1965.

Baudrillard, Jean. *America.* New York and London: Verso, 1988.

Blade Runner. Warner Brothers. Produced by Michael Deeley. Written by Hampton Fancher and David Peoples (based on the novel *Do Androids Dream of Electric Sheep?* by Philip K. Dick). Directed by Ridley Scott. 1982.

Cole, Max. "These Are Heroines?" *New York Times,* 30 June 1991.

Dick, Philip K. *Do Androids Dream of Electric Sheep?* Garden City, N.Y.: Doubleday, 1968.

Ellsworth, Barry. "It's All in the Context." *New York Times,* 30 June 1991.

Levin, Ira. *The Stepford Wives.* New York: Dell, 1979.

Maslin, Janet. "Lay Off 'Thelma and Louise.'" *New York Times,* 16 June 1991.

Namjoshi, Suniti. *The Conversations of Cow.* London: Women's Press, 1985.

Russ, Joanna. "When It Changed." In *The Norton Anthology of Literature by Women,* edited by Sandra M. Gilbert and Susan Gubar, 2262–69. New York: Norton, 1985.

Smith, Joan. "Road Testing." *The Guardian,* 9 July 1991.

Suvin, Darko. *Metamorphoses of Science Fiction: On the Poetics and History of a Literary Genre.* New Haven: Yale University Press, 1979.

Thelma and Louise. Percy Main Productions MGM–PATHE. Produced by Ridley Scott and Mimi Polk. Written by Callie Khouri. Directed by Ridley Scott. 1991.

Tiptree, James, Jr. "Houston, Houston, Do You Read?" In *Aurora: Beyond Equality,* edited by Vonda N. McIntyre and Susan Janice Anderson, 36–98. Greenwich, Conn.: Fawcett, 1976.

———. "The Women Men Don't See." In *Warm Worlds and Otherwise,* edited by Robert Silverberg, 131–64. New York: Ballantine, 1975.

2

ANNE McCAFFREY PORTRAYS A FEMALE ARTIST

*Such is the strength of women that, sweeping
away syntax, breaking that famous thread
(just a tiny little thread, they say) which acts for
men as a surrogate umbilical cord, assuring
them—otherwise they couldn't come—that the
old lady is always right behind them, watching
them make phallus, women will go right up to
the impossible.*

—Hélène Cixous, "The Laugh of the Medusa"

In a manner that aligns its author with Hélène Cixous and Tillie Olsen, *Dragonsong*, a deceptively simple science fiction novel, questions the subverting of a female artist's creativity. Anne McCaffrey's protagonist Menolly, like contemporary avant-garde French women writers, exemplifies that "women have been absent—in silence, in madness—that difference has been repressed and that consequently there has only been one voice, a male voice. . . . The repression of the feminine . . . was total" (Marks, 836). Menolly is a silenced artist whose name announces "men only," the absence of women artists, the presence of a male voice.[1] Because of her gender and the expectation that she should perform menial tasks, Menolly's struggle to create is nearly defeated. Similarly, economic necessity sometimes thwarted Tillie Olsen's art. The facts of Olsen's life, then, as well as two questions she posits in *Silences*—"What is it that happens with the creator, to the creative process in that time [of silences]?" and "What are creation's needs for full functioning?" (Olsen, 1)—articulate Menolly's story. Both women experience "unnatural silences," the "thwarting of what struggles to come into being but cannot" (Olsen, 1).

Menolly's accession to the world of forceful and eloquent feminine artistic discourse, what Cixous calls "la venue à l'écriture" (Burke, 845), is stymied for a precise reason: she is "only a girl" (McCaffrey, 1). The rules of her home, Half-Circle Sea Hold, dictate that art cannot be part of a female's role. Olsen illustrates how such rules function in our world: "Parasitism, individualism, madness. Shut up, you're only a girl. O Elizabeth [Barrett Browning] why couldn't you have been born a boy? For . . . women: roles, discontinuities, part-self, part-time: conflict, imposed 'guilt'; 'a man can give full energy to his profession, a woman cannot'" (Olsen, 27). Such differences between conceptions of males and females as creative professionals are so pervasive that women writers, especially women science fiction writers, have felt the need to adopt masculine names. Menolly could have benefited from resorting to this guise: Elgion, Half-Circle Sea Hold's new Harper (or songwriter), cannot imagine that a girl is the hidden source of musical talent in the Hold (McCaffrey, 46).

Ursula Le Guin's following description of James Tiptree is relevant to Elgion's behavior and Olsen's comment above:

He is a rather slight, fragile man of about sixty, shy in manner, courteous; . . . has lived in . . . some of the more exotic parts of the world; has been through the army, the government, and the university; an introvert, but active; a warm friend, a man of candor, wit and style. . . . The only thing better than Tiptree's letters is his stories. . . . The most wonderful thing about him is that he is also Alice Sheldon. . . . The army, the government, the university, the jungles, all that is true. Mr. Tiptree's biography is Dr. Sheldon's. (Le Guin, 180, 182)

How many contemporary readers would be comfortable with the fact that Alice Sheldon, a person who has experienced masculine institutions and adventures, a person who is a successful science fiction writer, was not born a boy? Present-day reactions to female artistry and professionalism bear some resemblance to those of Mrs. Browning's time. Hence, not unlike many of us, Elgion is blind to the talents of a young woman. Menolly's strong desire to create art generates conflicts with the predominant customs of her world—and our world—places where women artists are not welcomed, places where adopting a masculine pseudonym improves a woman artist's chance to achieve success. The Hold is a place where imposed guilt eradicates a part of Menolly's self.

Efforts to silence Menolly extend beyond mental coercion when she becomes the victim of her mother's insidious physical act: "Yet Mavi [Menolly's mother] was too skilled a healer not to have known that the knife had missed the finger tendons. It was painfully clear to Menolly that Mavi, as well as Yanus [Menolly's father], had not wanted her to be able to play again" (McCaffrey, 126). Menolly accidentally cuts herself because, instead of fulfilling the desire to use her hands to play musical scales, she is forced to scale fish. Mavi's purposefully improper care creates an inner and outer barrier to her daughter's artistic pursuits: bodily impairment is coupled with the aforementioned imposition of guilt. For Menolly, then, like "the gifted among women (and men) [who] have remained mute, or [who] have never attained full capacity, it is because of circumstances, inner or outer, which oppose the needs of creation" (Olsen, 17). For Menolly, a crippled hand is as devastating as bound feet or a clitoridectomy.

Today, with some exceptions, roles, rather than knives, cripple women. Like many females, Menolly is expected to invest all of her energy in "an endless round of tedious tasks"—women's work: "gutting, smoking, salting, pickling fish. Mending nets, sails, clothes. Cleaning dishes, clothes, rooms. Gathering greens, berries, grasses, spiderclaws. . . . Tend[ing] old uncles and aunts, fires, pots, looms, glowbaskets" (McCaffrey, 65). The needs of her elders and the need of her society to have her perform monotonous duties are thought to be more significant than cultivating her artistic voice. Menolly is an artist who is without "fullness of time, let alone totality of self," an artist who "must work regularly at something besides [her] own work" (Olsen, 13).

Even if Menolly's society showered female artists with encouragement, the expectation that women should perform menial tasks would rob her of the time she needs to devote to art. Because "women are traditionally trained to place others' needs first, to feel these needs as their own[,] . . . their sphere [and] their satisfaction [are] to be in making it possible for others to use their abilities" (Olsen, 17). Before thinking of her own needs, Menolly must satisfy and support others. She must also maintain a neat, ladylike appearance even though she is expected to gut, smoke, salt, and pickle: "Menolly hoped for a chance to speak to her mother to find out if the Harper had faulted her teaching, but the opportunity never arose. Instead, Menolly came in for another scolding from Mavi for the state of her clothes, unmended; her bed furs, unaired; her slothfulness in general" (McCaffrey, 38). Hence, *Dragonsong* is an addition to the "little [that] has been written on the harms of instilling constant concern with appearance; the need to please, to support, the training in acceptance, deferring" (Olsen, 28). No wonder Menolly welcomes the chance to exile herself from the repressive Sea Hold.

Bravely, in the manner of a stereotypic male hero, she leaves a protected enclosure and ventures into an environment where life-threatening "thread" falls from the sky. (The thread Cixous mentions in this chapter's epigraph is life threatening to women.) Once free of the Hold's restrictions, she can acquire full knowledge of the world; no longer is she denied "the kind of comprehensions which come only in situations beyond the private" (Olsen, 41). After Menolly survives alone and eventually enters the more liberal community of the dragonriders at Benden Weyr, she has opportunities to experience diverse situations that range beyond the private, female sphere of influence. The formerly homebound doer of domestic tasks becomes a worldly hunter. Instead of cutting fish—or cutting herself—she can aggressively use her knife to satisfy her own needs (McCaffrey, 89).

Most importantly, Menolly the hunter, the master of fire lizards, is free to follow her artistic inclinations. Her audience of adoring lizards makes no attempt to stifle her: "It was no trick at all to make one reed pipe, and a lot more fun to put five together so she could play a counter-tune. The fire lizards adored the sounds and would sit listening, their dainty heads rocking in time to the music she played. . . . Menolly sang . . . all the Teaching Ballads" (McCaffrey, 86). Menolly has found a place outside the confines of her society where she can play her music and define herself as an artist. This new existence as a creator of music outside her Hold corresponds with Verena Andermatt's description of Cixous's notion that "it is by means of their writing that women will be able to affirm themselves 'otherwise' than by the place assigned to them in and by the symbolic order" (Andermatt, 38). The opportunity to create as she sees fit enables Menolly to affirm herself in a fashion that differs from her assigned place within the Hold, and in accordance with this affirmation, she can no longer be silenced by the Hold's resistance to her creativity.

Like Erich Auerbach's experience while writing *Mimesis*, then, exile causes Menolly's art to flourish. Although it might seem rather impertinent to compare this science fiction character with Auerbach, the following comment from the epilogue to *Mimesis* is relevant to Menolly's situation: "I may also mention that the book was written during the war and at Istanbul, where the libraries are not well equipped for European studies. On the other hand, it is quite possible that the book owes its existence to just this lack of a rich and specialized library. If it had been possible for me to acquaint myself with all the work that has been done on so many subjects, I might never have reached the point of writing" (Auerbach, 587). Exile benefits both artists. Auerbach's presence in an unsatisfactory academic environment enhances his writing; Menolly discovers opportunities for self-expression after escaping from a culture that is, for her, devoid of artistic richness.

If Menolly had remained in the Sea Hold, she might never have reached the point of freely singing and writing songs. But even though Menolly's situation improves when she is exiled and alone, it is still not optimum. Her attentive fire lizards ultimately prove to be an unsatisfactory audience: "At first Menolly talked to her creatures to hear the sound of her own voice. Later she spoke with them because they seemed to understand what she was saying. They certainly gave every indication of intelligent listening, humming, or crooning when she paused" (McCaffrey, 92). Yet, indications of intelligent listening cannot fulfill an artist's need for supportive response. Since, according to the British ordinary language philosopher H. P. Grice, talking is "a special case or variety of purposive, indeed rational behaviour" (Pratt, 131),[2] it is purposeless—and indeed irrational—for Menolly to try to speak to her mute creatures. She must reenter society because an improved opportunity to express herself artistically cannot adequately compensate for the frustration of an isolated existence where all her speech acts must fail.

Menolly's solitary tuning contrasts sharply with the proud "self-songs" sung by the mutually supportive community of women in Suzy McKee Charnas's *Motherlines*: "The women had assembled as they had for the dancing, forming an oval of spectators surrounding the bedding chute. Here a voice rose in song, there another. The members of each Motherline sang all the self-songs of the past generation of their line. The singing of each Motherline unfurled like a banner against the paling sky" (Charnas, 173). There is no one to silence these free women who live in a matriarchal society. Both Menolly and contemporary female artists are limited because such an alternative is not open to them: men control most of the museums, publishing companies, art galleries—and halls that house Harpers. Unlike *Motherlines*, because Menolly's music is subject to male scrutiny, *Dragonsong* concerns the development of a female voice, not a feminist language—a language that Cixous believes begins, in Andermatt's words, "whence the written text supersedes the echo of a suppliant, tortured voice of a female held in the phallogocentric economies of representation" (Andermatt, 39).

Even though Harperhall, a phallogocentric institution, ultimately provides a forum for Menolly's art, the acceptance of her musical voice springs from a feminine mode of creative activity. She wins the prized lizards simply because she nurtures them during the first days of their lives. Menolly is a foster mother. Because the dragonriders of Benden Weyr respect Menolly's rapport with the lizards and because their respect helps her gain access to Harperhall, the final welcoming of Menolly's female voice is directly related to a "maternal" relationship. Interestingly, like Menolly, the unique characteristics of Cixous's voice also stem from a maternal process. As Andermatt explains: "Cixous' seemingly formless texts achieve that fluid status of change, we posit, more immediately, and effectively than any new novel of the last decade. For her, such a creation is a mother-born process by which the scriptor, in unity, finds a maternal drive within her, a force devoid of any and all Oedipal mechanics; closer to an unconscious than the writing of the male" (Andermatt, 43).

Thus, like Cixous, Menolly does not sacrifice her femininity to become an artist. When she feeds the lizards and sings to them, she calls upon all of her mother-born creative capacities. Once she cut fish while she was forbidden to create. Later, in the solitary company of the lizards, her music coincides with the clever idea to look toward the sea to ensure their comfort: "Cracks in the skin would be deadly for the young fire lizards. . . . She searched the coast for dead fish and found a packtail washed up during the night. She slit the carcass, carefully, always working the knife blade away from her, and squeezed the oil from the skin into a cup" (McCaffrey, 87). As opposed to her earlier repressive toil, Menolly is not alienated from her labor with a knife; she can sing and work and comfort other creatures. When she combines creativity with nurturing and with a reliance upon the sea, Menolly once again acts in accordance with Cixous's art. Andermatt explains: "The plenitude of a feminist writing has a biological explanation so convincing, Cixous suggests, that all writers of force and passage are those giving birth to words flowing in accord with the contractual rhythms of labor. . . . For this reason, we contend, she always projects her text to the sea. . . . Converse to the male who at best can only *spray* his words, the writer-as-mother gives birth to and 'nourishes' her text, at once giving milk and accouching it" (Andermatt, 43, 44). The lizards' sounds form a part of Menolly's musical text, and she nourishes them in fact.

Olsen is also concerned with the relationship between motherhood and creativity: "Balzac . . . described creation in terms of motherhood. Yes, in intelligent passionate motherhood there are similarities, and in more than the toil and the patience. The calling upon total capacities; the reliving and new using of the past; the comprehensions; the fascination, absorption, intensity" (Olsen, 18). In her opinion, however, this relationship retards accomplishment. It is "almost certain death to creation—(so far). . . . It is distraction, not mediation, that becomes habitual; interruption, not continuity; spasmodic, not constant toil. . . . Work interrupted, deferred, relinquished, makes blockage—At best, lesser accomplishment" (Olsen, 18). As opposed to this comment, and in accordance with Cixous's positive juxtaposition of art and motherhood, the intensity Menolly directs toward the role of nurturing protector enlivens, rather than kills, her creativity. *Dragonsong* fantastically eradicates the need for Olsen's use of the words "so far."

At the novel's conclusion, the phrase that echoes throughout the work—"but I'm a girl"—appears again and is dismissed. Regardless of Menolly's gender, she is finally able to satisfy fully her inclination to "want music more than anything else in the world" (McCaffrey, 175). As Menolly grasps the Masterharper's supporting hand, all the circumstances that caused her to be silenced are eradicated, and she, accompanied by the fire lizards, gladly follows him. Ensconced within this peculiar nuclear family—man, woman, and loving dragonlike creatures—Menolly is free to realize her full potential as a female and as an artist.

Dragonsong speaks out against repressing women's creativity by putting forth the idea that "woman must write her self: must write about women and bring women to writing, from which they have been driven away as violently as from their bodies—for the same reasons, by the same law, with the same fatal goal. Woman must put herself into the text—as into the world and into history—by her own movement. . . . Women should break out of the snare of silence" (Cixous, 875, 881). Both Cixous and Olsen would applaud the fact that McCaffrey is a woman who writes about a woman, a female artist who portrays a female artist. These feminist critics remind us to appreciate the good fortune of McCaffrey and her protagonist. They are women who have managed to escape the snare of silence. McCaffrey and Menolly break that famous thread; they go right up to the impossible.

NOTES

1. Because Menolly is a musician who creates her own music, the word *artist* will refer to both *musician* and *writer*.

2. H. P. Grice made this remark in his "Logic and Conversation," the 1967 William James Lecture at Harvard University.

WORKS CITED

Andermatt, Verena. "Hélène Cixous and the Uncovery of a Feminist Language." *Women and Literature* 7 (1979): 38–48.

Auerbach, Erich. *Mimesis*. Princeton: Princeton University Press, 1973.

Burke, Carolyn Greenstein. "Report from Paris: Women's Writing and the Women's Movement." *Signs* 3 (1978): 843–55.

Charnas, Suzy McKee. *Motherlines*. New York: Berkley, 1978.

Cixous, Hélène. "The Laugh of the Medusa." *Signs* 1 (1976): 875–93.

Le Guin, Ursula K. "Introduction to *Star Songs of an Old Primate*." In *The Language of the Night*, edited by Susan Wood, 179–84. New York: G. P. Putnam's Sons, 1979.

McCaffrey, Anne. *Dragonsong*. New York: Bantam, 1977.

Marks, Elaine. "Women and Literature in France." *Signs* 3 (1978): 832–42.

Olsen, Tillie. *Silences*. New York: Dell, 1965.

Pratt, Mary Louise. *Toward a Speech Act Theory of Literary Discourse*. Bloomington: Indiana University Press, 1977.

SUZY MCKEE CHARNAS, SALLY GEARHART, AND MARGE PIERCY DEPICT SEX AND THE SINGLE FEMINIST UTOPIAN QUASI-TRIBESPERSON

What a strangely attractive, almost erotic idea:
her beautiful . . . Stanley as a male mother.
The strange vision helped Lydia . . . to a fresh
reimagining of the world: gentle male mothers
. . . with healthy penises dangling freely beneath
loinclothes, but subjugating their male force to
the care of a small creature. But . . . Stanley's
vision seemed preposterous, even slightly obscene.
From where was the baby going to come out
of him? Would he still be able to have a penis?
What about breasts?

—*Gail Godwin,* A Mother and Two Daughters

A man with breasts? A gentle male mother? Unlike Gail Godwin's Lydia, some characters do inhabit worlds where such strange visions are true. In Marge Piercy's *Woman on the Edge of Time*, Connie Ramos encounters men who resemble Stanley's vision. The Hill Women in Sally Gearhart's *The Wanderground* see no reason for including a Stanley in their lives. Among the Riding Women in Suzy McKee Charnas's *Motherlines*, a mother and her two daughters look exactly alike. Lydia articulates a common response to the strangely attractive characteristics of these feminist utopian science fiction texts: preposterous, even slightly obscene. Maybe so; but one should not condemn these texts without remembering that real-world sexuality is also sometimes preposterous and obscene. The unusual biology and sexuality depicted in Piercy's, Gearhart's, and Charnas's utopias—men with breasts, babies who are not from women born, and women who mate with horses, for example—should be considered in light of the demeaning sexuality patriarchy sanctions. These texts link utopian sexuality with corresponding dystopian visions derived from negative aspects of sexuality in our world.

Most readers are not comfortable with the portrayal of sexuality in feminist utopian science fiction. Pamela Sargent notes that Joanna Russ's "When It Changed" "won the Nebula Award. . . . Yet it was also severely criticized in some science fiction publications. It is a bit odd that readers should feel threatened by a story in which well-characterized, likeable women can get along without men, when there is such an abundance of science fiction in which well-characterized, likeable men get along without women" (Sargent, liii). It is also more than a bit odd that readers should feel threatened by fiction in which likeable women choose to enjoy sex and reproduce without men when there is such an abundance of fiction in which thoroughly unlikeable—despicable— men choose to enjoy sex and reproduce in a manner that degrades or physically harms women. Hearing about these feminist novels, some people automatically express their distaste without realizing why fictitious portrayals of a different—and therefore threatening—sexuality deserve their attention. They prefer not to notice that rape, pornography, and other forms of sexual violence do not exist in these utopian societies, while such violence is a routine— almost normal—aspect of our daily lives. Although many people are entertained by images of women in dehumanizing sexual situations, they do not welcome imaginative visions of sexuality that enable women to enjoy dignity and freedom.

In *The Bleeding Heart*, Marilyn French's Dolores complains about the sexual abuse directed toward women daily: "Look at the world! Look at the cracks, the jokes, the whistles, the pawing hands, the rapes, the judgments, the ads, the movies, the TV, the books, the laws, the traditions, the customs, the economic statistics" (French, 257). The female characters who inhabit utopias created by Piercy, Charnas, and Gearhart never experience the circumstances Dolores catalogs as long as they remain within their utopian environments, where women are not treated as subhuman sex objects. Although the utopians these authors imagine sometimes choose to sleep with more than one lover, they would never consider entertaining themselves by watching hard- and soft-core pornography, sadistic movies, and television programming that denigrates the female body. They would dislike "Charlie's Angels." Because it is not linked with violence and exploitation, the sexuality feminist utopian science fiction characters enjoy is morally superior to sexuality sanctioned by patriarchy. Once they are reminded that real-world sexuality has many negative aspects, people more readily accept those portrayals of sexuality—both positive and negative—that appear in feminist utopian science fiction.

In "Recent Feminist Utopias," Joanna Russ explains why this literature is characterized by sexual permissiveness:

Classless, without government, ecologically minded, with a strong feeling for the natural world, quasi-tribal in feeling and quasi-family in structure, the societies of these [feminist utopian] stories are *sexually permissive*—in terms I suspect many contemporary male readers might find both unspectacular and a little baffling, but which would be quite familiar to the radical wing of the feminist movement, since the point of the permissiveness is not to break taboos but to separate sexuality from questions of ownership, reproduction and social structure. Monogamy, for example, is not an issue since family structure is a matter of parenting or economics, not the availability of partners. *Woman on the Edge of Time* is reproductively the most inventive of the group, with bisexuality . . . as the norm, exogenetic birth, triads of parents of both sexes caring for children, and all three parents nursing infants. Exclusive homosexuality . . . is an unremarkable idiosyncrasy. (Russ, 76)

Although Godwin's Lydia might welcome Russ's explanation and applaud the inventive reproduction and mothering *Woman on the Edge of Time* portrays, for her, as for many readers, accepting the sanctioned presence of lesbianism in these feminist utopias is quite a different matter. Unlike nursing male mothers, lesbianism is real—and, of course, threatens the patriarchal status quo. Hence, it is useful to know why some feminist utopias exclude men:

Since lesbianism is a charge routinely made against feminists . . . and since many men appear to believe that the real goal of all feminists is to get rid of men, it is important to investigate the reasons why these authors exclude men from their utopias. In the two-sexed utopian societies, lesbianism is one among many forms of freedom, but a world without men raises two questions: that of lesbianism (and lurking behind it) the question of separatism. I believe the separatism is primary, and that the authors are not subtle in their reasons for creating separatist utopias: if men are kept out of these societies, it is because men are dangerous. They also hog the good things of this world. (Russ, 77)

Charnas and Gearhart create separatist utopias, and Piercy's utopia includes men who differ markedly from real-world men.

Some women in *The Wanderground* leave the City, where they are hunted by men, and establish a feminist community in the surrounding hills. One of Gearhart's Hill Women, Ijeme, reacts with shocked disbelief when she encounters a City woman wearing ordinary attire: "Amazed as she was, Ijeme knew that she was in the presence of a woman—but not a woman as she knew women. This was the city edition, the man's edition, the only edition acceptable to men, streamlined to his exact specifications, her body guaranteed to be limited, dependent, and constantly available" (Gearhart, 63). Ijeme insists on differentiating between "woman as sex object" and "woman as person." Young Clana, another Hill Woman, responds similarly. Within the "remember rooms," she views images that could appropriately evoke the strident voice of French's Dolores: "covers from old magazines with women clad only in high-heeled boots and a thin crotch band or being whipped into apparent ecstatic submission by a masked man ready to enter her, photographs of women on their knees servicing men, women and men in a hundred varieties of sexual postures" (Gearhart, 157–58). Although not pretty, these images are certainly realistic examples of contemporary pornography. Yet Gearhart does not fail to mention another truth: not all aspects of sexuality the Hill Women learn about in the remember rooms are bad. The remember room guides "had said there was a difference between abusive sex between women and men and the kind which was a mutual expression of love. But Clana was still confused. How could you let someone enter your body that way and not be a victim?" (Gearhart, 158). Clana, the product of a lesbian society in which sex always functions as a mutual expression of love, cannot understand a society in which sex only sometimes functions as a mutual expression of love. She is confused by the notion of sexual intercourse between women and men as well as by sexual violence.

Sex in the world of the Hill Women, indeed their attitude toward everything in their world, is never linked to abuse and power. Their close connection to nature is part of their sexuality. Hill Women have "sex" with trees (Gearhart, 13) and with bushes (Gearhart, 97). They have group sex with the moon (Gearhart, 98–101) and with each other. They are free to express themselves sexually without experiencing any form of violence or exploitation, a freedom some feminists feel is impossible to experience with men. According to one Hill Woman (Betha), for example, "essential fundamental knowledge" includes the point that "women and men cannot yet, may not ever, love one another without violence; they are no longer of the same species" (Gearhart, 115). To Hill Women, such items as trees, bushes, and the moon—but not men—are of their species and are appropriate sex partners.

In addition to their innocence in regard to physical sexual violence, the Hill Women also do not experience the psychological violence that destroys friendships between heterosexual women. No matter how young and attractive a woman is in our culture, she learns never to forget that younger and more attractive women lurk just around the corner. The following image of sexually intertwined females offering each other comfort is much more positive than alienating sexual competition: "Gyna came down from the loft and crawled upon the mat among three sleeping women, all nestled close, all holding one another. She curled up among them and atop them, a breast for a pillow and a shoulder for a blanket. They sprawled together in outrageous tangles, soaking up warmth and comfort" (Gearhart, 132). The Hill Women's "outrageous tangles," with nature and with each other, are superior to the competitive sexual tangles encouraged by patriarchy. Even Pelagrine, an elderly Hill Woman who is near death, has "some things to share, some holding and rocking to do" (Gearhart, 92). Hers is a happier experience than that of people who languish alone and untouched in nursing homes.

In addition to such utopian descriptions of sexuality, Gearhart presents dystopian images extrapolated from contemporary life. During the Hill Women's past, women in the City were forced to adhere to extremely feminine roles. Those who refused to conform were "Shot. Gassed. Burned" (Gearhart, 153). Some were tracked down during "Cunt Hunts" when "small bands of men . . . packed up what gear they would need and set out for the day or weekend to see what womanflesh they could find in the hills" (Gearhart, 160). The men's gear includes guns, helicopters, and nets. This imaginative circumstance is not that different in essence from contemporary headlines, except that it is condoned. Groups of men do hunt for a vulnerable woman to rape. Furthermore, it is impossible to say that real women will never literally be hunted, that there can never be laws that sanction the murder of female nonconformists. The text reminds us that such heinous acts can—and do—occur outside science fiction: " 'We're all so fucking naive,' Shirley said. 'Who could believe it was really happening? We're as bad as the Jews in Germany' " (Gearhart, 153). I am a Jew who is writing this piece in the University of Düsseldorf's humanities building. Dachau is within excursion distance by train from where I now sit. If someone were to knock on my office door and advise me to run to the hills because all suspected feminists "had to get away from police and state militias" (Gearhart, 153), I would give serious thought to changing immediately into my jogging shoes.

Godwin's Stanley believes people will eventually have to run to avoid catastrophe, and his ideas inspire Lydia to imagine them running toward a better civilization. Stanley explains: " 'I think we're going to have to run for our lives. . . . I've got this feeling that we all may have to move pretty fast and be in the best shape we can.' . . . Lydia found herself entertaining fervid visions of a catastrophe . . . and imagined their two . . . bodies . . . running, swift as animals, on healthy, high-arched feet, toward a safe, quiet haven where they could begin to build a gentle civilization" (Gearhart, 241–42).

Alldera, the protagonist of Charnas's *Walk to the End of the World* and *Motherlines*, has lived through what Stanley and Lydia can only imagine. She is a skilled runner who joins the Motherline tribes after managing to run beyond the borders of the gynocidal Holdfast, a "concentration camp" for women that is the setting of *Walk*. *Walk* contains violent sexual acts of the same ilk as those described in *The Wanderground*—sans helicopters. Alldera summarizes her experience in the Holdfast to the utopian Riding Women: "While you rode and hunted and hugged each other here, men beat me and starved me, a man threw me down on my back in the mud and fucked me and made me eat dirt to remind me how much power he had over me" (Charnas, *Motherlines* 92–93). Hence, the Holdfast is analogous to Gearhart's City (and to Piercy's alternative to Mattapoisett). While Piercy and Gearhart include dystopias within their feminist utopian novels, Charnas places the alternative to her dystopian vision (*Walk*) in a separate novel (*Motherlines*).

Reproductive practices in *Motherlines* are more shocking than in *The Wanderground*. Although there are men in the City, Hill Women reproduce by parthenogenesis when they are "implanted" and exposed to a blast of "earthbreath" at a community gathering. Riding Women, who live in a world without men, are also "implanted" at their community gathering. Nenisi Connor, a black Riding Woman, explains: "'We mate with stallions.' Alldera was stunned. She could not think" (ibid., 100). Many readers would share Alldera's reaction—and would prefer not to encounter female characters who mate with horses and enjoy lesbian sex. Yet Nenisi argues that her method of reproduction is a logical and superior alternative to women's experience in the Holdfast. The women who survived the "wasting" of the world "perfected the change the labs had bred into them so that no men were needed. Our seed, when ripe, will start growing without merging with male seed because it already has its full load of traits from the mother. The lab men used a certain fluid [horse semen] to start this growth. So do we. "Simple and clean, compared to rape in the Holdfast" (ibid., 74).

Nenisi further explains that, in her opinion, voluntarily mating with a stud horse is an acceptable alternative to enduring the degradation of being forced to mate with a man: "The stud doesn't attack anyone, he means no harm, no abuse or degradation. He's innocent. He has to be led and coaxed and trained to do his part, with our help. It's nothing at all like a man overpowering a fem just to show her who's master" (ibid., 103). These passages illustrate that sexuality within Motherline tribes is far less brutal and exploitative than sexuality within the Holdfast—Charnas's exaggerated version of our culture's treatment and depiction of women. There is no rape or pornography—or any other form of sexual abuse—among the Riding Women. Lesbian sex is a natural and positive necessity in their world without men. So is mating with a horse.

Our culture routinely obscures the truth of women's sexuality by distorting it to sell products. Such distortions are absent from the Riding Women's society. For example, although menstruation is not routinely mentioned in novels, Charnas refers to it directly: "Alldera sat knotting the dry fibers spread on her knee into a menstrual plug. She could not yet turn out dozens of them during a conversation without looking down at her work, as the women did; but she could make enough for her own needs" (ibid., 59). Like a fisherman mending a net, Alldera is openly doing necessary work. The Riding Women have an appropriate attitude toward menstruation. They do not veil it in myth, secrecy, or blue and white flowered, unmarked cardboard boxes.

Motherlines depicts women's biological reality. The frankness of the novel is apparent, for instance, when the rawness of new mother Alldera's vagina is described after she urinates (ibid., 42). *Motherlines* does not define the vagina as an inferior version of men's genitals. In fact, in Charnas's world that excludes men because men are dangerous, male sexual organs are thought to be aberrant, threatening, encumbering, and ridiculous. To a Riding Woman named Sheel, a man's "sexual organs had seemed a ludicrous, dangling nuisance and hardly capable of the brutalities recounted by the escaped femmish slaves. Having everything external and crowded into the groin like that must make walking more uncomfortable for a man than riding at the gallop with unsupported, milk-full breasts would be for a plains woman" (ibid., 17). Alldera's young daughter thinks a description of a penis "sounds silly and clumsy, like carrying a lance around with you all the time" (ibid., 259). Riding Women believe that lesbian sexuality is normal and that heterosexuality is alien. This attitude, made possible by men's absence, enables both the Riding Women and the Hill Women to live in feminist utopian communities.

Piercy does not exclude men from Mattapoisett. Instead, she alters them. Men who live in Mattapoisett are not like the men we know: "He had breasts[,] . . . small breasts, like a flat-chested woman temporarily swollen with milk" (Piercy, 76). The content of the daydream of Gail Godwin's Lydia is a common occurrence in Mattapoisett, where both women and men lactate. As in the utopias created by Charnas and Gearhart, everyone is part of a sensual community: "Touching and caressing, hugging and fingering, they handled each other constantly" (Piercy, 134). Connie, Piercy's Mexican-American time traveler from contemporary Manhattan, shares Alldera's first reaction to feminist utopian sexuality: "She felt sick. . . . She felt angry" (Piercy, 134). She is shocked by things she never encountered before: men with breasts, babies born from machines, and group sex. Like Alldera, however, she accepts the sexual characteristics of her new utopian world when she realizes that they are better than those of her own world.

Her former world is our world. The abuse Connie suffers is endured by many women. Her ability to give birth is destroyed when she goes to a hospital to be treated for bleeding after having undergone first an abortion and then a beating. So that the hospital residents can get practice, she is unnecessarily given a complete hysterectomy. In addition, the state removes her daughter from her custody. These real-life occurrences are more shocking than the imaginary sexuality portrayed in feminist utopias.

In addition to presenting a realistic depiction of our world, Piercy —like Charnas and Gearhart—presents a dystopian counterpart to her feminist utopia. Connie confronts a society exaggerated in the manner of the Holdfast and the City when she meets Gildina, a woman who sells her sexuality. Like real prostitutes, Gildina has little control over her product and working conditions: "Contract sex. It means you agree to put out so long for so much. . . . Some girls got only a one-nighter or monthly, that's standard. . . . You can't get out of a contract unless you're bought out. . . . I never had a contract that called for a kid. Mostly the moms have them. You know, they're cored to make babies all the time" (Piercy, 289–90). Gildina's dystopian society is both an alternative to Mattapoisett and an exaggerated version of Connie's Manhattan. Although babies in Gildina's world emerge from mothers rather than from machines, Mattapoisett is superior to her world. "Mother the machine" (Piercy, 102) is a better mother than an exploited, powerless woman who is forced to become pregnant to survive.

Surrogate mothers were not in the headlines prior to 1976, when Piercy wrote this passage. This is one example of how these authors' dystopian visions can become part of reality. Instead of being outraged by the depictions of sexuality in feminist utopian literature, readers might direct their anger toward the real sexual abuses patriarchy sanctions. The creators of feminist utopias have something important to say. The years following 1984 are an appropriate time to listen.

In *A Mother and Two Daughters*, Lydia's sister Cate (who holds a Ph.D. in English) is listening, and she is impatient.

> Cate opened her book. . . . It was about a young woman who flees modern technology to rediscover her basic instincts in the honesty of the deep woods. In the past year, Cate had read at least three novels about women fleeing into the honesty of the woods. In the first book, the woman fell in love with a bear. . . .
>
> The women were fleeing into the wilderness. . . . What does that mean, thought Cate, as the woman in her book leaned against a tree and tried to imagine the act from the tree's side. . . .
>
> But at least these writers are trying to stretch the limits of communal imagination and envision new ways to live. . . . I don't knock these writers; how can I? . . . But I allow myself the right to be impatient with them, all the same. Why can't they come up with something marvelous to solve my life? (Godwin, 401–2)

Women who fall in love with bears and mate with horses, women who imagine the sex act from the tree's perspective, do not offer something marvelous to solve women's lives; however, they do live in worlds that, as Russ argues, "present not perfect societies but only ones better than our own," societies that are "conceived by the author as better in explicitly feminist terms and for explicitly feminist reasons" (Russ, 71). Although these societies cannot solve our problems, they do pose superior scenarios. They inspire people to imagine alternatives, and real solutions can stem from imagined alternatives.

WORKS CITED

Charnas, Suzy McKee. *Motherlines*. New York: Berkley, 1978.

————. *Walk to the End of the World*. New York: Ballantine, 1974.

French, Marilyn. *The Bleeding Heart*. New York: Summit Books, 1980.

Gearhart, Sally M. *The Wanderground: Stories of the Hill Women*. Watertown, Mass.: Persephone Press, 1979.

Godwin, Gail. *A Mother and Two Daughters*. London: Pan Books, 1983.

Piercy, Marge. *Woman on the Edge of Time*. New York: Fawcett Crest, 1976.

Russ, Joanna. "Recent Feminist Utopias." In *Future Females: A Critical Anthology*, edited by Marleen S. Barr, 71–85. Bowling Green, Ohio: Bowling Green State University Popular Press, 1981.

Sargent, Pamela. "Introduction to Women of Wonder." In *Women of Wonder: Science Fiction Stories by Women about Women*, edited by Pamela Sargent. New York: Vintage, 1975. Reprint. Watertown, Mass.: Persephone Books, 1979.

4

JESSICA AMANDA SALMONSON'S "THE PRODIGAL DAUGHTER" AND FEMINIST SCIENCE FICTION'S TRADITIONS

I have come to feel my own life as one in which women are an enormous delight.
—Louise Bernikow,
Among Women

After voyaging out from enclosed worlds, four female protagonists of feminist speculative fiction derive self-awareness from experiencing solitary adventure. Once their adventure ends, they are ensconced within a new, protected environment, safely—and sometimes literally—embraced by strong female support. In Anne McCaffrey's *Dragonsong*, for example, Menolly leaves the Sea Hold, encounters her fire lizards, and becomes the protégé of Lessa, Weyrwoman at Benden Weyr. Alldera, the hero of Suzy McKee Charnas's *Motherlines*, escapes from the Holdfast and journeys to female benefactors, members of the Motherline tribes. In Elizabeth A. Lynn's *The Northern Girl*, Sorren leaves the security of her home in Kendra-On-The-Delta and travels to Tornor Keep. Upon arrival she begins a loving relationship with Kedera, a fellow young woman.

World Fantasy Award winner Jessica Amanda Salmonson's "The Prodigal Daughter" continues this tradition. Unise leaves Castle Green, pursues adventure in the outside world, and returns home to the welcoming arms of her lover, Jonathon, the female stable master. To exemplify the directions of contemporary feminist speculative fiction, in this chapter I discuss Salmonson's story in terms of the three previously mentioned texts. References to Louise Bernikow's *Among Women* will link these works to feminist reality.

In addition to female adventurers' exploits, the four imaginative works I have chosen share the following plot elements: the positive portrayal of love between women, the support—or rescue—of young females, and attention to the damage women inflict on one another. There is also one important difference between "The Prodigal Daughter" and the other texts. Women in *Motherlines* and *The Northern Girl* live in worlds without patriarchy, and Menolly at first develops her talents in isolation from men. Unise, however, functions within patriarchy. She is indispensable to her grandfather Arlburrow, patriarch of Castle Green, and, because of his assistance, she vanquishes the evil spirit Hophaetus. Unlike feminist speculative fictions that obliterate patriarchy, "The Prodigal Daughter" presents a positive—and ultimately possible—cooperative solution: patriarch and feminist are two fully realized mutually dependent individuals.

In the manner of Menolly, Sorren, and Alldera, Unise experiences isolation and growth before reentering society. "Had she never ridden from these comfortable confines in pursuit of adventure, she might still retain a degree of her lamented innocence—or ignorance" (Salmonson, 120). She returns as the rightful possessor of a designation that was never given to women: "Arlburrow and the knight [Unise] appeared" (Salmonson, 142). Because Unise is the knight, this metalinguistic phrase is as fantastic as the following sentence from Ursula Le Guin's *The Left Hand of Darkness*: "The king was pregnant" (Le Guin, 99). Another gender-related metalinguistic occurrence appears in the following exchange between Unise and her young cousin: " 'You would do a weary knight a favor, Miranna?' 'Anything, Lady' " (Salmonson, 121). This "Lady"— who happens to be a knight—is the antithesis of Robin Lakoff's description of "lady".[1]

Because they are not metalinguistic and fantastic, the following sentences might disturb some readers: " 'I missed you every night' [says Jonathon to Unise]. . . . 'Have you had other lovers?' Jonathon asked [Unise]" (Salmonson, 126–27). Love between women is also a part of *Motherlines* and *The Northern Girl*, and, as Louise Bernikow reminds us, it is also a part of reality that threatens many people: "Love between women is not permissible. Men grow resentful of exclusion, women become frightened. . . . She loved her. A hundred things happen when I write that sentence, when you read it. It depends on who I am, where you are, where you read it" (Bernikow, 157). The above conversation between Jonathon and Unise communicates "She loved her." It is potentially more threatening than "The king was pregnant." Feminist speculative fictions are dangerous visions.[2]

Such potential danger arises when fiction mirrors reality. Hence, the working life of Unise the knight might also be thought of as threatening. When Unise prepares to fight Hophaetus, Arlburrow cautions that she must be "Better . . . than any warrior [read male warrior]" (Salmonson, 137). She must be better than a man.

Unise, who adheres to characteristics of real women's working lives, does not act like a fellow fantastic woman. Although, like Pandora, she is responsible for the presence of evil—"it was her hand which broke the ancient seals of sorcery against the fiend [Hophaetus]" (Salmonson, 135)—"The Prodigal Daughter" indicates that Unise is a feminist version of that mythic character.

However, the story never directly says why, how, or when she provoked the demon's release. Its final line provides information by implication: "Hophaetus was locked away, a hauntingly lifelike statue of fey and sorrowful beauty, to await some other hapless hero who might draw the argent sword from his chest" (Salmonson, 150). As opposed to Pandora's negative feminine traits, Unise releases evil because of that which is positive and masculine: she draws the sword because she is impressed by the authority it symbolizes.

Young Miranna is also impressed by swords. When Unise sees old women preventing Miranna from dueling with boys, she "remembers her own girlhood, . . . the powerlessness she felt in frills and petticoats while boys leapt in tights" (Salmonson, 132). Like Miranna, Unise probably unsheathed swords in defiance of frills and petticoats when she was very young. One such sword might have been held by the statue of Hophaetus.

Because she fights against gender restraints, unlike the lady in traditional fantasies, Unise is not locked away; she is not a hauntingly lifelike statue of fey and sorrowful beauty who awaits the appearance of some hapless male hero. Unise is the antithesis of the female passivity represented by Pandora, Sleeping Beauty, and Galatea. She is a female controller, a female Prospero or Pygmalion, whose assertiveness directs the "life" of a male statue.

Unlike Pandora, Unise takes responsibility—life-threatening responsibility—for her actions. Yet she does not act alone. Jonathon plunges into Unise's battle with Hophaetus. Behaving counter to the stereotypical patriarch, Arlburrow plunges in too, serving as Unise's squire.

In contrast to the insidious older Holdfast men (Charnas), the scheming male member of Kendra-On-The-Delta's royal house (Lynn), and Menolly's destructive silencing father (McCaffrey), Arlburrow is a very positive figure: "For all his aloofness and mystery, he was a kind man deep inside, the living cornerstone of an ancient clan" (Salmonson, 122). Unise wins her battle against Hophaetus because she and Arlburrow cooperate with each other. Arlburrow wields a decisive blow to the demon's spine; Unise is the only person who can contain the demon. In addition to supporting a woman's actions, Arlburrow suffers a fate alien to literary patriarchs. It is he, not a helpless woman, who sacrifices himself. "It would be like Arlburrow, . . . to sacrifice himself, to make sure he, and not Jonathon, was the price read in the stars. . . . Arlburrow was blind. It seemed a terrible price indeed, . . . for the codger's life revolved around the library" (Salmonson, 147–48). Not only does the patriarch pay the price of victory, his presence also gives

Unise freedom. Because Arlburrow survives, Unise is spared the responsibility of ruling; she is not yet "bound to Castle Green" (Salmonson, 149).

While positive images of patriarchs are absent from *Motherlines*, *Dragonsong*, and *The Northern Girl*, Salmonson's story emphasizes such images. In addition to Arlburrow, Jonathon's father is also a very supportive figure. Jonathon explains: "Pa had three more sons, and more daughters, but I was the eldest and his pride" (Salmonson, 128). Surprisingly (in this feminist story) while men support women, women damage other women. The story's portrayal of old patriarchs is exceedingly positive; its portrayal of old matriarchs is exceedingly negative. This point is exemplified by the aforementioned old women who reprimand Miranna for effectively handling a sword. Unise's imaginary solution: "The squealing jabber of these . . . these *hens* coiled in her system. . . . She envisioned herself with sword to hand, hacking down foes—old ladies and their smug daughters—until the main room was astrew with piles of fancy clothes bloodied by the folded corpses within" (Salmonson, 132). These women—not the patriarch—enforce the repressive rules associated with patriarchy.

McCaffrey and Charnas also create women who harm other women. When she purposely withholds proper treatment for her daughter's injured hand, Menolly's mother retards the young girl's ability to be a musician. Holdfast women repress each other no less vehemently than Holdfast men repress women. Jonathon's reaction to such damaging—and pitifully powerless—women: "Put it up your arse, biddy" (Salmonson, 149). Feminist speculative fiction asserts that women's enemies are not limited to those who don't share their gender.

Unise's defense of Miranna signals a recurrent theme in this genre: "the rescue of the female child" (Russ, 79–80). Alldera saves her daughter, Sorrel, from the fate women suffer in the Holdfast. Sorren, a girl without a family, is welcomed within the house of Arré Med, ruler of Kendra-On-The-Delta. Menolly is sheltered and cared for by the women of Benden Weyr. Like these women, when Unise interacts with Miranna, she is the antithesis of the evil female, the evil stepmother or stepsister. Women who support other women are emerging presences in literature. Bernikow explains that they are also emerging presences in our society: "What happens to the project Ann has in mind, whether she gets the money that will enable her to do it or not, is something we will draw a lesson from. We are neither saints nor martyrs. We know it to be in our best interest to support Ann's progress in the world. We are not the terrible stepsisters. This is a happy ending. Somehow, we have come to this" (Bernikow, 38). In examples of contemporary feminist speculative fiction this "happy ending" applies to relationships between a woman and her female mentor. Alldera is especially close to Nenisi Connor. Sorren experiences the love of both Kedera and Yardmaster Paxe. Unise is intimate with a stable master who closely resembles Paxe. These women all engage in relationships with other women whom they like and respect.

Bernikow describes a relationship that mirrors the one Jonathon and Unise enjoy:

> Two women are alone in a room. One is content to sit near the hearth, stirring the evening's meal. Perhaps she is not really content, only appears so. . . . The second woman is restless. She wants to do something else, go elsewhere, take up a bow and prowl the woods, ride a horse. What will happen depends on how closely each woman feels compelled to translate her own preferences into prescription to say *all* women should stay near the hearth, or *all* women should reject the hearth. Do these women grant or withhold approval for differences? Will one chain the other to the hearth? (Bernikow, 31)

Jonathon is content to sit by the "hearth" acting as Castle Green's stable master. The hearth is not the proper place for Unise, however. Neither says that *all* women must live as they live; neither tries to chain the other to her own preference. Because their relationship is so close to the reality Bernikow describes, I quote the story's description of it at length:

> "I [Jonathon] am comfortable; no *man* could want for more. Nor offer it. I am good at what I do—as you are at what you do." . . .
>
> "You were content in my absence?" The idea hurt Unise who had never been content. . . . "Now that I see you I say, 'Jonathon-girl! You erred in staying here!'" . . . Unise could scarcely comprehend a human being so devoid of bitterness. . . .

"No longer my father's son—I was your woman then. . . . I wished to be my *own* woman, and that, dearest Unise, is why I did not go with you. I was your slave.

"I [Jonathon] was glad to be free, for all the pain of it."

"You were no more free than I."

"It did not lessen our love." (Salmonson, 126, 127, 129)

Regardless of their differences, Jonathon and Unise approve of each other. They are both androgynous wholes who share mutual positive characteristics. Unise the restless adventurer is quite womanly: "She was clad now, after a bath, in a blouse with fluffed sleeves, lace at wrists, a tightly buttoned velvet vestcoat over this. Her figure, her womanhood, was less in doubt thus clad" (Salmonson, 130). The hearth-bound Jonathon is certainly not "feminine," in the negative sense of the word. Because of their interesting characteristics, like Alldera and Nenisi, like Sorren and Paxe, like Menolly and Lessa, Jonathon and Unise think that they are "the most interesting people around." Women in the real world think the same of each other: "The man walking beside me observes the great numbers of women out for the evening together. I have ceased to think of this as remarkable. I have come to think of this as a period in history . . . in which women find each other the most interesting people around, in which women find new thinking, new ways of looking at the world, in other women far more than they do in men. . . . The man beside me is envious. He does well, I think, to be so" (Bernikow, 153). Although the man is rightly envious, feminists—and the creators of feminist speculative fiction—should not forget that his presence does not coincide with an enemy attack. After experiencing the negative depictions of patriarchy in *Motherlines*, *The Northern Girl*, and *Dragonsong*, I welcome Salmonson's positive portrayal of a patriarch.

Women have much to learn from Unise—and from her relationships with Jonathon and Arlburrow. Although Unise is successful in love and work, patriarchy supports her, and she saves the day—like the women of the Motherline tribes—she is not perfect; she is not superwoman. After vanquishing Hophaetus, Unise "lay . . . in bed like a sick old nanny" (Salmonson, 149). Here, when Unise is close to abandoning adventure, Jonathon drags her out of bed. These women can depend on each other during times when they are weak.

Unlike the feminist speculative fiction that stresses the mutual support of women in isolation from the patriarchy, "The Prodigal Daughter" couples this support with patriarchal sanction. As the text tells us, compromise is the key to cooperation between father and feminist. Unise momentarily puts aside an important object to please Arlburrow: "Unise unbuckled her sheath and, placing the sword within it, set it out of sight. Then she bent to her grandfather's cheek and left a kiss" (Salmonson, 124). He, in turn, sacrifices his sight for her benefit. Their compromise benefits the whole of society.

Some brief comments about the authors' presentations of animals form an appropriate coda to this chapter. Mite, the grey lynx who appears in "The Prodigal Daughter," symbolizes its crux: women's strength and mutual cooperation. Animals play a similar role in the other works of contemporary feminist speculative fiction I have discussed: Menolly's fire lizards represent her artistic success; horses are responsible for the presence of the Motherline tribes; Sorren's close relationship with Kedera is signaled by the growling of a dog. Mite, Unise's parting gift to Arlburrow when she first leaves Castle Green, pads through the story. The animal is a feline doppelgänger of Unise and Jonathon. For example, Salmonson provides a "lynx-like" description of them: "'What a strapping strong thing [Unise] you are!' The livery woman had landed with feline grace" (Salmonson, 125). Like these characters, like real women, the lynx "had grown tremendously" (Salmonson, 122). Such growth causes women's refusal to act like, in Jonathon's words, "some king's poor catamite" (Salmonson, 126). (Because the lynx is named Mite, "catamite" textually emphasizes the animal's presence.) Mite points to those women who are not content to be "mites"—infinitesimal parasites, small entities of small value—in society.

Mite participates in the battle with Hophaetus: "The cat's hackles raised from neck to haunches, back arched high: he spat and snarled at the evil killer. . . . Mite meowed monstrously" (Salmonson, 147–48). No purring domestic house cat here, nor are Jonathon and Unise purring domestic housewives who treat each other—and other women—in a catlike manner. In "The Prodigal Daughter," "cat," whose derogatory meaning is never directed at men, connotes the positive in reference to women. Like Mite, Unise and Jonathon are the possessors of beauty and grace—and deadly force. The presence of these female characters in feminist speculative fiction bodes well for their existence in feminists' reality.

NOTES

1. Lakoff says, "The point . . . is that unless we start feeling more respect for women, and at the same time, less uncomfortable about them and their roles in society in relation to men, we cannot avoid *lady* any more than we can avoid *broads*. For at least some speakers, the more demeaning the job, the more the person holding it . . . is likely to be described as a *lady*. Lady carries with it overtones recalling the age of chivalry. . . . This makes the term seem polite at first but we must also remember that these implications are perilous: they suggest that a 'lady' is helpless and cannot do things for herself" (Lakoff, 21, 23, 25).

2. Harlan Ellison coined the term "dangerous visions."

WORKS CITED

Bernikow, Louise. *Among Women*. New York: Harper and Row, 1980.

Charnas, Suzy McKee. *Motherlines*. New York: Berkley, 1978.

Lakoff, Robin. *Language and Woman's Place*. New York: Harper and Row, 1975.

Le Guin, Ursula K. *The Left Hand of Darkness*. New York: Ace Books, 1969.

Lynn, Elizabeth A. *The Northern Girl*. New York: Berkley, 1980.

McCaffrey, Anne. *Dragonsong*. New York: Atheneum, 1976.

Russ, Joanna. "Recent Feminist Utopias." In *Future Females: A Critical Anthology*, edited by Marleen S. Barr, 71–85. Bowling Green, Ohio: Bowling Green State University Popular Press, 1981.

Salmonson, Jessica Amanda. "The Prodigal Daughter." In *Elsewhere*, edited by Terri Windling and Mark Allen Arnold, 119–50. New York: Ace Books, 1981.

5

SCIENCE

FICTION'S

INVISIBLE

FEMALE

MEN

I am an invisible man. No, I am not a spook like those who haunted Edgar Allan Poe; nor am I one of your Hollywood-movie ectoplasms. I am a man of substance, of flesh and bone, fiber and liquids—and I might even be said to possess a mind. I am invisible, understand, simply because people refuse to see me. Like the bodiless heads you sometimes see in circus sideshows, it is as though I have been surrounded by mirrors of hard, distorting glass. When they approach me they see only my surroundings, themselves, or figments of their imagination—indeed, everything and anything except me.

—Ralph Ellison, Invisible Man

The two feminist science fiction stories I wish to discuss in this chapter concern protagonists of substance whose presence is distorted or made invisible because people refuse to see properly. The invisible man in Joanna Russ's "When It Changed" and James Tiptree's "The Women Men Don't See," however, cannot be categorized under the umbrella definition of the word *man*. In *The Female Man*, Russ challenges the supposition that *man* includes all human beings by arguing that *man* and *mankind* are improper synonyms for *person* and *human*. Joanna, one of Russ's protagonists, neatly explains:

"If we are all mankind, it follows to my interested and righteous and right now very bright and beady little eyes, that I too am a Man and not at all a woman, for honestly now, who ever heard of cave Woman and existential Woman. . . . I think I am a Man; I think you will . . . employ me as a Man and recognize child-rearing as a Man's business. . . . I *am man*. . . . Listen to the female man.

"If you don't, by God and all the saints, *I'll break your neck*" (Russ, *Female Man*, 140).

According to Joanna's terms, Janet, the narrator of "When It Changed" (which shares this narrator as well as its setting on the planet Whileaway with *The Female Man*), and Ruth Parsons, the protagonist of "The Women Men Don't See," are both female men. In this chapter I explore the worlds these female men inhabit. I illustrate how Russ and Tiptree create new feminist versions of old science fiction plot formulas, and I explain how they manipulate words to convey patriarchy's distortion of their female characters (and real women), how patriarchy routinely transforms women of substance into invisible female men.

Both stories open with the purposeful presentation of invisible women. When Tiptree's narrator, Don Fenton, first encounters Ruth Parsons and her daughter, Althea, he sees "a double female blur" (Tiptree, 176–77). Althea is individually described as "the near blur" (Tiptree, 177). Why does a feminist story open with a male narrator's description of two female blurs? Tiptree uses Fenton's male perspective to exemplify how men routinely erase individual women. Just to be fair, however, Tiptree admits that sometimes men do choose to see women quite clearly: "I [Fenton] see the girl [Althea] has what could be an attractive body" (Tiptree, 178). In order to be seen, a woman must be attractive.

Instead of creating a male narrator, Russ, in "When It Changed," chooses to distort the facts of women's lives by playing with our definition of specific words. She uses language to poke fun at immediate cultural responses. For example, when she begins the story with a description of an unnamed narrator's "wife" (Russ, "When It Changed," 227; unless otherwise indicated, all subsequent Russ citations refer to "When It Changed"), she wishes readers to assume that the narrator is male. She wishes readers to assume that the following sentence alludes to a divorce: "Katy [Janet's wife] and I [Janet] have three children between us, one of hers and two of mine" (Russ, 228). These conclusions are harmless enough, but not so for readers' mental picture of Janet's eldest child, who "dreams of love and war: running away to sea, hunting" (Russ, 228). Upon learning that these dreams are accomplished by someone called "she," readers are abruptly plunged into the world of Whileaway. That single personal pronoun signals that readers have a false view of the story's beginning, that they have fallen into Russ's prearranged linguistic trap. The glaringly inappropriate use of "she" announces that on Whileaway women have wives.

Like readers of both sexes, the male characters in Russ's story view the women of Whileaway in terms of figments of their imaginations. Even though these men take pains to emphasize the reestablishment of sexual equality on earth, they still insist on falsely viewing Janet and Katy according to patriarchal conceptions of proper power relationships: *"Which of you plays the role of the man?* As if we had to produce a carbon copy of their mistakes! I [Janet] doubt very much that sexual equality has been reestablished on Earth" (Russ, 238). These women—women who live in a society that does not include men—are expected to behave as if men are present. According to the male astronauts from earth, their special status as independent female men is unimportant and unseen.

Ruth's and Althea's special characteristics are also irrelevant to Don. Don, accompanied by women who are willing to move beyond earth's boundaries, cannot move beyond the boundaries of his male ego. He insists on falsely defining and seeing the Parsons women. For example, he would like to have sex with Ruth's body even though he does not know or care about *her*. "The woman doesn't mean one thing to me, but . . . the defiance of her little rump eight inches from my fly—for two pesos I'd have those shorts down and introduce myself" (Tiptree, 191). Ruth has designs on voyaging to the stars; Don speculates, "I wonder if Mrs. Parsons has designs on me" (Tiptree, 198).

When Don denies Ruth's agenda and her humanity, he acts according to a fundamental principle of our world: men are people and women are the Other, the invisible mistress, helpmate, wife, mother. Russ exemplifies this situation through the use of humor. Soon after arriving on a planet populated by women, the male astronaut asks, "Where are all your people?" (Russ, 231). When he looks at the inhabitants of Whileaway, he sees mere women, not people. Similarly, Don does not see Ruth as a person when he first meets her. In addition to treating her as a sex object, he believes he knows her because she can be defined as one of the army of faceless female government clerical workers: "Of course, I know her now, all the Mrs. Parsonses in records, divisions, accounting sections, research branches, personnel and administrative offices" (Tiptree, 185). Yet, in Don's eyes, Ruth can be separated from this female herd. He believes that she deserves to be seen because she is not ugly and not old: "Who was that woman . . . who coped with my perdiem for years? . . . But dammit, Ruth is a lot younger and better looking. Comparatively speaking" (Tiptree, 197). This differentiation is temporary. All women face growing old—invisible, separate, Other.

Tiptree, like Russ, also uses humor to exemplify the distinction between *women* and *people*. She seems to say, Okay, if women aren't people, we should call them something else. So she invents science fiction's invisible female human opossum: "Think of us [women] as oppossums, [*sic*] Don [says Ruth]. Did you know there are oppossums living all over. Even in New York City?" (Tiptree, 205). In the manner of opossum, women must somehow survive by inhabiting unseen places within man's world: "What women do is survive. We live by ones and twos in the chinks of your world-machine"[1] (Tiptree, 205). It is sobering to realize that even though Whileaway is not a part of our world-machine, it too is yet another such chink.

Regardless of Janet's and Katy's independence, achievements, and good life—their substance—when men come to Whileaway Ruth's following words are applicable to its feminist utopian society: "Women have no rights, Don, except what men allow us. Men are more aggressive and powerful and they run the world. When the next real crisis upsets them, our so-called rights will vanish. . . .

We'll be back where we always were: property" (Tiptree, 204). Janet is aware of the consequences of men's aggression and power, the truth of Ruth's statement: "Men are coming to Whileaway. When one culture has the big guns and the other has none, there is a certain predictability about the outcome. . . . I will remember all my life those people [Earth men] I first met who were muscled like bulls and who made me—if only for a moment—feel small" (Russ, 237). The men Janet describes are dangerous invading enemies. When men come to Whileaway, the rights of female men vanish. Earth men define residents of Whileaway as adjacent, aberrant, not quite fully human—something Other than *man* and *people*. Janet realizes that her achievements will be distorted and that she will soon be analogous to a circus sideshow: "And I'm afraid that my own achievements will dwindle from what they were—to the not-very-interesting curios of the human race, the oddities you read about in the back of the book, things to laugh at sometimes because they are so exotic[,] . . . charming but not useful. I find this more painful than I can say" (Russ, 238). I find the possibility of Janet—a proud, independent woman of achievement—becoming something freakish to be more painful than I can say.

I also find it painful to realize that "When It Changed" and "The Women Men Don't See" insist that women live better without men. Ruth does not reside with a man, and she gave birth out of wedlock. "There isn't any Mr. Parsons, Don. There never was" (Tiptree, 201–2). Her independence proves to be insufficient. Although her personal life does not include men, she is still desperate to escape from patriarchy. Her frantic attitude is justified because, despite her solitary, self-supporting existence, she is still not free. Don is even threatened by the amount of freedom she does possess: "A mad image blooms in my mind: generations of solitary Parsons women selecting sires, making impregnation trips" (Tiptree, 202). An even madder image bloomed in Russ's mind: generations of women who exist without men, who marry and give birth, and who live perfectly complete lives. "I miss nothing," says Katy (Russ, 235). Janet's daughter's reaction is less controlled. Her response after being asked whether she could fall in love with a man: "With a ten-foot toad!" (Russ, 238).

This child does not think that men are a part of her species. Further, according to her elders, men are rather analogous to rancid tuna fish salad: "They [men] are obviously of our species but *off*, indescribably off, and as my [Janet's] eyes could not and still cannot quite comprehend the lines of those alien bodies, I could not, then, bring myself to touch them. . . . I could only say they were apes with human faces" (Russ, 230). The word "alien" is all-important here. Russ revives the grand cliché of science fiction plot formulas, the alien encounter. Her feminist version of the alien encounter tale gives new meaning to common words. When human males are aliens in a feminist community, according to the residents of that community, females are defined as people and males become the Other.

Like Janet, Ruth also sees males as aliens, and like Russ, Tiptree uses the old alien encounter plot formula to make a new feminist point. When the spaceship lands, Don panics while Ruth remains calm: " 'For Christ's sake, Ruth, they're *aliens!*' " " 'I'm used to it,' she says absently" (Tiptree, 213). Ruth has been living with aliens throughout her life. For Ruth, males are aliens, and extraterrestrials are a source of salvation. Hence, according to Russ's and Tiptree's feminist version of the alien encounter, human males are the bug-eyed monsters. This is a fair fantastic reaction to our reality that routinely defines women as different, as the Other—as aliens.

Through the use of a new version of a worn plot formula, Russ and Tiptree turn the tables on language and create a fantastic situation where it is appropriate to define males, not females, as the Other. In terms of the title of Robin Lakoff's book, they toy with our conceptions of language and women's place. Here is another example of Russ's response to sexist language: " 'Man' is a rhetorical convenience for 'human.' 'Man' includes 'woman.' Thus: 1. The eternal feminine leads us ever upward and on (Guess who us is)" (Russ, *Female Man*, 93).

Russ's ideas encourage a new reading of Tiptree's title. Since "men" does not really include "women," "The Women Men Don't See" can be read as "The Subhumans People Don't See." This title more explicitly points to the crippling impact of sexist language and patriarchy. On one level, Tiptree's story tells us that the women men don't see are those women who do not appear to be good sex objects. When the title is read in Russ's more direct terms, it announces the deeper meaning of the story: the difference between "women" and "people," the existence of invisible female men.

In Janet's society, men's superiority, their hegemony over all aspects of life, is irrelevant—"For-A-While" (Russ, 239). "When It Changed" takes place during a moment when men are absent and women are visible. How does its title reflect this fantastic occurrence? Does "When It Changed" refer to the time when men on Whileaway were killed by disease or to the time when men returned to Whileaway in the role of a disease that will infest a healthy society? Since the story does not specify which of these two interpretations is correct, I offer a third. I think "it" refers to the time when the universal masculine personal pronoun became an anachronism. Janet's following comment hints that "it" refers to language: "*He* turned *his* head—those words have not been in our language for six hundred years" (Russ, 230). The definition of "woman" changes in Russ's story. "It" refers to the temporary time when "woman" became a rhetorical convenience for "human." Sadly, after the men arrive, the people of Whileaway again become invisible female men. "He" will again supposedly include "she."

Ruth and Janet wish to be defined as people, to be seen correctly and clearly. They strive to be female men instead of invisible women. Don fails to understand why Ruth believes that an unknown world could be better than earth: "How could a woman choose to live among unknown monsters, to say good-bye to her home, her world?" (Tiptree, 217). A feminist would answer his question with another question: How could a woman fail to take advantage of the opportunity to leave a world dominated by those who call her the Other, a world that is not her own? Ruth and Althea are not doing something that has not been done before. After all, Europeans who desperately desired to escape oppression entered ships bound for a new world. The Parsons women are journeying toward an unknown world that might possibly be a new nonsexist United States. They are attempting to create their own Whileaway. They hope the new world they encounter will be more effective than Whileaway. More specifically, if future "generations of solitary Parsons women" (Tiptree, 202) succeed in living decently and well away from earth, unlike Janet and her fellows, may they manage to avoid an alien encounter with earth men.

These stories do not give a positive account of relationships between women and men. They tell us that, under patriarchy, women of substance become analogous to opossum. Reality is more sobering than the texts, however. Real women cannot leave earth permanently. Whileaway does not exist for them. Real women have but one alternative: they must remain and fight to widen their particular chink in the male world-machine. They must remain and struggle to be seen.

NOTE

1. Tiptree's phrase "in the chinks of your world-machine" has resonated for critics of feminist science fiction. Sarah Lefanu named her book *In the Chinks of the World Machine: Feminism and Science Fiction* (London: Women's Press, 1988; Bloomington: Indiana University Press, 1989). Anne Cranny-Francis ended *Feminist Fiction Feminist Uses of Generic Fiction* (New York: St. Martin's Press, 1990) by citing the phrase.

WORKS CITED

Ellison, Ralph. *Invisible Man*. New York: Random House, 1947.

Lakoff, Robin. *Language and Woman's Place*. New York: Harper and Row, 1975.

Russ, Joanna. *The Female Man*. 1975. Reprint. New York: Gregg Press, 1977.

————. "When It Changed." In *The New Women of Wonder: Recent Science Fiction Stories by Women about Women*, edited by Pamela Sargent, 227–39. New York: Vintage, 1977.

Tiptree, James. "The Women Men Don't See." In *The New Women of Wonder: Recent Science Fiction Stories by Women about Women*, edited by Pamela Sargent, 176–217. New York: Vintage, 1977.

6

MARGE PIERCY,

THOMAS BERGER,

AND THE END OF

MASCULINITY

MEN IN

FEMINIST

SCIENCE

FICTION

*Men, some men, now— and perhaps by way
of repeating an age-old habit—are entering
feminism, actively penetrating it (whatever "it"
might be, either before or after this intervention),
for a variety of motives and in a variety of
modes, fashions. . . . Perhaps the question that
needs to be asked, then, by these men, with
them, for them, is to what extent their irruption
(penetration and interruption) is justified? is it
of any political use to feminism? to what extent
is it wanted?*

—Paul Smith, "Men in Feminism:

Men and Feminist Theory"

Literary gender war is not new. Jane Tompkins describes the battle between women's nineteenth-century domestic novels and men's Westerns:

> This point for point contrast between a major popular form of the twentieth century and the major popular form of the nineteenth is not accidental. The Western *answers* the domestic novel. . . . And so, just as the women's novels which captured the literary marketplace at mid-century had privileged the female realm of spiritual power, inward struggle, homosociality, and sacramental household ritual, Westerns, in a reaction that looks very much like a literary gender war, privilege the male realm of public power, physical ordeal, homosociality, and the rituals of the duel. (Tompkins, 371, 374)

The war Tompkins describes rages in science fiction. Feminist utopias answer male-authored sex-role-reversal novels—and discussions of men in feminist theory can contribute to this bellicose conversation. In "*Amor Vincit Foeminam*: The Battle of the Sexes in Science Fiction," Joanna Russ responds to men's sex-role-reversal fictions by declaring postmodern generic gender war. Russ's article and Alice Jardine and Paul Smith's *Men in Feminism* proclaim an announcement pertinent to both feminist science fiction and feminist theory: the men are coming! the men are coming!

Jardine and Smith's acquiescent tone is not at all a part of Russ's response, however. She is combative and dismissive toward male-authored sex-role-reversal fictions, the works she calls flasher novels: "The male ignorance betrayed by such fiction is appalling; the male wishes embodied in them are little short of soul-killing. But consider the title I almost used . . . : *The Triumph of the Flasher* (Russ, "*Amor*," 13). After considering Russ's comments in light of Paul Smith's and Stephen Heath's contributions to *Men in Feminism*, I conclude that Russ too hastily chastises flasher novels. These novels can be read as men's attempts at flashes of feminist insight rather than as ignorant invasions of the territory of feminist science fiction. In other words, when Smith states that men's involvement with feminism "is often looked upon with suspicion: it can be understood as yet another interruption, a more or less illegal act of breaking and entering . . . for which these men must finally be held to account," he addresses Russ's response to flasher novels. In the epigraph to this chapter, he asks questions that can serve as alternatives for Russ's hostility.

I pose similar questions through a reading of a flasher novel, Thomas Berger's *Regiment of Women*, in terms of a feminist utopia, Marge Piercy's *Woman on the Edge of Time*. Although much inferior to *Woman on the Edge*, *Regiment* shares a great deal in common with this feminist utopia and is really not all that negative. A point by point contrast between the two novels reveals that a female feminist author and a male author (a male who would not exist in some feminist utopias) both use science fiction to explore the real world's gender-related cultural problems. I argue that rather than being viewed as the despised penetrators of science fiction's feminist sanctum, Berger and his fellow creators of flasher novels might be welcomed by science fiction's feminist readers.

After all, the science fiction flashers do follow Smith's suggestions for men who wish to engage with feminism: they "undertake to write and speak as if they were women . . . [and] mime the feminist theoretical effort of undermining the male economy" (Smith, 37). Men who use the science fiction sex-role-reversal convention necessarily view the world from female perspectives and confront questions raised by feminist science fiction and feminist theory. Men in feminist science fiction are useful; the genre's female and male feminists both posit alternatives to patriarchy—the end of masculinity.

A FLASHBACK TO THE GENERIC BATTLEGROUND

Science fiction's gender war is being waged between individual tales as well as between the tales' individual characters. On one side of the OK Corral stands the subject of Russ's article, the sex-role-reversal stories about powerless men. Feminist utopias stand on the other side as they form a rebuttal to male flashers' powerful—but inept—women and downtrodden men who always win in the end. For example, Suzy McKee Charnas's *Motherlines*, Joanna Russ's *The Female Man*, and James Tiptree's "Houston, Houston, Do You Read?" present feminist utopian worlds that exclude men. Although these feminist works are, of course, much more complex than the flasher sex-role-reversal tales, they fail to answer a question important to women who are not separatists: how do men and women live together with dignity and equality? In fact, some feminists may find that the all-female utopias have little to say to them.[1]

Although the all-female feminist utopias certainly are useful, in order to interest readers who insist on reality, their creators may have to move a little closer to earth. Marge Piercy is one writer who has done so. As I point out in chapter 3, instead of eradicating men, *Woman on the Edge* changes them. Men in Mattapoisett—like men in Berger's Manhattan—have bodies and attitudes that differ from those of real, contemporary men. In Mattapoisett, men mother babies who have been gestated within machines; in Berger's Manhattan, men assume the social constructions reserved for women and become new-gendered beings. Piercy and Berger change human biology (and these are possible changes) by attaching breasts to men and embryos to machines. Piercy's feminist utopia does not exclude men; Berger's flasher novel does not exclude feminism. Georgie Cornell, Berger's protagonist, is a feminist who could be at home in Mattapoisett.

Both novels articulate "the real point at which change must come[,] . . . the end of 'masculinity'—which, of course, is the end of 'woman' too" (Heath, 5). The male mothers in *Woman on the Edge* and the male feminists in *Regiment* reflect changes signaling the end of gender roles—the end of marginalized women and the end of masculinity.

REPRODUCTION ON THE EDGE OF CHANGE

When Berger creates Georgie's world, he adheres to Heath's criteria regarding the most any man can do to engage feminism. *Regiment* reveals its author's desire "to learn and so to try to write or talk or act in response to feminism, and so to try not in any way to be anti-feminist, supportive of the old oppressive structures" (Heath, 9). Although *Regiment* is far from a flawlessly feminist work, the gender role reversals Berger imagines certainly show his mastery of what Heath suggests men learn from feminism: "One of the things men learn from feminism is that women have had enough of being marginal, marginalized: patriarchal society is about marginalization, keeping women out or on the edges of its economy, its institutions, its decisions" (Heath, 24). Berger is sensitive to the marginal woman's plight; Georgie has certainly had enough of being marginalized.

Georgie experiences the marginalized position usually reserved for women because he, like male residents of Mattapoisett, inhabits a society characterized by the end of men's masculinity. In Piercy's and Berger's novels, women no longer have to give birth and, if they so desire, men can burn their bras. Georgie acquires silicone breast implants because they are fashionable. Like some real women, he spends money and experiences pain to please the opposite sex: "Not only had the silicone injections cost him a pretty penny; the operation had been much more painful than promised; surely taking them [silicone breasts] off would be even less pleasant" (Berger, 128). His breasts, which do not have a natural function, are degrading fashion accessories. Stanley, a male liberation movement member, explains this degradation to Georgie while they are both in the Manhattan movement headquarters: "When women produced young, the mammary glands were functional, secreting milk. Is it not degrading, now that tits are useless, that we are the sex who wears them?" (Berger, 128–29). Men's breast implants exemplify how the novel's fantastic role reversals emphasize real sexist attitudes.

In contrast to Georgie's useless breasts, as I mention in chapter 3, men in Mattapoisett have breasts that are quite functional. Connie Ramos, Piercy's protagonist, is appalled when she learns about male nursing mothers: "She felt angry. Yes, how dare any man share that pleasure. These women thought they had won, but they had abandoned to men the last refuge of women. . . . They had let men steal from them the last remnants of ancient power, those sealed in blood and in milk. . . . She could almost hate him [Barbarossa] in the peaceful joy to which he had no natural right; she could almost like him as he opened like a daisy to the baby's sucking mouth" (Piercy, 134–35). Despite Connie's—and our own—immediate adverse reaction to a nursing male, Barbarossa's ability is a possible future alternative to present sex roles. The end of masculinity has been constructed in Mattapoisett; the end of masculinity is a potentially constructive aspect of our reality.

Georgie is also "milked"; but his version of the end of masculinity is not positive, and his milk is not extracted from his breasts. Men in his Manhattan, a society that labels "normal" heterosexual intercourse a criminal act, fulfill their reproductive function in a very mechanistic fashion. Like so many cows, they are herded to hosed sperm-collecting apparatuses that force them to ejaculate. The men's bodies, then, are literally controlled by machines.

A mandatory sperm service where the delicate sensibilities of men are jolted by forced ejaculation in a "laboratory full of machines attended by women in white uniforms" (Berger, 198) is really quite humorous. Not so for Connie's experience of becoming analogous to a machine: "How could anyone know what being a mother means who has never . . . borne a baby in blood and pain, who has never suckled a child. Who got that child from a machine the way that couple, white and rich, got my flesh and blood. All made up already, a canned child, just add money. What do they know of motherhood?" (Piercy, 106). Georgie's sperm is appropriated against his will; Connie's child is appropriated against her will.

In our society, women's reproductive role sometimes becomes analogous to a biological machine whose product can be purchased. This fact helps to make the fantastic baby-making machines in *Woman on the Edge* and *Regiment* appear to be more positive. In Georgie's world, birth has nothing to do with a woman's body. Watching a new life emerge is analogous to visiting a General Motors factory: "From a glass-enclosed balcony he [Georgie] and the visitors, all male, looked down on the ranks of stainless-steel incubating tanks. . . . A high spot of the tour had been the actual delivery of a baby. A technician checked the dials, threw a lever, opened a glass porthole of the type found in front-loading washers, and slid out a newborn child. Then she snipped off the plastic umbilicus that attached it to the tray" (Piercy, 245). Residents of Mattapoisett would believe that this cut-and-dried procedure is a necessary and liberating sacrifice.

Luciente, Connie's link to Mattapoisett, explains that when women no longer give birth, when everyone—males as well as females—can become mothers, women enjoy equal relationships with warm, nurturing men (Piercy, 105). Hence, in Mattapoisett, as in Georgie's world, *mother* does not necessarily signify *female*. *Birth* becomes synonymous with *machine*: "He [Bee] pressed a panel and a door slid aside revealing seven human babies joggling slowly upside down, each in a sac of its own inside a larger fluid receptacle. Connie gaped, her stomach also turning slowly upside down. All in a sluggish row, babies bobbed. Mother the machine" (Piercy, 102). "Mother the machine" is a good alternative to "woman the machine." The latter phrase is also a good alternative to Connie's "blood and pain." She—and readers—can be reassured because although *birth* means *machine* in Mattapoisett, *nurture* does not mean *nonhuman*. Luciente explains: "Everyone raises the kids. . . . Romance, sex, birth, children . . . isn't women's business anymore. It's everybody's" (Piercy, 251). While Berger fails to explain exactly who raises children, Piercy creates an elaborate ritual where three "mothers" publicly express their desire to accept and raise a child. One particular baby is mothered by an elderly woman, a lactating male, and Connie—a woman who cannot give birth (Piercy, 250). As more men realize that they should be responsible for more mothering, society will slowly move toward realizing Piercy's feminist utopian vision.

Mother the machine is a useful feminist version of the biological manipulation that is already a routine method to ensure social control. Berger and Piercy reflect upon oppressive uses of changed human biology. Men in *Regiment* fear that they will be castrated by those in power; Connie and her fellow inmates in the mental hospital fear that they will be lobotomized by those in power. Those in power do perform castrations and lobotomies. The potentially frightening specter of the fictitious—and liberating—baby-making machine pales beside the truth of existing brutal biological manipulation.

PEOPLE AS REGIMENTED AS ANIMALS

Aviva Cantor, another feminist voice, enters this section's discussion of the link between exploiting women, minority groups, and animals. In her article in a popular feminist magazine, Cantor points out that vivisection and hunting trains men to act as oppressors: "Hunting animals for sport is a training ground for callousness, cruelty, and insensitivity: it teaches men not to feel anything when they kill or maim a living creature" (Cantor, 27). Such training might have made the power to castrate and lobotomize more acceptable to the novels' respective female and male psychiatrist-villains, Berger's Doctor Prine and Piercy's Doctor Redding. Cantor explains that doctors have the power biologically to alter patients because of a system analogous to patriarchy's oppression of animals:

Nowhere is patriarchy's iron fist as naked as in the oppression of animals, which serves as the model and training ground for all the other forms of oppression.

Its three basic strategies—the club, the yoke, and the leash—operate similarly in the oppression of women and minorities. The club strategy is to kill animals for gain. . . . It is domination through brute force. The yoke strategy is to domesticate animals to carry burdens. . . . It is domination through enslavement. The leash strategy is to tame animals to provide the psychic benefits of direct rule of master over pet. It is domination through deceit. (Cantor, 27)

The biological oppression suffered by Connie and Georgie can be understood in terms of Cantor's three categories.

A doctor maims Connie to practice hysterectomies. Another doctor imprisons Connie to practice a new brain electrode implantation procedure. Doctor Prine sexually abuses Georgie because she believes men should experience orgasm when women rape them with dildos. She rapes him, violates him in terms of the club strategy: "Another example of the club strategy of brute male power applied to human females is, of course, rape. Rape . . . strikingly resembles hunting" (Cantor, 27).[2] Both Georgie and Connie suffer from a form of the yoke. Cantor explains: "Enclosing animals as prisoners in fenced-off areas led to the eventual loss of their survival skills. Limitation of movement produced similar results for the domestication of women" (Cantor, 28). Connie is enclosed within her brother's house and within the mental hospital. After she manages to escape, like a stray dog, she is not equipped to survive in the outside world.

In addition to being imprisoned in a sperm-collection facility, Georgie experiences limited freedom of movement on dark Manhattan streets. Further, he is "leashed" and treated as a pet when he becomes the "mattress" (read "mistress") of an older female artist. Women of color, like Connie, however, are usually not treated as "the pet-woman" by patriarchy. She does not have a male master to be her "provider, protector, rescuer." Rather, Connie and her fellow inmates receive treatment analogous to Cantor's description of obedience training: "The pet . . . requires obedience training in order to be responsive to *individual* owners. One of the thrills of being a pet owner is to show off 'tricks'" (Cantor, 29). Connie watches a patient who has undergone an electrode brain implantation perform "tricks" according to a doctor's commands. Doctor Redding explains the procedure: " 'We can electrically trigger almost every mood and emotion. . . . We can monitor and induce reactions through the microminiaturized radio under the skull. . . . That concludes our little preview demonstration' " (Piercy, 204). Connie, whose body has been used as a reproductive machine, faces the possibility of having a similar electrode implanted within her head.

She visits an alternative to Mattapoisett (the home of Gildina, a character I discuss in chapter 3) that is a direct outgrowth of such casual abuses of individual patients' bodies. People in this second future are literally analogous to experimental animals: " 'It's not like they're people. They're diseased, all of them, just walking organ banks[,] . . . and even half the time the liver's rotten. . . . Some are pithed for simple functions, but they live like animals' " (Piercy, 291). In contrast, people in Mattapoisett respect animals and communicate with them through sign language (Piercy, 99). Harriet, who eventually becomes Georgie's lover, shares this respect. She realizes that vivisection leads to the biological alteration of people. She understands the relationship between degrading animals and degrading women: " 'You know why even a lot of women who have no objection to fishing disapprove of hunting? . . . We don't like to kill animals, . . . because they remind us of ourselves' " (Berger, 335).

JUGGLING GENDER IN MANHATTAN AND MATTAPOISETT—AND IN FEMINIST THEORY

Georgie and Connie at once reflect aspects of female marginalization and inhabit different feminist spaces. Connie, whose experiences coincide with those of real, disadvantaged minority women, is a part of feminist practice; Georgie, whose position as a literal feminized man is as yet possible only within the pages of science fiction, is a part of feminist theory. Georgie is a female impersonator who shares much in common with Stephen Heath's notion of a male theorist who reads as a feminist: "There *is* a female impersonation in a man reading as a feminist" (Heath, 28).

Georgie, Berger, and male feminist theorists all act as female impersonators. When Berger creates a fictitious female impersonator, he functions as an imperfect feminist reader, as Heath's male theorist reading as a feminist. Georgie's role as the fictive incarnation of a male feminist reader is more crucial than his role as an imperfect feminist woman. This character illustrates that male feminists are doomed to remain outside the female feminist perspective. Like the men in feminist theory, the men in feminist science fiction are outside, Other, alien. They impersonate women experiencing patriarchy.

Paul Smith articulates the role reversal he shares with Berger and Georgie, the role of a subordinate male engaging dominant female discourse: "We're [men in feminism] not able to do quite the right thing. Even the fact that I'm perceived as understanding feminist theory . . . proves 'difficult' for this female feminist [Jardine] because, finally, I do not have the right intonation and syntax. I don't have the native accent; I'm an alien" (Smith, 36). Georgie, in Smith's terms, is analogous to a real male theorist entering feminism, not to a real woman. Further, according to Smith's terms, Russ's hostility toward flasher novels is an example of a female feminist's difficulty accepting a male feminist. Russ defends feminist science fiction from being penetrated by a voice with the wrong intonation and syntax, the voice of the male feminist alien. Again, as men "in" feminism, Georgie, Smith, and Berger experience gender role reversal when they assume a marginalized position within a discourse system they do not control. Georgie is simultaneously a perfect impersonator of the male feminist as feminist reader and an imperfect impersonator of a female feminist.

Heath and Smith lead me to conclude that flasher novels can be understood best in terms of subordinate male feminism, not in terms of female feminism. Feminist science fiction is most appropriately read in terms of female feminist theory; flasher novels are most appropriately read in terms of male feminist theory. Berger's sex-role-reversal plot provides an occasion for a science fiction text to merge with male feminist theoretical texts: Georgie and male feminist theorists (such as Smith and Heath) speak with one voice. Feminists (such as Russ) should refrain from completely dismissing flasher novels. After all, Berger and his fellow male authors of flasher novels—and male feminist theorists—have voluntarily reversed their customary dominant roles. They have chosen to become subordinate aliens who listen to female feminism. If Berger were given the opportunity to respond to Russ's

"Amor Vincit Foeminam," his comments might resemble Smith's following thoughts about a male feminist's situation: "These feelings, these fears, are in a large part the result of having to engage with a discourse whose laws I can never quite obey. I recognize that such a discourse has its reasons for . . . not taking me in. . . . It seems to me that it could still be useful to have men in feminism" (Smith, 38).

When they choose to venture outside patriarchal discourse, male feminist theorists voluntarily discard dominance. Female feminist theorists, in contrast, are as subordinate as the science fiction genre itself. Ursula Le Guin has discussed "the feminization of science fiction" (Berkley, 2). Because female feminist theorists and the science fiction genre are both marginalized (or feminized), when "men in feminism" is brought to bear upon "women and men in feminist science fiction," gender merges with genre. Voluntary reversal enables male feminist theorists to assume the position shared by both women and science fiction: the feminized, inferior Other. This analogy between men in feminism, feminism, and science fiction is, in the words of Heath, a discussion of "matters of place and . . . exclusion or inclusion, [which] finishes in a series of ironic reversals in which men now occupy the dark continent, are the excluded other" (Heath, 43).

Women assume a dominant position within the realm of feminist discourse; men become the excluded Other in feminist theory and in feminist science fiction. The male feminist—who is welcomed in Piercy's novel and barred from the feminist utopias created by Russ, Tiptree, and Charnas—can be understood according to Russ's female man. A series of ironic reversals allow the male feminist—like Georgie—to become the male woman, the reversal of Russ's female man: "We must listen to the female man" (Russ, *Female Man*, 140); science fiction's feminists should listen to the genre's male women.

FEMINISTS, FLASHERS, AND CHANGED HUMAN BIOLOGY

The act of being reminded of oneself is one reason why flasher novels should be read by feminists. These novels' gender role reversals can help to illuminate patriarchal oppression that is routine and, hence, often invisible. Although Russ justifiably believes that flasher novels contain appalling male ignorance and soul-killing male wishes, I argue that these novels can be useful to feminists. I shall momentarily rely on transactive criticism, my personal response, to explain further why my assertion is true.

Much science fiction has been characterized as male power fantasies. My own response signals that *Regiment* can be called a power fantasy for women. I enjoy entering a world where women have the upper hand. I am drawn to a novel that questions feminine behavior: "How men painted, adorned, and even mutilated themselves—for women?" (Berger, 149). I have wondered about such feminine behavior while viewing the televised graphic details of face-lifts or, more frequently, while noticing pregnant women wearing panty hose during the heat of summer.

I do resent the implication in *Regiment* that women cannot run the world: "The tyranny of women was exceeded only by their inefficiency" (Berger, 175). However, *Regiment* also provides a clear picture of how men use gender as an excuse to deny women power. I sympathize with the fact that Georgie, who becomes a real man in the end, does not want to dominate anyone: " 'I don't want to be a boss,' Cornell shouted. 'Can't you understand? I just don't want to be bossed' " (Berger, 249). This attitude qualifies Georgie to participate in Mattapoisett's shared governmental power. If, in the closing sex scene, he desires to "be boss once in a while" (Berger, 349), well, that's all right. Similarly, it is justifiable for Connie to commit murder. She wants to be the boss once in a while, too. Georgie and Connie speak with and for each other.

Heath could be speaking for Berger:

> So there I am between a male writing as oppression and a male writing as utopia, and still I am . . . a male writing. All I can do is pose each time the question of the sexual positioning of my discourse, of my relations to and in it, my definition as man, and then through it to the practice and reality of men and women, their relations in the world. To do this . . . is, at least, to grasp writing as an involvement in an ethics of sexual difference, which is a start today towards another male writing. . . . We [male theorists] can learn to read as feminists; that is, we can learn women's readings, feminist readings, we can make connections that we never made before, come back critically on our point of departure. (Heath, 26–27)

Regiment is one start toward another male writing. Berger has learned feminist readings; feminists who read *Regiment* with an accepting rather than a rejecting approach make connections with a new male writing that they have never made before.

Russ concludes her article by stating, "Strikingly, no Flasher book I was able to find envisioned a womanless world (or dared to say so); about half the feminist Utopias matter-of-factly excluded men" (Russ, "*Amor*," 14). Those feminist utopias that, like *Woman on the Edge*, include and tolerate both sexes, do not lean on the fantastic to eradicate a fundamental truth of our reality: our world consists of both feminists and flashers—and the potential for biological change that will alter gender roles. Women's lives, men's new roles, and feminist fiction and theory authored by women and men must meet the challenges of these differences and changes. Connie's and Georgie's similar experiences exemplify that it is quite unnecessary to continue the literary gender war Tompkins describes. Feminists and flashers can logically ride off into the sunset, the realm of the Western world's penchant for changed human biology and the new social roles resulting from these changes, together.

NOTES

1. Carolyn G. Heilbrun articulates this attitude: "It is the Utopian mode that separates science fiction from the other categories of popular feminist fiction. Russ has brilliantly summarized the features of female Utopias: 'the communal nature of the societies portrayed, the absence of crime, the relative lack of government, and the diffusion of the parental role to the whole society.' These are, indeed, longings from many female hearts, including mine. But I live here, where I must find the language to incarnate these things: whether through weakness of intellect or paucity of imagination, I am not content, nor even able, to dream them" (Heilbrun, 119).

2. In the discussion following Jane Tompkins's presentation of "West of Everything: The Rise of a Male Mass Cultural Genre" (delivered at the Duke University Center for Critical Theory Conference, "Convergence in Crisis: Narratives of the History of Theory," 24–27 Sept. 1987), Tompkins asserted that women who derive power and status through the ability to inflict harm are not necessarily negative. Tompkins explained that the female discourse of love and peace is ignored, that powerful women sometimes have to be evil, that the good woman is powerless. Her argument

supports the idea that Berger's powerful—and evil—women do not have to be seen as antifeminist. She provides an alternative view to the notion of some feminists that powerful women should not act like powerful men. Unlike the good women in Westerns, Berger's evil women have an opportunity to act. Furthermore, the protagonists of some feminist utopias are not always good women. For example, the feminist tribes in *Motherlines* do not always behave peacefully, and the feminist government in Katherine Forrest's *Daughters of a Coral Dawn* is not completely democratic.

WORKS CITED

Berger, Thomas. *Regiment of Women*. New York: Simon and Schuster, 1973.

Berkley, Miriam. "Ursula K. Le Guin." *Publisher's Weekly*, 23 May 1986, 72.

Cantor, Aviva. "The Club, the Yoke and the Leash—What We Can Learn from the Way a Culture Treats Animals." *Ms.*, Aug. 1983, 27–30.

Charnas, Suzy McKee. *Motherlines*. New York: Berkley, 1978.

Forrest, Katherine. *Daughters of a Coral Dawn*. Tallahassee, Fla.: Naiad Press, 1984.

Heath, Stephen. "Male Feminism." In *Men in Feminism*, edited by Alice Jardine and Paul Smith, 1–32. New York: Methuen, 1987.

Heilbrun, Carolyn G. "Why I Don't Read Science Fiction." *Women's Studies International Forum* 7 (1984): 117–19.

Jardine, Alice, and Paul Smith, eds. *Men in Feminism*. New York: Methuen, 1987.

Piercy, Marge. *Woman on the Edge of Time*. New York: Fawcett Crest, 1976.

Russ, Joanna. "*Amor Vincit Foeminam*: The Battle of the Sexes in Science Fiction." *Science-Fiction Studies* 20 (1980): 2–15.

———. *The Female Man*. New York: Gregg Press, 1975.

Smith, Paul. "Men in Feminism: Men and Feminist Theory." In *Men in Feminism*, edited by Alice Jardine and Paul Smith, 33–46. New York: Methuen, 1987.

Tiptree, James. "Houston, Houston, Do You Read?" In *Aurora: Beyond Equality*, edited by Vonda N. McIntyre and Susan Janice Anderson, 36–98. Greenwich, Conn.: Fawcett, 1976.

Tompkins, Jane. "West of Everything." *South Atlantic Quarterly* 86 (1987): 357–77.

7

SUZY MCKEE

CHARNAS,

ZOË FAIRBAIRNS,

KATHERINE MARCUSE,

AND KATE WILHELM

BLUR GENERIC

CONVENTIONS

PREGNANCY
AND POWER
IN FEMINIST
SCIENCE
FICTION

*I would like to believe this is a story I'm telling.
I need to believe it. I must believe it. Those who
can believe that such stories are only stories have
a better chance.*

It isn't a story I'm telling.

*It's also a story I'm telling, in my head,
as I go along.*

—*Margaret Atwood,* The Handmaid's Tale

Discussions of pregnancy and power in feminist science fiction do not adhere to Darko Suvin's well-known definition of science fiction as "a literary genre whose necessary and sufficient conditions are the presence and interaction of estrangement and cognition, and whose main formal device is an imaginative framework alternative to the authors' empirical environment" (Suvin, 7–8). The depictions of reproductive technology in feminist science fiction reflect existing conditions in the authors' empirical environment and, thus, do not satisfy Suvin's requirements. These visions spring from blurred science fiction conventions, the reality of what is presently happening to women on reproductive technology programs. When feminist science fiction turns its attention to reproductive technology, the differences between fiction and fact become indistinct.

Images of reproductive technology found in feminist realistic novels closely resemble their counterparts in feminist science fiction. Here, for example, is the experience of Zelda Harris, the protagonist of Elizabeth Baines's British mainstream novel *The Birth Machine*:

> The machine is measuring, measuring the contractions, the rate at which her womb gathers itself up, gradually retracts. . . .
>
> They decided to do this to her. Lay her out and strap her up and pump a synthetic drug into her blood. . . . They could kill her. She turns back, strains, letting out her breath again, to look at the tube leading from the bottle. . . . Her breath comes . . . and she isn't ready, she isn't in control. The contraction seizes her, a giant hand descending and grabbing round the middle and crushing the life out; she like a rubber doll, helpless. (Baines, 67–68)

Zelda Harris is described as attached to a machine that controls her body. Synthetic drugs delivered by mechanical tubes determine the timing of her pregnancy's final stages. *The Birth Machine* centers on a practice of the medical establishment: inducing labor for the doctors' convenience. Baines thus describes what began in the 1960s when women in labor became increasingly helpless, their bodies controlled by machines and (usually) male doctors. This signaled a future stage of modern technology's cooption of women's reproductive power that is today carried further by such new practices as test tube fertilization and surrogate mothering.

Feminist science fiction writers have responded to this merging of mother and machine, to the mixture of mother's blood and synthetic drug. Some, in the manner of Baines's realistic novel, create texts about women made powerless by the act of giving birth. Others portray all-powerful mothers who are not subjected to technological intervention.[1] In this chapter I discuss the powerless mothers in four works categorized as science fiction: Kate Wilhelm's *Where Late the Sweet Birds Sang*, Suzy McKee Charnas's *Walk to the End of the World*, Katherine Marcuse's "Twenty-first Century Mother," and Zoë Fairbairns's *Benefits*. I juxtapose and compare passages from these works with nonfiction by critics of the new reproductive technologies.

This pairing of imaginative texts with nonfictional texts supports my notion that feminist discussions of reproductive technology blur the usually distinct discourse patterns characterizing feminist science fiction, feminist realistic fiction, and feminist nonfiction. In an environment that includes the reality of woman as birth machine, it becomes increasingly difficult for feminist science fiction writers to address reproductive technology in terms of science fiction; their imaginative frameworks regarding this technology are components of reality rather than alternatives to reality. Hence, when feminist science fiction writers confront reproductive technology, they do not create true science fiction. I argue that (1) because depictions of reproductive technology issues in feminist science fiction are so close to reality, feminist science fiction becomes blurred as a genre when it explores these issues and (2) feminist critics and feminist science fiction writers are raising analogous concerns about reproductive technology that should be heeded. These points are underscored in my concluding remarks about Margaret Atwood's *The Handmaid's Tale*.

THE END OF REPRODUCTIVE FREEDOM IN THE WORLD

In texts where women's anatomy literally becomes women's destiny, basic reproductive freedoms—contraception and abortion, for example—become impossibilities, feminist utopian dreams. Women are reproductive prisoners in Charnas's *Walk to the End of the World* and Wilhelm's *Where Late the Sweet Birds Sang*. They are birth machines whose individuality lacks significance. Reproductive freedom does not exist in the worlds posited by these novels.

Molly, an inhabitant of Wilhelm's postholocaust society, is an incarcerated birth machine. Against her will, she spends over a year in a semiconscious state undergoing conditioning to become a "breeder." Molly is older than her fellow breeders, who were first conditioned when "they had been children, easy to condition into breeding machines who thought it wasn't that bad a life" (Wilhelm, 115). These breeders, who are "given soporifics at bedtime and stimulants at breakfast" and who spread their "legs obligingly when they [doctors] approached with their instruments, with the carefully hoarded sperm" (Wilhelm, 114), are barred from controlling their lives. Like the realistic protagonist Zelda Harris, they address doctors with powerless, uninformed voices: "Yes, Doctor, or No, Doctor" (Wilhelm, 116). Furthermore, both Zelda and Molly become birth machines who do not receive nurses' respect. Molly experiences the following ordeal:

> Four times they had put her in the breeders' hospital ward and installed a constant temperature gauge, and when the temperature was right, Nurse had come in with her tray and said cheerfully, "Let's try again, shall we, Molly?" And obediently Molly had opened her legs and lain still while the sperm was inserted with the shiny, cold instrument. "Now, remember, don't move for awhile," the Nurse said, still cheerful, brisk, and had left her lying unmoving, on the narrow cot. And two hours later she was allowed to dress and leave again. Four times, she thought bitterly. A thing, an object, press this button and this is what comes out, all predictable, on cue. (Wilhelm, 117)

Like many real women, she is victimized by the institutionalized power to deny her the control of her own body.

The novel's vision of the powerless woman becomes even more extreme when the breeders are used as hosts for clones: "We'll use them [breeders] to clone those children who are particularly intelligent. We'll go to implantations of clones using the breeders as hosts to ensure a continuing population of capable adults" (Wilhelm, 187). These breeders are doubly dehumanized. They are powerless sperm receptacles as well as receptacles for clones who are not genetically their own.

In Wilhelm's novel, the individual female breeder's well-being is sacrificed for the benefit of humanity as a whole. Suzy McKee Charnas's *Walk to the End of the World* presents an even more drastic version of this situation. Women in the novel, the "fems," are treated as subhumans who, in order to produce sons, are forced to copulate with men in breeding rooms. The sacrifice of the individual fem to ensure the survival of the species is twofold: her children result from rape and her breast milk is used as the primary ingredient of curdcake, a food source for other fems. Collecting the mothers' milk is an institutionalized ritual. In the same way, as the breeders in Wilhelm's novel automatically open their legs, the fems automatically bare their breasts: "Some of the sleeping fems sat up, reaching for the swaddled cubs beside them or for the clay pitchers kept under their beds. Each of the cubs was put to the breast for a moment only, then handed on to the nearest waking fem who had no cub of her own to start her milk. Some of the fems didn't even open their eyes as they went through the motions of what was obviously a well-established routine. The pitchers, now containing fresh milk, were set on the floor to be picked up by fems who pushed carts down the aisles between the beds" (Charnas, 62).

These near-comatose mothers are inferior to farm animals. Necessity forces them to feed not only on their breast milk, but also on their children and their fellows: "The milk wouldn't be plentiful enough to go around unless it were stretched; and what more nutritious additive than the flesh of dead fems and of fem-cubs who did not survive the milkery?" (Charnas, 64). The fems, whose bodies are used to produce sons, must themselves use their bodies to produce food. They are forced to farm themselves and to harvest the fertile fields of their fellow fems' bodies.

Ghastly as this situation appears, women are farmed in reality. Wilhelm's and Charnas's powerless mothers who become analogous to farm animals certainly exist outside the pages of science fiction. Philosopher Julie Murphy and journalist Genoveffa Corea explain why this is so. Murphy uses the term "egg farming" to designate "the entire scope of patriarchal reproductive techniques that remove our bodies from our . . . lives" (Murphy, 69). In "Egg Farming and Women's Future" she states that reproductive technology causes women's bodies to be used as commodities:

Women are defined in patriarchy as "reproductive bodies." Our bodies are regarded as potential carriers of unborn generations. . . . We are constantly discouraged, forbidden to use our bodies for ourselves. . . .

Reproductive technology, in the service of patriarchy, assumes that women's bodies are fertile fields to be farmed. Women are regarded as commodities with vital products to harvest: eggs. Egg-farming thereby limits female bodies to reproductive bodies, more systematically than ever before. (Murphy, 68–69)

Murphy shows us that the female body used as a commodity is part of our world as well as Charnas's fictional world. The exaggerated patriarchal society in *Walk* forces women to use their bodies as commodities, as nutritional products, as life-sustaining protein. Wilhelm's breeders are not used as a food source. Like the fems, however, the drugged breeders produce offspring who bear no relationship to them. Their bodies are separated from their lives.

Corea's reaction to egg farming technology is more personal than Murphy's response. In her following comments, which also apply to the two science fiction texts, she places herself in the role of a laboratory animal:

I watched a television news show (NBC, 1980). The man interviewed was Dr. Richard Levine, an artificial inseminator of breeder women and founder of Surrogate Parenting Associates of Louisville, Kentucky. The woman was . . . the first of Levine's surrogates.

"That's what I do: make babies," said the man.

"I think of myself as a human incubator," said the woman.

Man is possessing woman's procreative power. She is losing it. She is a thing. She is a vessel for the babies men make. . . .

I read Kathleen Barry's *Female Sexual Slavery* (1979), an account of the traffic in women, and thought: just as man has a perfect right to probe, puncture and irradiate the bodies of laboratory animals, so may he violate the bodies of women. Both women and animals are objects to be bought, seized, used and discarded. . . .

I entered the laboratory. . . . I saw rabbits, mice, rats, monkeys in stainless steel cages. I felt like an imposter. The biologist and the technician spoke to me as though I were one of them. But I was one of the animals. (Corea, 45, 47–48)

The televised conversation Corea heard might have been lifted from the pages of Wilhelm's novel, and her interpretation of the interview coincides with Charnas's and Wilhelm's images of mothers who are reproductive vessels. In both novels, mothers are analogous to laboratory and farm animals.

Murphy and Corea underscore the point that science fiction's catastrophic portrayal of motherhood is neither fictitious nor exaggerated. As Corea so simply and correctly explains, real women are treated like animals. It is possible for us (or our female descendants) to become Wilhelm's and Charnas's characters.

SPURIOUS BENEFITS

Another science fiction work, Katherine Marcuse's "Twenty-first Century Mother," discusses *mother* as birth machine and guinea pig. Marcuse's story mirrors the points raised by Australian psychologist Robyn Rowland: "Ultimately the new reproductive technology will be used for the benefit of men and to the detriment of women. Although technology itself is not always a negative development, the real question has always been—who controls it? Biological technology is in the hands of men" (Rowland, 356). Because Mike, a laboratory technician, secretly adds chemicals to food eaten by his pregnant wife (Marcuse's protagonist Amuri), she loses the ability to control her pregnancy. The chemicals entering Amuri's body without her consent enable her fetus to be taken out of her body and to be sustained by a machine. When Amuri learns that her husband has surreptitiously violated her body, she exclaims, "You've been dosing *me*—same as your monkeys and rabbits!" (Marcuse, 22). Instead of being left to develop in her body, Amuri's fetus is stolen by a man who wishes to use technology to bring it to term. A man's machine, not a woman, is expected to create life.

The story sets woman and nature in opposition to man and machine. Mike believes that machines can provide the best developmental environment for fetuses: "We can set up an artificial environment that *improves* on nature. Because it's fool-proof and under constant automatic control. There's an electroanalyzer in the circuit that gets a continuous feed-back from the detectors in the development tank. It's got 300,000 valves, Amuri. And that many can't go wrong!" (Marcuse, 23). The ideology behind this intervention is that women's bodies are faulty, that men can improve on women's ability to produce life. Men use technology in an attempt to become better than women at giving birth to children.

Amuri refuses to allow patriarchy to coopt her ability to create life. She concludes that if she is no longer defined as mother, the fetus in the machine is no longer defined as child. "No. Not her *son*. Not now. Her *problem*" (Marcuse, 24). She solves the problem. She breaks the mechanical circuits that support the fetus's development. Amuri believes it is correct for her to destroy the potential life that is no longer located within her body: *"But she knew the answer. The only true, human answer, even if it were not the logical one. For she was a mother, not a machine"* (Marcuse, 25).

Amuri concludes that death provides the only true, human answer to the following question: how do women preserve their individual humanity and power in the face of patriarchal biological tyranny? She finds killing her child preferable to colluding with patriarchy and thus regains control as the causer of potential death, rather than as the giver of life. In this text, the end of human life results from the clash between patriarchal technology and feminist biological self-determination. Marcuse creates a woman who derives power from functioning as an equal and opposite force to patriarchal values. She acts in opposition to the image of woman as mother and nurturer. For her, the proper definition of *mother* becomes synonymous with death and destruction.

In *Benefits*, Zoë Fairbairns creates a female character who derives power from opposing patriarchy. Enraged by the government's invasion of the building that houses a feminist community, Marsha, a lesbian feminist, shoots David Laing, the government official who was once her lover. Marsha's action epitomizes the frustration that causes female science fiction characters to view murder as an appropriate offensive weapon against those who wish to separate motherhood from female control. David, who promotes governmental legislation that enforces this separation, is reduced to literal nothingness by the shot from Marsha's gun. The male government official who creates laws detrimental to the interests of mothers is reduced to soundless vapor; the female scream is omnipresent. "She closed her eyes but the pillars of flames that David had become glowed through their lids, vapourising [*sic*] him as he stood. . . . Not a sound from David, not a scream. The screaming she heard was all hers" (Fairbairns, 164–65). Marsha's scream is a warning directed to other women, a warning that has also been articulated by Corea: "Sitting at my typewriter night after night, I see my writing on the new reproductive technologies as a scream of warning to other women" (Corea, 48).

Fairbairns's *Benefits* warns against those who wish to use motherhood to control women socially and to remove motherhood from women's influence. She envisions a government that forces women to become mothers by making motherhood a prerequisite for women's economic survival: "All mothers, regardless of race, marital status or domestic competence would be eligible for the weekly payment, so long as they stayed at home and looked after children under sixteen. . . . The explosion of job opportunities that would result from the economic upturn and women leaving work, would ensure that no man need be unemployed; Benefit mothers would not need social security or income supplements. . . . Motherhood . . . was not a misfortune to be insured against; it was a national service to be paid for" (Fairbairns, 56). Only mothers can collect "benefits," the one livelihood available to women. As the novel progresses, the government adopts an even more efficient method to wrench control of motherhood from women: artificial technological methods of contraception and conception.

The questions posed by this science fiction text coincide with real-world questions posed about motherhood. For example, Nancy Chodorow's following comments about mothering and economic change are applicable to the economic situation that sets the stage for the benefits Fairbairns's novel describes:

> Contemporary problems in mothering emerge from potential internal contradictions in the family and the social organization of gender. . . . Changes generated from outside the family, particularly in the economy, have sharpened these contradictions.
>
> At present, new strains emerge as women enter the paid labor force while continuing to mother. Women today are expected to be full-time mothers and to work in the paid labor force, are considered unmotherly if they demand day-care centers, greedy and unreasonable if they expect help from husbands, and lazy if they are single mothers who want to receive adequate welfare payments in order to be able to stay home for their children. (Chodorow, 213)

The benefit payments eradicate these strains. This fictitious social welfare plan removes the expectations about mothers who work in the paid labor force by removing their access to the paid labor force. New strains take the place of the old in an economic system that forbids mothers to work outside the home: mothers who receive the benefit are not free to be "unmotherly."

Robyn Rowland's work analyzing scientific attitudes toward motherhood makes it clear that some events described in *Benefits* are indistinguishable from reality. Here, for example, is her description of Nobel laureate William Shockley's view of the relationship between women and reproduction:

> He suggests that all girls be sterilized on entering puberty by an injection of a contraceptive time capsule which seeps contraceptives into the girl until it is time for her to conceive. At marriage she is issued with deci-child certificates, payment of which will enable her to have a doctor remove the capsule. It is replaced when the child is born. If the state deems it desirable that a couple have two children, the appropriate number of certificates would belong to the couple. . . .
>
> And who would control this dystopian bleak future? The state would ultimately have to organize and run things, with particular expertise from medical researchers. . . .
>
> The fact is that *all* women are guinea pigs in this exercise. We have not been included in the decisions about the technology, not asked if we want it. Are we again to collude with patriarchy because our own momentary needs or desires blind us to the social responsibilities we must have to our daughters; to those who come after us and want the experience of natural conception and childbirth? (Rowland, 366–67)

Rowland's description resembles the method used by the government in *Benefits* to control reproduction.

Benefits confronts Rowland's question of whether or not women will cooperate with patriarchy. The resisters Fairbairns portrays, radical feminists as well as women who advocate women's traditional role in the family, are more numerous and vocal than their real counterparts. The novel applauds its female characters who refuse to collude with patriarchy, and as in the story by Marcuse, women who wish to prevent patriarchy from controlling reproduction do so by refusing to be nurturing, life-sustaining mothers.

Fairbairns's feminists fight against the government by going on strike, refusing to nurture children (Fairbairns, 136–37).

Her most vehement outcry against the technological manipulation of motherhood, however, occurs when she imagines that such manipulation becomes responsible for women's inability to reproduce. Like Zelda Harris, Astrid (a mother in *Benefits*), has her labor controlled by a machine: "She was sedated. Wires from the machines sent her body into spasms at intervals. . . . Fluids dripped into tubes, cylinders disgorged their contents into Astrid's supine body" (Fairbairns, 194). Despite the supposed efficiency of such technology, because of the combined effects of contraceptive chemicals and antidotes placed in the water supply, Astrid's baby—and every baby born in Britain—is stillborn. British women become "unsuitable as vehicles for the carrying of unborn children" (Fairbairns, 196). *Benefits* questions removing reproductive control from women by positing the end of women's ability to give birth.

It faults doctors who dismiss women's complaints about contraceptive side effects. Although the novel's doctors refuse to listen to women's complaints about contraceptives, they absolutely cannot deny the fact of babies "being born with deformities so gross as to make some of them unrecognizable as human" (Fairbairns, 196). Feminist theorist Scarlet Pollock comments about what happens when women attempt to discuss contraceptive side effects with their doctors: "Women found that their doctors did not consider their symptoms, even when they were recognised to be side effects[,] as serious because they did not seem to present life-threatening hazards. Thus for the majority of women little attention was paid to their symptoms (Pollock, 149–50).

BLURRING WOMB AND WORD

Such failure to respond adequately to women's descriptions of their symptoms reflects a lack of respect for women's words and experiences—silences women. In Margaret Atwood's *The Handmaid's Tale*—a dystopian future vision in which a few fertile women become "breeders," surrogate mothers—pregnancy also coincides with the silencing of women. Fertile women are forbidden to speak freely, to read, and to write. Atwood's handmaids "learned to whisper without a sound" (Atwood, 4). As she holds her prohibited pen, the narrator (an escaped breeder) comments on her lack of access to powerful words: "The pen between my fingers is sensuous, alive almost, I can feel its power, the power of the words it contains. Pen is envy" (Atwood, 186). The pen between her fingers is impotent. She inhabits a society that juxtaposes sexuality with textuality, a world where the combination of silenced woman and word results in sexual titillation. (The handmaid sexually arouses a man by agreeing to play *Scrabble* with him.) In the future Atwood imagines, women who have the power to become pregnant lose free access to the power of words.

Women who have viable ovaries are condemned to a silenced existence as handmaids. Successful reproduction becomes a handmaid's only official reason for living and her sole permitted means of self-expression. Handmaids are analogous to an indistinct genre, women forced to function as a juxtaposition of the human and the mechanistic. Their bodies become birth machines, reproductive technology composed of female flesh. The dehumanized handmaids result from an extreme version of equating fertility with powerlessness.

Like Wilhelm, Charnas, Fairbairns, and Marcuse, Atwood creates a science fiction text about women's relationship to reproduction that is congruent with the developing reality of new reproductive technologies. As I have argued, the real world is replete with aspects of women's reproductive and sexual roles that could be gleaned from the pages of these writers' fictions. My final example: Atwood's merger of sex, reproduction, and silence is very much a part of popular American culture. Television viewers are sexually titillated nightly by Vanna White, the handmaid hostess of the country's most popular game show, "Wheel of Fortune." Vanna, a sexually potent woman, arouses the audience as she silently turns letters while lacking the power to control those letters. Handmaids are silenced potential mothers who are themselves components of reproductive technology; Vanna is a silenced, unmotherly component of television technology. Her televised image speaks to Atwood's image of the silenced woman-as-reproductive technology. Vanna, a mechanical, wordless woman who reproduces sexist images rather than her ideas, is but one symptom of society's possible transformation into feminist science fiction writers' dystopian vision of women's future.

The writing of women's dystopian science fiction is intimately related to the realities of reproductive technologies and their threat to women's autonomy. The battle between the sexes over the control of women's fertility and, correspondingly, infertility, as represented in these texts, should serve as a warning. These texts are not only stories.

NOTE

1. The following works portray women as powerful mothers: Vonda McIntyre, *Dreamsnake* (New York: Dell, 1978); Joanna Russ, *The Two of Them* (New York: Berkley, 1978); Joanna Russ, *We Who Are about To . . .* (New York: Dell, 1975); Pamela Sargent, *Cloned Lives* (New York: Random House, 1976); Sydney J. Van Scyoc, *Star Mother* (New York: Berkley, 1976); Joan D. Vinge, *The Snow Queen* (New York: Dell, 1980).

WORKS CITED

Atwood, Margaret. *The Handmaid's Tale*. Boston: Houghton Mifflin, 1986.

Baines, Elizabeth. *The Birth Machine*. London: Women's Press, 1983.

Charnas, Suzy McKee. *Walk to the End of the World*. New York: Ballantine, 1974.

Chodorow, Nancy. *The Reproduction of Mothering: Psychoanalysis and the Sociology of Gender*. Berkeley: University of California Press, 1978.

Corea, Genoveffa. "Egg Snatchers." In *Test-Tube Women*, edited by Rita Arditti, Renate Duelli Klein, and Shelley Minden, 37–51. London: Pandora Press, 1984.

Fairbairns, Zoë. *Benefits*. London: Virago Press, 1979.

Marcuse, Katherine. "Twenty-first Century Mother." In *Marriage and the Family through Science Fiction*, edited by Val Clear, Patricia Warrick, Martin Harry Greenberg, and Joseph Olander, 21–25. New York: St. Martin's Press, 1976.

Murphy, Julie. "Egg Farming and Women's Future." In *Test-Tube Women*, edited by Rita Arditti, Renate Duelli Klein, and Shelley Minden, 68–75. London: Pandora Press, 1984.

Pollock, Scarlet. "Refusing to Take Women Seriously." In *Test-Tube Women*, edited by Rita Arditti, Renate Duelli Klein, and Shelley Minden, 138–52. London: Pandora Press, 1984.

Rowland, Robyn. "Reproductive Technologies: The Final Solution to the Women Question." In *Test-Tube Women*, edited by Rita Arditti, Renate Duelli Klein, and Shelley Minden, 356–69. London: Pandora Press, 1984.

Suvin, Darko. *Metamorphoses of Science Fiction: On the Poetics and History of a Literary Genre*. New Haven: Yale University Press, 1979.

"Wheel of Fortune." NBC/CBS/Syndicated. Produced by Nancy Jones, David Williger, and Paul Gilbert. 1975– .

Wilhelm, Kate. *Where Late the Sweet Birds Sang*. New York: Pocket Books, 1974.

After Feminist Fabulation

Space Dust by James Rosenquist
© 1989 by James Rosenquist/Tyler Graphics Ltd.
Photo: Steven Sloman

8

OCTAVIA

BUTLER

AND

JAMES

TIPTREE

DO NOT

WRITE

ABOUT

ZAP GUNS

*Q: But you don't change your nature
by changing your name, surely?
A: Oh yes, you do.*
—*Fay Weldon,* Darcy's Utopia

I want to discuss my rationale for arguing that feminist science fiction is part of the larger whole I call feminist fabulation. To accomplish this objective, in the first part of this chapter I associate gender and race with science fiction by focusing on Octavia Butler's and James Tiptree's depiction of aliens. Their aliens are alienated women, not interplanetary monsters. Yet, despite this truth, Butler and Tiptree are categorized with writers who focus on zap guns and dinosaurs devouring cities, not writers who focus on race, class, and gender. The designation *science fiction* causes a group of important feminist writers who address familiar feminist concerns to be made unfamiliar. Tiptree is almost never mentioned in discussions about major contemporary feminist fiction writers; Butler has not received the recognition accorded to contemporary black women authors. Associating writers such as Butler and Tiptree with science fiction devalues them. Hence, I argue that feminist science fiction should be incorporated within feminist fabulation. In the second part of this chapter, I support this argument by addressing feminist fabulation's connection to publication, reading, and writing practices.

ALIENS

Women—especially black women—who are alien in relation to patriarchal society, alter fiction's depiction of the alien. Robert Crossley makes this point when he explains that Butler's and Tiptree's aliens do not resemble the stock science fiction invader:

> The alien in many of the new fictions by women has been not a monstrous figure from a distant planet but the invisible alien within modern, familiar, human society: the woman as alien, sometimes more specifically, the black woman, or the Chicana, or the housewife, or the lesbian, or the woman in poverty, or the unmarried woman. Sheldon's famous story "The Women Men Don't See" (1974), about a mother and daughter who embark on a ship with extraterrestrials rather than remain unnoticed and unvalued on earth, is a touchstone for the reconception of the old science-fictional motifs of estrangement and alienation. . . . As American women writers have abandoned the character types that predominated in science fiction for a richer plurality of human images, they have collectively written a new chapter in the genre's history. (Crossley, xvi)

Feminist fabulators rewrite the story of the human vanquishing the alien (a story epitomized in the film *Alien* when Sigourney Weaver's character is pitted against the monster). Science fiction's new feminist chapter expresses a longing for a richer plurality of human images by portraying women as gendered or racial aliens who embrace, rather than quell, the invading monster. Butler and Tiptree, who oppose racism and sexism when shattering science fiction stereotypes, write in the tradition of feminist awareness of the Other—not the Hollywood grade-B science fiction monster movie.

Barbara Christian explains that in "every society where there is the denigrated Other whether that is designated by sex, race, or class, or ethnic background, the *Other* struggles to declare the truth and therefore create the truth in forms that exist for her or him" (Christian, "Creating," 160). The denigrated *Other* that Butler and Tiptree imagine struggles to declare and create the truth and insists that women "are not just stereotypes, for stereotype is the very opposite of humanness" (Christian, "Images," 16). The female protagonists in Tiptree's "The Women Men Don't See" and Butler's *Kindred* and *Dawn*,[1] in opposition to science fiction stereotypes about vanquishing aliens, join with or are assisted by the aliens they could be expected to view as epitomizing the very opposite of humanness. These female characters, who are themselves the Other, do not oppose the Other.

Butler and Tiptree turn to the fantastic to depict merging with the Other when they describe species transformation as a method to eradicate both sexism and racism. I have written elsewhere that Tiptree (in *Up the Walls of the World*, for example) equates hope with the human race's change into a "new biological something."[2] Species transformation, the nonhuman newness resulting after humans merge with aliens, causes racism and sexism to become impossible. Tiptree's imaginative visions often portray the disappearance of race and gender coinciding with the disappearance of racism and sexism.

Butler describes this newness as a blurring of racial difference. In *Kindred*, she emphasizes the combined racial characteristics of children born as the result of sexual encounters between social and cultural aliens: white masters and black slaves. In *Dawn*, a more fantastic work than *Kindred*, Butler describes the end of human racial difference achieved after humans procreate with extraterrestrial aliens. Dana, the black protagonist of *Kindred*, is married to a white man. Lilith Iyapo, the black protagonist of *Dawn*, has sexual intercourse with the extraterrestrial Oankali. Both novels are concerned with a new biological something, the third kind resulting from black women's close encounters with aliens.

Butler's third kind, the child born of black and white—or human and extraterrestrial—parents, exemplifies contemporary black literature's version of what Barbara Christian describes as "the tragic mulatta theme" that characterizes late nineteenth-century black literature. According to Christian, the "tragic mulatta theme reveals the conflict of values that blacks faced as a *conquered* people" (Christian, "Images," 3). Christian continues: "In her very being, the mulatta called up the illicit crossing between cultures. She is American in that she emerges out of the sexual relationship between a black slave mother and a white slave master, a sexual relationship denying the most basic philosophical concept of slavery—that blacks were not human beings. Do humans mate with nonhumans, and if they do, what is the product, human or nonhuman? As the white slave master entered the body of countless black women, he knew of her being, her humanness" (ibid.). *Kindred* draws upon the tragic mulatta theme according to science fiction tropes. (Again, I argue that these tropes should not be used as a reason to marginalize Butler.) Dana time travels to a plantation to rescue her white great-grandfather, slave owner Rufus Weylin. Dana's presence in the past involves a conflict derived from the fact that sexual relations between a female slave (Alice Greenwood) and a white man (Rufus) make her life possible. (Dana's survival depends on ensuring that Rufus will live and father Alice's child, Dana's grandmother Hagar Weylin.) Dana functions as the agent responsible for a mulatta's birth. She makes it possible for Rufus to know of Alice Greenwood's "being, her humanness." However, in addition to being transformative, "the illicit crossing between cultures" *Kindred* portrays is fraught with inescapable contradiction and pain. Rape makes Dana's life possible.

Dawn depicts a more fantastic version of the sexual encounter between racial aliens *Kindred* describes. In *Dawn*, humans are forced to mate with nonhumans and to produce nonhuman offspring. Lilith's Oankali/human son is Dana's fantastic racially mixed counterpart who evokes the biological end of humanity's present form. This "mulatto" child eradicates the need for "alien," a word eliminated when *Dawn* (and Tiptree's *Up the Walls of the*

World) positions the human race as an obsolete species newly incorporated within a larger extraterrestrial communal whole. *Dawn* and *Up the Walls* emphasize that eradicating humanity is in humanity's best interest.

In a similar vein, I argue that rethinking the term *feminist science fiction*, incorporating this literature within the larger whole of postmodern feminist fabulation, is in this literature's best interest. When Butler, Tiptree, and their colleagues are no longer stigmatized by the label *science fiction*, they will no longer be literary aliens. For example, if Butler were not associated with science fiction, Christian might have commented on her fiction while discussing "placing" contemporary African American women's fiction. Butler's work, after all, certainly conforms to Christian's point that "thematically and stylistically, the tone of the fiction of the early eighties communicates the sense that women of color can no longer be perceived as marginal to the empowerment of all American women and that an understanding of their reality and imagination is essential to the process of change that the entire society must undergo in order to transform itself" (Christian, "Placing," 185). Christian's understanding of the relationship between women of color and all American women is applicable to feminist science fiction writers. Feminist science fiction writers, whose imaginations and recast versions of patriarchal reality are crucial catalysts for achieving social change, are not marginal to the empowerment of all American women writers—and to the empowerment of all American women.

NAME CHANGE

The category of women's writing called feminist science fiction remains virtually invisible. When I cited Crossley's description of "Sheldon's famous story 'The Women Men Don't See'" (Crossley, xvi) above, I did so with the immediate realization that neither the story nor Sheldon/Tiptree are famous. Because Tiptree is categorized as a science fiction writer, she is invisible to most members of the academic community. Hence, to correct this situation, I suggest, in addition to her pseudonym, a second name change for Tiptree. Tiptree and her colleagues should be called postmodern feminist fabulators, not science fiction writers.

In a lecture drawn from his *Thinking through Cultures: Expedi-*

tions in Cultural Psychology, anthropologist Richard A. Shweder stated that postmodernism "re-values the past, present, and future as art or artifice" and concerns "diversity, multiplicity, and resortings" (Shweder, *Thinking*, 1). As we all know, even though female authors bring diversity and multiplicity to postmodern fiction, they have been sorted out of the postmodern canon. To link feminist fabulation with postmodern fiction, it is necessary to unmask the artifice used to devalue women's present fictional art about feminist futures. It is also necessary to revalue this contemporary literature by associating it with noncontemporary literature. As I indicated when discussing Butler and Tiptree, this revaluation can best be accomplished by changing the name feminist science fiction (fantastic feminist fabulation might be a better alternative), a move conforming to Joanna Russ's description of women's avant-garde science fiction.

According to Russ, women's avant-garde science fiction is "part of the recent rapprochement between the most experimental of the science fiction community and the most avant-garde of what is called 'the mainstream.' This takes us out of the field of science fiction altogether" (Russ, 88–89). I wish to take the literature known as feminist science fiction out of the science fiction field altogether. This call for the loss of a particular literary female specificity— integrating ostracized feminist science fiction within postmodern fiction—circles back to the above discussion about absorbing the alien. Since it is not in the best interest of a cadre of feminist writers to have their work defined as different from respected work, I want to bridge the separation of feminist science fiction from canonical postmodern literature, to recast feminist science fiction as a disappearing self. Ironically, although Naomi Schor tells us that Myra Jehlen "forcefully" argues that "difference does have a future" (Schor, 57), this future lacks positive implications for the supposed difference that continues to make feminist science fiction invisible. The claim of difference relegates feminist literature about the alien Other to alien Otherness.

Jehlen's statement that the claim of difference "represents a new understanding that if the other is to live, it will have to live as other, lest the achievement of integration be crowned with the fatal irony of disappearance through absorption" (Schor, 57–58; Jehlen, n.p.), applies to the relationship between feminist science fiction, feminist fabulation, and canonical postmodern literature. In the real world, disappearance through absorption entails a subordinate group's loss of its unique characteristics after adopting a hegemonic group's supposedly universal norm. The hegemony is strengthened at the minority's expense. This is not the case in regard to feminist novels (such as *Dawn* and *Up the Walls of the World*) that portray a new entity resulting from the fusion between humans and extraterrestrials. The new entity inhabits a space resembling what Schor calls "the promised utopia of sexual indifferentiation . . . [where] there will no longer be any place or need for sexual difference, it will simply wither away" (Schor, 57). The at once human and extraterrestrial being Tiptree envisions in *Up the Walls* eradicates both sexual difference and the alien. Within this novel, a true exercise in human equality occurs when humanity and an alien race are absorbed within a second alien race. All humans merge with the extraterrestrials and benefit from the merger. Similarly, Butler's *Kindred* describes a less fantastic picture of indifferentiation resulting in equality. *Kindred* asserts that the achievement of integration might best be realized by the example the positive mulatta epitomizes: reciprocal darkening and lightening of races.

Isolation as a subgenre, not absorption into a larger literary whole, has been and will continue to be fatal to feminist science fiction. Although feminist science fiction proliferates through the efforts of such publishers as the Feminist Press, Virago, and the Women's Press, no matter how many feminist science fiction works feminist presses produce, this literature will continue to be marginalized. Recognition is still accorded to women writers in terms of tokenism; in science fiction, only one female writer, Ursula Le Guin, has achieved widespread respect. Through no fault of her own, Le Guin's prominence works against other female science fiction writers. Nancy K. Miller offers a general comment that explains why this particular situation is so: it "is, after all, the Author anthologized and institutionalized who by his (canonical) presence excludes the less-known works of women and minority writers and who by his authority justifies the exclusion" (Miller, 4). Le Guin's science fiction, which has won designation as "literature," positions her as the Author who keeps less-known women science fiction writers in their generic place. This tokenism is contrary to Le Guin's generosity to her fellow writers—and all too effective.[3]

If the type of writing Le Guin and her colleagues create continues to be designated as feminist science fiction, then Le Guin will continue to be the token anthologized, institutionalized female science fiction Author. Furthermore, the science fiction produced by such luminaries as Atwood, Lessing, and Piercy will continue to be disconnected from the work of unrecognized feminist science fiction writers who are, in addition, isolated from their modernist predecessors. Carroll Smith-Rosenberg's observations about feminist modernist novels seem to point to the particular violence done to feminist science fiction by criteria that both sever its connection to modernism and situate it outside the postmodern canon. Smith-Rosenberg explains that "feminist modernists set their novels in 'unnatural' worlds and unstructured situations, beyond the threshold of conventional order"; that their "plots violate the restrictions of time (*Orlando*), of day and night (*Nightwood*), of conventional literary forms (Gertrude Stein's novels)"; and that in "surrealistic and expatriate worlds, New Women float between genders and violate divisions between appearance and reality" (Smith-Rosenberg, 118). Although positing unnatural worlds, violating time restrictions, and transcending gender and reality in surrealistic worlds are surely pertinent to feminist science fiction, feminist science fiction writers are not routinely associated with Djuna Barnes, Gertrude Stein, and Virginia Woolf. Hence, the term *feminist science fiction* blinds people to connections between feminist fiction's recent past and present. Name change can assuage this situation.

Name change will allow ostracized feminist science fiction writers to be recognized as respected feminist fabulators, the rightful postmodern daughters of modernist mothers. Within literature, token female writers who work in many genres—such as Isabel Allende, a token female figure within magic realism; Maxine Hong Kingston, a token female figure within nonwhite ethnic American literature; and Grace Paley, a token female figure within American Jewish literature—can assist female writers through their association with as yet unrecognized science fiction authors who, like themselves, transform patriarchal fables. Tokenism and marginality are cast aside when diverse writers are recognized as feminist fabulators. Writers such as Butler and Tiptree are not designated as Other within feminist fabulation. Feminist fabulation can generate a new order within the world of contemporary fiction.

Molly Hite's *The Other Side of the Story* maps the differences between women's and men's contemporary writing. When Hite states that she is not trying to admit a group of female and feminist writers to the postmodern canon (Hite, 2), she relegates female and feminist specificity to the other side of the tracks. Instead of emphasizing difference and placing women outside the male postmodern literary domain, feminist fabulation generates "webs of inclusion" (Sally Helgesen's term for women's distinctive leadership style). These webs form when postmodern fiction incorporates the agenda of women writers, when feminist science fiction is absorbed within canonized feminist fabulation. In order to become a part of the web of inclusion existing within feminist fabulation, texts—regardless of their authors' gender, race, or culture—must unmask the fictionality of patriarchal master narratives, rewrite patriarchal tales, and be feminist metafiction—fiction about patriarchal fictions. I argue that feminist fabulation involves a reading practice that engages diverse texts and that feminist fabulation is worthy of a prominent place in pedagogical and theoretical literary institutions.

I hear Schor's warning when I call for a name change that involves the disappearance of *feminist science fiction* through absorption into the postmodern canon. Schor states that before "tearing down the cultural ghetto where the feminine has been confined and demeaned, we need to map its boundaries and excavate its foundations in order to salvage the usable relics and refuse of patriarchy" (Schor, 58). I have spent more than a decade exploring the science fiction ghetto in which women writers are confined and demeaned. I know that *feminist science fiction* is a usable relic that can motivate people to construct a society "which will not simply reduplicate our own" (Schor, 58) patriarchal society. I know, too, that the practice of frequently taking feminist science fiction texts out of print turns valuable feminist thought into the refuse of patriarchy. After mapping the boundaries and excavating the foundations of the feminist science fiction ghetto, I know that the time has come to tear down this ghetto's walls. I want the literary establishment to define the science fiction component of feminist fabulation as an integral part of the postmodern canon, not as an extraneous textual alien.

Some members of the literary establishment do not wish to acknowledge feminist literature that imagines alternatives to patriarchal social constructions. The term *feminist fabulation* makes it difficult to justify such deliberate marginalization. Feminist fabulation nullifies the argument that feminist science fiction shares the inferiority of grade-B science fiction films. Writers such as

Butler and Tiptree produce regenerative texts that are appropriately connected to canonical modernist and postmodernist texts. Their work should not be ignored because it is called science fiction. Their work shares nothing in common with the hypothetical grade-B science fiction film "The Dinosaur Who Ate Metropolis."

NOTES

1. *Dawn* is the first volume in Butler's Xenogenesis series. The subsequently published volumes are *Adulthood Rites* (New York: Warner, 1988) and *Imago* (New York: Warner, 1989).

2. See Marleen S. Barr, *Alien To Femininity: Speculative Fiction and Feminist Theory* (Westport, Conn.: Greenwood Press, 1987), and " 'The Females Do the Fathering!': James Tiptree's Male Matriarchs and Adult Human Gametes," *Science-Fiction Studies* 13 (1986): 42–49.

3. I have benefited from Le Guin's generosity. I wish publicly to thank her.

WORKS CITED

Alien. Brandywine–Shusett/Fox. Produced by Gordon Carroll, David Giler, and Walter Hill. Written by Dan O'Bannon (based on a story by Dan O'Bannon and Ronald Shusett). Directed by Ridley Scott. 1979.

Butler, Octavia E. *Dawn*. New York: Warner, 1987.

———. *Kindred*. 1979. Reprint. Boston: Beacon Press, 1988.

Christian, Barbara. "Images of Black Women in Afro-American Literature: From Stereotype to Character." In *Black Feminist Criticism: Perspectives on Black Women Writers*, by Barbara Christian, 1–3. New York: Pergamon Press, 1985.

———. "Creating a Universal Literature: Afro-American Women Writers." In *Black Feminist Criticism: Perspectives on Black Women Writers*, by Barbara Christian, 159–63. New York: Pergamon Press, 1985.

———. "Trajectories of Self-Definition: Placing Contemporary Afro-American Women's Fiction." In *Black Feminist Criticism: Perspectives on Black Women Writers*, by Barbara Christian, 171–86. New York: Pergamon Press, 1985.

Crossley, Robert. Introduction to *Kindred*, by Octavia Butler, ix–xxvii. Boston: Beacon Press, 1988.

Helgesen, Sally. *The Female Advantage: Women's Ways of Leadership*. New York: Doubleday, 1990.

Hite, Molly. *The Other Side of the Story: Structures and Strategies of Contemporary Feminist Narrative*. Ithaca and London: Cornell University Press, 1989.

Jehlen, Myra. "Against Human Wholeness: A Suggestion for Feminist Epistemology." Paper presented at Seminar on Women and Society, Columbia University.

Miller, Nancy K. "Changing the Subject." In *Coming to Terms: Feminism, Theory, Politics*, edited by Elizabeth Weed, 3–16. New York and London: Routledge, 1989.

Russ, Joanna. "The Image of Women in Science Fiction." In *Images of Women in Fiction: Feminist Perspectives*, edited by Susan Koppelman Cornillon, 79–94. Bowling Green, Ohio: Bowling Green State University Popular Press, 1972.

Schor, Naomi. "Dreaming Dissymmetry: Barthes, Foucault, and Sexual Difference." In *Coming to Terms: Feminism, Theory, Politics*, edited by Elizabeth Weed, 47–58. New York and London: Routledge, 1989.

Shweder, Richard A. "Collective Representations and the Post-modern Self." Paper presented at Anthropology Colloquium, New York University, 18 Apr. 1991.

——— . *Thinking through Cultures: Expeditions in Cultural Psychology*. Cambridge, Mass.: Harvard University Press, 1991.

Smith-Rosenberg, Carroll. "The Body Politic." In *Coming to Terms: Feminism, Theory, Politics*, edited by Elizabeth Weed, 101–21. New York and London: Routledge, 1989.

Tiptree, James, Jr. "The Women Men Don't See." In *Warm Worlds and Otherwise*, edited by Robert Silverberg, 131–64. New York: Ballantine, 1975.

——— . *Up the Walls of the World*. New York: Berkley, 1978.

Weldon, Fay. *Darcy's Utopia*. New York: Viking, 1990.

9

Antipatriarchal Fabulation; or, The Green Pencils Are Coming, the Green Pencils Are Coming*

> "But I [George Darling] refuse to allow that dog to lord it in my nursery for an hour longer." The children wept, and Nana ran to him beseechingly, but he waved her back. He felt he was a strong man again. . . . He was determined to show who was master in that house.
> —*J. M. Barrie*, Peter Pan

> *Now, as you well know, it is not seldom the case in this conventional world of ours—watery or otherwise; that when a person placed in command over his fellow-men finds one of them to be very significantly his superior in general pride of manhood, straightway against that man*

*In James Rosenquist's original full-color work Space Dust, *the pencils are bright green.*

he conceives an unconquerable dislike and

bitterness; and if he have a chance he will pull

down and pulverize that subaltern's tower, and

make a little heap of dust of it.

—*Herman Melville,* Moby Dick

The patriarchal United States is governed by men who, when given the chance, pulverize their subalterns' towers. Instead of constructing alternatives to this dominating behavior—instead of attempting to make life better for disadvantaged people—individual men usually struggle to be superior to other men, to make so many heaps of dust. In the contemporary United States, pulverizing takes precedence over nurturing. David Leverenz alludes to this situation when he describes Melville's term *pride of manhood,* an ethos that continues to form the foundation of the U.S. government and economy. According to Leverenz, "Anyone preoccupied with manhood, in whatever time or culture, harbors fears of being humiliated, usually by other men. . . . Competition for dominance and the fear of being humiliated by a stronger man constitute the ideology of entrepreneurial manhood" (Leverenz, 72–73, 200).[1] Maintaining this ideology is no longer in the best interest of the United States. America, a country preoccupied with entrepreneurial manhood, is being humiliated economically by Japan and Germany. Although American men may feel antagonistic toward their Japanese and German rivals, pulverizing these rivals acts out an exhausted story. In order to remain competitive in the postmodern world, Americans need to rewrite old stories, to create alternatives to the exhausted tale of entrepreneurial manhood. To my mind, retelling this tired tale is one way to, in the words President Clinton used to begin his inaugural address, "celebrate the mystery of American renewal."

Harriet Beecher Stowe created one such alternative. Leverenz explains that Stowe's portrayal of motherhood in *Uncle Tom's Cabin* opposes Melville's portrayal of manhood: "Only the men with lots of mother in them . . . have some potential to transcend their drive for power" (Leverenz, 191). Life in the contemporary United States unfortunately mirrors Melville's, rather than Stowe's, art. Many of the country's myriad problems can be attributed to disdain for mothering and to valorization of men's drive for power. Sons of Melville, men who author social and economic policies in the United States, are captains of congressional chambers and corporate boardrooms. Daughters of Stowe, women who imagine fantastic alternatives to this conventional patriarchal world of ours, are not, with very few exceptions, part of the ship of state. Women are not often welcome in boardrooms and seldom wield power in the literary world. For example, female feminist fabulators who turn to science fiction to depict maternal males and matriarchal societies have been branded noncanonical genre fiction writers. Their imagined alternatives to manhood are marginalized, nullified, and silenced— jettisoned from the mainstream. Feminist science fiction writers are lost in space.

James Rosenquist's *Space Dust* (1989) might picture their current location. This paper-pulp work with lithographic collage elements, a part of the series "Welcome to the Water Planet," seems to represent an alternative to Melville's watery conventional world, to the little heap of dust resulting after one man pulverizes another. Rosenquist draws a counterpart to the male pen/penis that writes the patriarchal world: what I view as alien green feminist space pencils orbiting the patriarchal world—green pencils that, I think, represent the feminist science fiction texts branded as alien and marginal. (Associating the color green with the science fiction alien is a cliché. When a spaceship lands on the White House lawn, for example, the aliens who emerge from the ship are usually little green men.) Patriarchy regards these green pencils as a bug-eyed monster. Patriarchy constructs a vehicle (the conservative literary establishment) to ostracize this monster, to eject it from literary worlds/canons. The alien space pencils produce writing that can be erased easily. Instead of having an impact on American life, feminist science fiction is in orbit. I am happy to report, however, that the patriarchal vehicle that removes feminist science fiction from earthly influence is slowly backfiring. According to my interpretation, *Space Dust* depicts vibrant female space dust, particles of feminist insight that are alternatives to little heaps of patriarchal dust. While it is true that the alien green feminist pencils—implements that can represent feminist science fiction—are currently lost in orbit, they might eventually be found as a part of postmodern literary canons. Rosenquist, after all, attaches the pencils to a reentry vehicle. With red heat-shield pointed toward earth's patriarchal atmosphere, the space capsule launched to jettison encapsulated feminist alternative stories is on its way home.

Meanwhile, the conservative literary establishment still views this writing as alien and monstrous—something "extra" in relation to terrestrial literary canons. Furthermore, the space capsule carrying the feminist green pencils lands in Melville's ocean. An alternative reentry mode to falling in the conventional watery world has not been constructed for the particular vehicle Rosenquist depicts. (American space shuttles, not space capsules, use a landing strip.) Despite this situation, males can facilitate the reentry of jettisoned feminist science fiction. Male-generated alternatives to stories of manhood can begin to nullify these patriarchal stories and facilitate welcoming feminist science fiction home. New male stories that decry tales of manhood can rendezvous with feminist fabulation. As I will point out, these new male stories, examples of antipatriarchal fabulation, are major components of American popular culture.

Antipatriarchal fabulation is authored by men who bash manhood even though they are ensconced within patriarchy's powerful positions. Antipatriarchal fabulation involves different behavior patterns, not the different worlds Robert Scholes refers to in his definition of fabulation (see introduction). Antipatriarchal fabulation's male protagonists behave in a manner that is clearly and radically discontinuous from male behavior patterns patriarchy sanctions: male leaders cooperate with rather than try to dominate each other; business executives embrace their roles as fathers; starship captains are paternal rather than combative. In other words, men who wield patriarchal power confront the usual definition of manhood by deviating from it. However, antipatriarchal fabulation, which involves men who question male systems while positioned within male systems, is not feminist. I argue, nonetheless, that antipatriarchal fabulation, a challenge to American manhood, facilitates the eventual acceptance of feminist fabulation. If the story of American manhood is pulverized, then feminist science fiction can become a found female voice of postmodern literature, a valued diamond of the postmodern canon. I posit a cooperative model for change in which examples of male-centered

American popular culture (the works I call antipatriarchal fabulation) can supplement the efforts of feminist science fiction to be no longer lost in space.

LINKING ANTIPATRIARCHAL FABULATION TO EDGAR ALLAN POE, STEVEN SPIELBERG, ANITA HILL, AND CLARENCE THOMAS

Antipatriarchal fabulation, like the story of powerful motherhood and entrepreneurial manhood, is rooted in nineteenth-century American literature. (Stowe, for example, emphasizes that "brutal men are lower even than animals" [Stowe, 370–71].) While Leverenz respectively links these stories to Stowe and Melville, I want to connect antipatriarchal fabulation to Edgar Allan Poe. I suggest that, in addition to creating the detective story, Poe defined manhood as a horror story. "The Cask of Amontillado" portrays manhood trapping and nullifying itself. Montresor seeks revenge because Fortunato humiliates him. In turn, since Fortunato wishes to emphasize his manhood by displaying his knowledge of wine, he insists on walking into Montresor's trap.

Montresor, knowing that Fortunato will act as a protagonist in the tale of manhood, constructs (with trowel in hand) a means to entomb manhood—in the person of Fortunato attired in a fool's costume. Fortunato, like Ahab, a "captain of the good ship *Manhood*," too late "discovers that he has been sailing toward the ultimate in manly humiliations" (Leverenz, 297). Poe emphasizes that the good ship *Manhood* is a ship of fools, an evil deserving to be trapped, enclosed, and ended. I think that the most horrible aspect of "Amontillado" is revealed when it is read as a rewritten Pandora fable. According to this reading, only Fortunato, not the story of manhood he epitomizes, remains buried in the Montresor family vault. Manhood deconstructs Montresor's wall; manhood emerges from the vault and predominates in the world. "Amontillado" is antipatriarchal fabulation about the horror of manhood, a horror that remains unabated after burying an individual man. As long as manhood continues to be venerated, people are less likely to reside in feminist utopias.

There is nothing feminist about the antipatriarchal fabulation in "Amontillado." Montresor acts according to his family motto, *"nemo me impune lacessit"* (Poe, "Amontillado," 1444), "No one insults me with impunity." In other words, no one compromises his manhood. When Montresor encloses Fortunato, manhood vanquishes itself, or according to a recognized tenet of postmodernism, the system critiques itself from within. Contradicting manhood in terms of manhood brings a contemporary antipatriarchal fabulator to mind: Steven Spielberg. According to a kinder, gentler version of Montresor vanquishing Fortunato, Spielberg exemplifies Hollywood entrepreneurial manhood critiquing itself. Like Montresor, Spielberg nullifies manhood in terms of manhood. Both Spielberg's own words and a reporter's observations about him support this point:

> "I don't see myself as a businessman," he [Spielberg] says. . . . At points, Mr. Spielberg even seems worried about what his achievements might say about him. "People who don't know me think I'm just motivated by money or success," he says. "But I've never been motivated by that. I've never based a decision on money." . . . Amblin [Spielberg's production company] is housed in a two-story Santa Fe–style adobe mansion. Inside, there is a game room, a candy counter and a kitchen stocked with popcorn and ice cream. . . . Within the protective confines of his company, Mr. Spielberg has probably nurtured more talent, and fiercely loyal talent, than any other director. But he is also a hard negotiator. (Andrews, 20)

Spielberg, a man who amassed a fortune, says that he is not motivated by money. His corporate empire is housed in an amusement park space. His enactment of manhood involves functioning as both a nurturer and a businessman.

According to another example of the juxtaposition of masculine and feminine, Poe is sometimes relevant to contemporary women's, as well as contemporary men's, response to manhood. "The Black Cat" evokes the voices of contemporary women confronting men who treat them violently. Many violent men try to bury the abuse they inflict while acting according to the requirements of manhood. Poe's murderous wall builder in "The Black Cat" does not succeed in this attempt. This male narrator is exposed by the black cat trapped within the wall where he has hidden his wife's corpse. The cat's cry—"a wailing shriek, half of horror and half of triumph, such as might have arisen only out of hell, conjointly from the throats of the damned in their agony and of the demons that exult in the damnation" (Poe, "Black Cat," 1424)—is a voice that, on the site of buried Woman, challenges and retells the male narrator's false story of innocence. The shriek ensures that the narrator will face the consequences of the crime he denies committing.

I hear the cat's shriek as an exaggerated version of female voices that attempt to reveal the violence against women men perpetrate and conceal. I hear the cat's shriek anticipating Anita Hill speaking out against the sexual harassment I believe she endured. In Poe's antipatriarchal fabulation, the cat's "informing voice" (ibid., 1425) is effective; in contemporary American social systems, which invalidate women's challenges to manhood, women's voices are usually ineffective. As Clarence Thomas's appointment to the Supreme Court makes clear, in American reality the story of manhood almost always prevails after women's words question it.

"The Black Cat" can be read as an indication that this situation might change. Pluto, the cat Poe's narrator kills, is not lost in space. This cat becomes a constellation, a visible sign on a wall created by fire and ammonia (ibid., 1421), an indelible reminder of the narrator's crime. The narrator becomes a reader who interprets signs of his own guilt; he reads the white mark on the second cat's chest as an image of the gallows: "It had . . . assumed a rigorous distinctness of outline. It was now the representation of an object I shudder to name[,] . . . the monster[,] . . . the image of a hideous— of a ghastly thing—of the GALLOWS!" (ibid., 1422). Perhaps he sees the death of patriarchal stories, the alternatives to patriarchal fictions written with monstrous alien green pencils.

Poe's narrator incorrectly assumes that he will never encounter the "monster" cat again: "The monster, in terror, had fled the premises forever! I should behold it no more! My happiness was supreme! The guilt of my dark deed disturbed me but little" (ibid., 1424). Perhaps the patriarchal literary establishment, ignoring the possibility of reentry, thinks the same thing in regard to relegating feminist science fiction to being lost in space. In terms of my metaphor, the happiness the patriarchal literary establishment derives from possibly not having to behold monstrous feminist science fiction in the canon might be short lived; or, in regard to a real-world nullification of a woman's words, perhaps in the future an Anita Hill, rather than a Clarence Thomas, will be placed in the position of power. I hope sexual harassers will eventually be seen as monsters who deserve to be "walled . . . up within the tomb" (ibid., 1425) of manhood and patriarchal stories. Then, women's words will no longer be regarded as "the hideous beast whose craft had seduced" men (ibid.), the craft of women's stories launched outside the canon.

ALTERNATIVES TO MELVILLE'S GOOD SHIP *MANHOOD*: A NURTURING *ENTERPRISE* AND FRITZ LANG'S FEMININE SPACESHIP

A female character in Fritz Lang's 1929 film *Woman in the Moon (Frau im Mond)* asks, "Helius in these last moments are you trying to say that we women are not brave enough to try this venture?" This comment about traveling to the moon, a woman's questioning of femininity, addressed to a man named Helius, concerns the flight of the first realistic spacecraft in movie history. *Woman in the Moon* depicts a ship that Hermann Oberth describes in *Ways to Spaceflight* (1929), a revised edition of *The Rocket into Planetary Space* (1923).[2] The model E rocket, first proposed in the earlier study, embarks, in the later study, on a fictional flight around the moon (on 14 June 1932). The ship is a three-stage rocket launched from the Indian Ocean. Its pilots are housed in "a small cabin, an oblate spheroid in shape, contained in the nose of the third stage" (Ordway and Liebermann, 62). The spaceship *Friede*, which appears in Lang's film, is based on Oberth's model E rocket. Because the *Friede* is fragile and made from delicate material, it is launched from a large tank of water. This "birth" of the wide ship emerging from the water tank is a feminine alternative to the land-based thrust of thinner, more phallic, real rockets. The watery world surrounding the *Friede* is more akin to contained amniotic fluid than to Melville's masculine sea. The *Friede*, a rounded maternal ship pregnant with passengers, rises from a female component of man's watery world.

Woman in the Moon is a story of entrepreneurial manhood juxtaposed with components that are not manly. The film is about the lunar adventures of a professor who, because he believes there is gold on the moon, attracts investors to develop a ship capable of traveling there. The ship's occupants are no more manly than the circumstances regarding its launching. Its crew consists of a boy, an elderly man accompanied by a caged bird, two middle-aged men who wear sweaters (one has a receding hairline), and a woman. These are no supermen, no dashing exemplars of manhood who resemble the young Wernher von Braun or the male American astronauts. The bird's presence on the ship, an unexpected coupling of technology and nature, brings to mind the kudzu vines growing in the women's spaceships James Tiptree imagines (in "Houston, Houston, Do You Read?"). The caged bird does not signify manliness.

As the female crew member's comment to Helius (mentioned above) shows, she refuses to be constrained (or caged) by patriarchal stories about female frailty. After Helius asks her to reconsider her decision to participate in the flight, she responds by insisting that women are indeed brave enough to venture to the moon. This female astronaut who crosses out femininity is a cross-dresser: she travels to the moon wearing a tie and trousers. Her words and her clothes announce that she is as brave as men. Women's efforts to challenge femininity's restrictions are a part of Lang's vision. The first realistic spaceship in cinematic history carries the alien green pencil: women's words that counter patriarchal stories. *Woman in the Moon* portrays an androgynous vision—and is no story of manhood.

Another ship accompanies Lang's and Rosenquist's vessels as alternatives to Melville's "good ship *Manhood*." I refer to the starship *Enterprise*, *Star Trek*'s ship of nurturing that ventures into the sea of space to explore, not to vanquish. Aspects of *Star Trek* revise aspects of *Moby Dick*. Unlike Captain Ahab, Captains Kirk and Picard preside over a crew of women and men who form a family; their decisions are not based on "manly rage and rivalry" (Leverenz, 287). The *Enterprise*, counter to Leverenz's observation that "as the male workplace became quite separate from the home, competition intensified, and men defined manhood much more exclusively through their work" (Leverenz, 72), is at once a workplace and home governed by cooperation. The *Enterprise*, then, differs from Melville's depiction of American enterprise: "the sex-segregated world of American capitalism in its most predatory individualistic phase" (Leverenz, 281).

Star Trek's new generation is even less manly than the old. Picard's *Enterprise* contains classrooms for schoolchildren run by female and male teachers. The extremely feminine counselor, Deanna Troi, a Betazoid who can sense emotions, is often integral to the success of *Enterprise* missions. Captain Picard bears little resemblance to the physically combative, womanizing Kirk. He is more fatherly than Kirk and, instead of joining "away teams," usually chooses to remain behind in the ship/home. This Frenchman simply does not conform to American manhood. Even Commander Will Riker, who is more like Kirk than like Picard, is not as macho as Kirk. Furthermore, Data, unlike his counterpart Spock, respects human emotion. In comparison with Data, Spock more closely resembles Ahab, who "becomes dead to human feelings" (Leverenz, 298).

Perhaps Data and engineering officer Geordie La Forge epitomize a postmodern version of what Leslie Fiedler describes as "the mutual love of *a white man and a colored*" (Fiedler, 146). Perhaps they exemplify a contemporary version of "the Sacred Marriage of males" (Fiedler, 148) Ishmael and Queequeg, and Huck and Jim, experience. Data and Geordie seem to retell Jim's comment— "Come back to the raft ag'in, Huck honey"—when they ask each other to report back to the ship's engineering section. According to *Star Trek*, "the American Dream of isolation afloat" (Fiedler, 148) occurs on a starship populated by an interdependent multiracial community of women and men, not by a black man and a white man sailing on a raft or a whaling vessel.

Data, who does not fully understand humans, is the most isolated *Enterprise* crew member sailing in space. His friendship with Geordie assuages his isolation. In Fiedler's words, "Our dark-skinned beloved will take us in, we assure ourselves, when we have been cut off" (Fiedler, 150). Like Data, Geordie the dark-skinned "beloved" is not completely biologically human. One part of Geordie's body, the visor that enables him to see, is a mechanical sense organ. Hence, Data's and Geordie's relationship is not a relationship between two men. Their version of the archetype Fiedler describes does not focus on manhood. Instead, a white android shares a close relationship with a black partially mechanical human, a human who is part android.

Marge Piercy addresses my point when she writes, "We're all cyborgs. . . . You're [the cyborg named Yod] just a purer form of what we're all tending toward" (Piercy, 156). On the *Enterprise*, "come back to the engineering room again" is uttered by two cyborgs, the beings Donna Haraway describes as "a cybernetic organism, a hybrid of machine and organism, a creature of social reality as well as a creature of fiction." Instead of evoking images of homosexuality, Data's and Geordie's close relationship calls to mind "cyborg 'sex' [that] restores some of the lovely replicative baroque of ferns and invertebrates (such nice organic prophylactics against heterosexism)" (Haraway, 174).

Although Data himself cannot experience human feelings, in one episode he acts as a father figure who assuages a boy's emotional trauma. The boy, in order to cope with the fact that a starship explosion has left him orphaned, mimics Data's android behavior. Data is an effective substitute father to this boy. Dr. Beverly Crusher and Lieutenant Worf also nurture children. Crusher routinely interacts with her son; an entire episode concerns Worf's response to parenting. Worf is an alien who behaves in a manner foreign to American manhood: he resolves not to allow his work to retard his ability to be a parent. Instead of sending his son away, Worf lets him know that he is welcome to remain on the *Enterprise*. Worf, then, ultimately does not act like the "American men [who] tend to define their self-respect much more stringently through their work than through any other aspect of their lives" (Leverenz, 89).

Maternal principles govern aspects of both the old and the new crews' behavior. Captain Kirk, for example, encounters a creature (called a Horta) who threatens a mining colony. The situation is resolved when Kirk recognizes that the Horta is a mother wishing to protect her children. When the Horta's children are no longer threatened, she assists the miners by digging tunnels. The relationship between the Horta and the miners bears upon Leverenz's reading of *Uncle Tom's Cabin*. According to Leverenz, "*Uncle Tom's Cabin* insists that what white men do to black people can be changed if men can be brought to feel what any mother feels" (Leverenz, 190). The Horta episode insists that what white men do to an alien can be changed if men can be brought to feel what any mother Horta feels. This story about men understanding a maternal viewpoint relates to Stowe's emphasis in *Uncle Tom*: "salvation through good mothering" (Leverenz, 301).

The new *Enterprise* itself functions as a good surrogate mother who makes it possible to reunite an orphaned infant alien with its fellows. A large, white, amoebalike baby imprints with the starship and follows "mother" *Enterprise*. Like *Uncle Tom*, this episode's rhetorical impact concerns "the separation of child from mother" (Leverenz, 301). The baby alien is a "whale" who is rescued, not hunted. The same holds true for the real whales who figure in the film *Star Trek IV: The Voyage Home*. *Star Trek* revises Melville's portrayal of the manly American mind's "zest for exploration, its awe at pain, its rapture at the hunt for whales and ideas" (Leverenz, 305). *Enterprise* crew members continually explore—and they attempt to assuage pain. They hunt for ideas; they mother whales.

PETER PAN GROWS UP AND CRITIQUES MANHOOD

Steven Spielberg acts according to the effective parenting *Star Trek* portrays. Like Worf, to function as a good father, Spielberg does not direct all of his attention to work. He acknowledges "that it was once his ambition to build the kind of company Walt Disney built. . . . Mr. Spielberg turned down the jobs [offers from studios that would enable him to become the new Disney] because he had found something in life that was more important to him. 'I became a father,' he says. . . . 'After [his son] Max was born, the ambition wasn't there as much. It became, in some ways, a real choice. I realized that I could be Disney, but that I would be a terrible father, or I could forget Disney and be a great father" (Andrews, 21). The choice between becoming a superlative businessman or a terrible father forms the crux of *Hook*. Spielberg's film reflects J. M. Barrie's critique of manhood. George Darling, as this chapter's epigraph indicates, feels like a strong man after he shows his maternal dog who is master. Asserting his manhood places George in the dog house: "He went down on all fours and crawled into the kennel. . . . In the bitterness of his remorse he swore that he would never leave the kennel until his children came back. . . . There never was a more humble man than the once proud George Darling, as he sat in the kennel of an evening talking with his wife. . . . Every morning the kennel was carried with Mr. Darling in it to a cab, which conveyed him to his office, and he returned home in the same way at six" (Barrie, 164). *Hook* insists that men who crawl into their office and seem never to leave are barking up the wrong tree.

While Stowe's "Cassy regains her motherly nature by reuniting with her long-lost daughter Eliza" (Leverenz, 198), Spielberg's Peter Banning regains his fatherly nature by reuniting with his twice-lost children (Maggie and Jack) who, before they are kidnapped to Neverland, are lost to Peter (a father who never places parenting before working). Spielberg's version of *Peter Pan* rewrites the role of the corporate executive who flouts fatherhood. Further, Maggie, an outspoken little girl who is close to her mother, defines Captain Hook in terms of women—as a man without a mother. Neverland's Lost Boys are potential future lost men engulfed by corporations that view domestic concerns as neverlands for businessmen. Despite Maggie's strength and the Lost Boys' presence, *Hook* concerns a fight for a biological son waged between two combatants: Peter, the repentant failed father, and Hook, who, in the guise of a critic, pans Peter's performance as a parent.

Hook advocates making *manhood* synonymous with *family responsibility*. When Peter is presented with an opportunity to have an affair with a seductive, full-sized Tinkerbell, he chooses to remain loyal to his wife, Moira. Instead of, according to the story of manhood, making love to Tinkerbell, Peter is attracted to a story about motherhood: Wendy's attention to orphans. He himself ultimately disregards manhood and becomes a nurturer. His most important swordsmanship involves breaking his mobile phone connection (an extension of the hand that functions as a businessman's sword), not severing Hook's hand. Peter's attention to cutting deals is replaced by his newfound ability "to fly, to fight, and to crow." Neverland functions as Peter's rehabilitation clinic, the place where he learns to control his addiction to entrepreneurial manhood. Soon after his arrival there via a stretcher transported by Tinkerbell-as-ambulance, Peter, who was formerly drowning in manhood, falls into a sea. He is resuscitated by mermaids, fantastic women who breathe new life into him.

Hook addresses the possibility that such fantastic alternatives to patriarchal reality might be real. Peter Banning, after all, lives the *Peter Pan* story that, according to the elderly Wendy, is no fairy tale. *Hook*—a rewritten version of American manhood—opens a window to antipatriarchal fabulation. Such openness, shared by other alternative-to-manhood films such as *Regarding Henry* and *The Doctor*, implies that antipatriarchal fabulation might replace manhood as the American man's most appropriate story. As *Hook* announces, homes and workplaces in the United States need nurturing men who emphasize community well-being, not domineering men who emphasize gratifying their own egos.

The leader of the Lost Boys, the chief executive officer of a male group who epitomizes the corporate edict about men avoiding family responsibilities, dies. Peter's son, who learns to love his nonpatriarchal father, lives. The Lost Boys' new leader conforms to no patriarchal image of a male leader: he is black, he is fat, and he bounces. He resembles Bouncing Boy, a member of the Superman comics' Legion of Super Heroes popular during Spielberg's youth. Like Bouncing Boy, the Lost Boys' new leader shows that someone Other in relation to manhood can be super.

Upon his return to Wendy's London home, Peter literally opens a window to the potential arrival of something Other than patriarchal reality. He unhooks the hook-shaped window clasp and grants access to whatever may fly in to supplant reality. Perhaps he expects Rosenquist's green pencils. Regardless of what particular newness appears, Peter opens the potential for something else— new master narratives about gender roles—to replace the story of entrepreneurial manhood. *Hook* is itself a new narrative of leadership that, because Peter no longer allows entrepreneurial manhood to encompass his life, defines him as a flying superman.

Spielberg's no longer young versions of Barrie's characters themselves show that the story of manhood should be retired. Hook's wig symbolizes this point about the literature of exhaustion. When the wig is removed from Hook's head and he is revealed to be an elderly, white-haired man, patriarchy appears as an old story. Although Jack temporarily wears a smaller version of Hook's wig, he will not continue to present himself according to either Peter's or Hook's stories. Hook, by motivating Jack to don the wig, does not crown him as a new scion in the line of ongoing aggression between men. Jack chooses not to continue Hook's vendetta against Peter. *Hook* shows that like Uncle Tootles, one of Barrie's Lost Boys whom Spielberg portrays as a senile old man residing in Wendy's house, manhood has lost its marbles.

Tootles finds his marbles, and despite its critique of manhood, *Hook* finds its patriarchal voice. This voice applies to the Lost Boys who remain in Neverland. Because Peter's rescue attempts are directed toward his biological children, the Lost Boys remain lost in space. His son receives first priority; his daughter is an afterthought; the Lost Boys, who cannot inherit the name of the father, remain lost. With his biological children in tow, Peter leaves the Lost Boys in Neverland, the land of fatherless sons. The boys never have a chance to find a mother. Although Wendy is honored for her attention to orphans, she never nurtures the Lost Boys. Wendy's lost opportunity to assist the Lost Boys shows that women in *Hook* are lost girls. Wendy's, Maggie's, and Moira's stories are the film's lost stories. These female characters, like the fake crocodile who kills Hook, are props—plastic beings.

Even though Wendy does not save the Lost Boys, their situation is not hopeless. Feminist fabulation provides an appropriate refuge for boys who are perfectly suited to be protagonists of postseparatist feminist utopias. These utopias would welcome men who are tribal, ecologically aware, and adept at killing male pirates. Furthermore, if the nonmanly Peter cannot find a comfortable niche in the real world, he might consider emigrating to a feminist world. He would, for instance, particularly enjoy Doris Lessing's Zone Three. Like Ben Ata, a protagonist of Lessing's *The Marriages between Zones Three, Four, and Five*, Peter reassesses his role in relation to manhood. The point is that *Hook*, a male-centered tale that critiques manhood, presents male characters who could comfortably reside in the feminist utopias patriarchy views as neverlands.

This situation can be attributed to the fact that American children, at the dawn of the postmodern age, learned about androgyny. Every baby boomer knows that Peter Pan is a woman—that Mary Martin is Peter Pan. While watching *Hook*, I wished that Martin would fly through Wendy's London window. (I refrained, however, from clapping my hands and saying, "I do believe Mary Martin will appear.") I wished that I could hear Martin sing about reconciling with Tiger Lilly, the female Indian chief. I believe that my fellow baby boomers who watch *Hook* share my response. Spielberg, Dustin Hoffman, and Robin Williams probably miss Mary Martin too.

They might not agree with other aspects of my response, though. I, for example, do not think a human-sized, sexy Tinkerbell improves on the original. I do not think *Hook* improves on the televised *Peter Pan*. I would like to see a new version of Barrie's story in which Peter focuses on a feisty daughter. *Hook* might be rewritten to emphasize Wendy's attention to nurturing. This new version of *Hook* could appropriately be called *Darling*.

Mary Martin's son Larry Hagman, the star of an exhausted television story, epitomizes the need for new stories such as *Darling*. After all, *Hook*, an example of antipatriarchal fabulation, functions as a nail in "Dallas"'s coffin. Peter Banning learns to dismiss J. R. Ewing's definition of manhood as obsessive attention to capitalism.

The television audience grew tired of the son who emulates his entrepreneurial daddy. Feminist fabulation, a literature of replenishment, provides an old—and presently uninteresting—question with a newly relevant answer. The old question: who shot J. R.? The new answer: the exhausted patriarchal story of manhood, Hook's successful new nemesis. Feminist fabulation, relegated to ostracized noncanonical neverland, is journeying back to fill the space this exhausted story vacates. *Darling* might be one particular contender poised to occupy this space. In *Darling*, a pregnant female crocodile kills Hook. Her presence in the story implies that the word *hook* should be read differently. A hook is a crooked phallic symbol. It is also a question mark. The word *hook* questions phallic power and male-centered stories.

NEW NARRATIVES AND THE NEW WORLD ORDER

The postmodern political world questions formerly sacrosanct stories. German and Japanese economic success stems from redefining and rebuilding Germany and Japan. The former Soviet Union and its former satellites are redefining themselves; western Europe is becoming one monetary entity. During the Reagan/Bush years, the United States, in contrast, remained mired in fixed meanings.[3] George Bush's January 1992 trip to Japan (he was accompanied by auto industry executives who wished to convince the Japanese to buy American cars) exemplifies this point. Adhering to expected characteristics of American businessmen, Bush and the executives did not deviate from self-definitions relating to entrepreneurial manhood. In fact, alternatives to American manhood make many powerful American men ill. When Bush vomited on the Japanese prime minister, he not only displayed his human characteristics: his illness epitomizes the response of an American male leader of the World War II generation encountering versions of manhood that differ from his own.

Anthony Lewis, in a *New York Times* op-ed piece about Bush's trip to Japan, hints that American manhood is a metaphor for failure. He observes that "Bush's visit to Japan this week, with his entourage of business executives, is a metaphor for what ails America. There in a neat package are symbols of corporate failure, social division and lame political response." The United States, instead of communicating a willingness to change the story these symbols represent, brought to Japan the individuals responsible for "the record of the American automobile chiefs in lining their own pockets while they run their companies into the ground." These chiefs, in accordance with American manhood, strongly resisted adopting a behavioral alternative: the Japanese business practice that requires that "managers whose companies do so badly resign. The ethic is personal responsibility—which does not seem a bad idea for any society" (Lewis, 13).

Although Bush and the executives who accompanied him to Japan would never, of course, use these terms, they could not stomach the notion that antipatriarchal fabulation is an appropriate story for the post–cold war era. Russian men no longer threaten to humiliate American men. Khruschev's desk-pounding at the United Nations has ultimately been muffled by a new era of "friendship and partnership" between the United States and the former Soviet Union. Yet, despite this era's inception, most powerful American men have not declared that the definition of American manhood is an exhausted story. (President Clinton's willingness to showcase Hillary Rodham Clinton's talents is a very welcome exception to this statement.) They have not declared that, because the main military U.S. rival no longer exists, this story should be revised.[4] American manhood, in other words, does not usually participate in the postmodern questioning of master narratives.

This adherence to old pervasive stories is epitomized by the current response of the United States to Germany and Japan. To cope with German and Japanese economic success, the United States goes back to the future by reevoking the World War II era (the modern golden age of American manhood). The American media routinely emphasizes "Japan bashing" and dwells on Nazism.[5] Most news reports about contemporary Germany discuss attacks on foreigners. Yes, Nazi-era history should, without question, remain part of the public consciousness. Yes, racism most certainly exists in contemporary Germany. However, in addition to dwelling on Nazism and contemporary German racism, the American media should inform people about positive aspects of present German life. These include superb secondary school systems, respect accorded to teachers and professors, tuition-free universities, efficient public transportation, and clean, safe cities. Perhaps the American media does not emphasize the high quality of life Germans enjoy because many powerful American men would turn a deaf ear to these positive aspects. The examples I list, after all, have nothing to do with manhood.

In addition to perpetuating negative images of Germany that ignore the positive achievements of the present and evoke the Nazi past, the American media positions Japan as a scapegoat for America's problems. Placing blame on Japan substitutes for admitting that the recession is caused by America's failure to remake itself. Clinton's call for American renewal addresses this failure and, I think, advocates formulating alternatives to tired, fixed definitions of American manhood. During Reagan's and Bush's administrations, in contrast to many examples of American popular culture, the U.S. government failed to embrace antipatriarchal fabulation. While the world changed before their eyes, most powerful American men vehemently rejected changing themselves. Perhaps the American electorate's vote for change is a vote against manhood. The White House is now occupied by a brilliant, participatory first lady and a president who—counter to stereotypical images of manhood—hugs his vice-president in public. The White House is now occupied by antipatriarchal fabulators.

The business world, as well as the government, is calling for renewal. Donald E. Petersen and John Hillkirk express this view in *A Better Idea: Redefining the Way Americans Work*, a book that endorses a system of employee involvement with corporate management espoused by W. Edwards Deming, an American statistician and management consultant. Petersen, the former chairman and chief executive officer of Ford Motor Company, and Hillkirk, a *USA Today* business writer, describe the teamwork used to design the Taurus, a 1986 car that proved profitable for Ford. One reviewer of the book, however, indicates that this example of cooperation between American workers and managers is the exception rather than the rule. The reviewer responds to Petersen and Hillkirk by stating that "it may strain credulity to think that American managers will willingly relinquish some authority in the belief that it would improve their companies' products" (Strom, 14). Men who relinquish authority do not often play important roles in the story of American manhood.

This prevailing situation might explain why Americans celebrate war rather than peace. New York City staged the largest ticker tape parade in history to honor Gulf War soldiers; not one sliver of paper was thrown to celebrate the end of hostilities with the former Soviet

Union. On the contrary, the media presented peace as a new problem. At the start of 1992, for example, "Sixty Minutes" discussed the complexities relevant to disposing of the nerve gas peace makes superfluous. Surely the threat of the gas's potential use is more unnerving than the happy circumstance of its obsolescence.

Instead of being euphoric about the end of the cold war, Americans' response to peaceful former Soviets mirrors Captain Kirk's response to peaceful Klingons: "I was used to hating Klingons" (Brinkley, 10). Americans are used to hating Soviets. Americans are, according to Robert Jay Lifton (director of John Jay College's Center on Violence and Human Survival), "confused." Lifton continues: "People no longer know how to view the world or how to understand our own national problems, which have to some degree been subsumed by the cold war" (Brinkley, 1). Americans are bewildered by life without Soviet rivalry. More specifically, removing the Soviet menace threatens American manhood. The boys are lost: "Politicians, intelligence officials, foreign policy experts, military analysts along with military-industry scientists all say they realize that the major force that has directed them these last four decades no longer exists. But few of them have clear ideas of what their new missions should be" (Brinkley, 10). The forty-year-old cold war force that fueled American manhood is no longer with these officials.

A woman clearly articulates the new mission of the United States, which counters manhood. According to Adele Simmons (president of the John D. and Catherine T. MacArthur Foundation), "If we're going to be a world leader, we need to be able to say we have some values and we want to take some leadership in an area like children's needs. . . . We have an enormous opportunity to provide leadership in the area of . . . nurturing genuine democracies in many parts of the world. . . . The old 'we have the answers' style is not one that will serve us well in the future. . . . I don't think it's possible for us to remain a world leader long into the future if we don't get our domestic house in order" (Simmons, 11). The old "we have the answers" style communicated in terms of manhood serves the United States no better than it serves Poe's Fortunato. Simmons's new answer—which echoes the Clintons' new answer—advocates emphasizing children's needs and other domestic priorities. She seems to imply that, to remain a world leader, the United States must imprison Fortunato and release Stowe's voice about the importance of motherhood. If we fail to do so, our white whale—the pursuit of selling American products—will be transformed into a white elephant. The United States is now poised to replace Melville's view of manhood with Stowe's view of mothering; White House power is wielded by a couple who emulates Cassy, not by a man who emulates Ahab.

Bush emulated Peter Pan when he decided not to remove Saddam Hussein from power. A mustachioed villain who looks like Captain Hook, Hussein gives American men the chance to proclaim that they can still fly, fight, and crow. He functions as American manhood's needed adversary. He provides an excuse for the United States to proclaim itself Neverland, a land that never deviates from behaving according to manhood. While the world abandons fixed meanings of "center" (Moscow is now merely the capital of one country in a commonwealth; German power is divided between Bonn and Berlin; Japan manufactures cars in Tennessee), most American men continue to center on manhood. They continue to refuse to exchange this old and tired story for new models: antipatriarchal and feminist fabulation.

Their refusal is not necessarily permanent. In the face of startling worldwide change, American adjustment is not impossible. For example, unlike Bush, when Clinton travels to Japan, his entourage might consist of open-minded teachers, sociologists, and economists. It is not impossible for antipatriarchal fabulation (and even feminist fabulation) eventually to replace manhood as the most influential narrative in the United States.[6] If this change occurs, I suggest to American conservatives a replacement for the warning "the Russians are coming, the Russians are coming": the green pencils are coming, the green pencils are coming. Now that Americans have stopped fearing the Reds, we might see the green pencils as new go-ahead signals. Americans might view Rosenquist's *Space Dust* as picturing feminist fabulation's needed reentry vehicle that returns from space and leaves manhood in the dust. When this vehicle lands on the White House lawn, the Clintons will set out a welcome mat.

"LOST IN SPACE"

The alternatives to manhood advocated by Adele Simmons and the Clintons were addressed—during the height of the cold war—

by the television show "Lost in Space." In the program's unaired pilot, Will Robinson voices a complaint to his sister Penny. "You women are always getting lost," he says. (Penny becomes lost while chasing her alien pet, a pointed-eared chimp named Debby. The possibility that Debby might be a chimp from Vulcan would not occur to the Robinsons.) Will chastises Penny, a brilliant girl interested in zoology, for nurturing. Despite Will's criticism, "Lost in Space" applauds good parenting undertaken by female and male professionals, cooperation between men, and maternal technology.

Dr. Maureen Robinson, played by none other than Lassie's "mother" June Lockhart, is a distinguished biochemist from New Mexico College of Space Medicine. John Robinson, a professor of astrophysics, is routinely assisted by Don West, a graduate student. Instead of behaving as John's younger rival, Don, through his attachment to John's daughter Judy, eventually becomes a part of the cohesive Robinson family. John has no desire to pulverize his subaltern's tower. John and Don, who do not threaten each other, are accompanied by benevolent technology. The robot (which does not appear in the pilot) is an androgynous maternal machine, a female body whose male voice routinely announces "danger." Like the Darling family's Nana, the robot is a combination watchdog and mother. It guards the Robinsons and their home, the spaceship that is an extremely technologically sophisticated camping vehicle.

"Lost in Space" reflects the awareness that women's talent becomes lost in patriarchy. In addition to emphasizing that the Robinson women are smart and accomplished, the narrator of the show's pilot episode states that they exemplify the "first time anyone but an adult male passed the test" required for acceptance into the space program. Despite this awareness, however, "Lost in Space" is not feminist. When biochemist Maureen Robinson first arrives on the unknown planet, she runs a washing machine, not experiments. (Although this washing machine resembles the ones we all know, it transforms dirty clothes into clean, plastic-wrapped garments.) Despite Penny's IQ of 147, Will, not Penny, is touted as the child genius. Will does not tell his sister that her talent is always getting lost in gender stereotypes.

Don and the Robinson men, not the Robinson women, deviate from these stereotypes; the men are not manly. A "real" American man would fault the cooperative relationship John and Don share.

A "real" American boy would call Will a nerd. This is not to say that manhood is absent from the show. Dr. Zachary Smith, the saboteur of the control system who becomes lost with the Robinsons and Don, functions in terms of manhood. (Like the robot, Smith does not appear in the pilot episode.) Smith, Will's bad "father," acts as a businessman who constantly tries to make deals that serve his self-interest. He attempts to use negotiation with aliens as a means to return to earth without the others. Smith's silly and selfish plans are always thwarted by the adults, Will, or the robot. (The aliens' response to his designs resemble Japanese reactions after Bush told Japan to buy our inefficient cars.) "Lost in Space" applauds familial cooperation and defines manhood as a villain.

This show, then, centers on a family unit thwarting the selfish intentions of a lone male entrepreneur. Although Smith is a pompous, cowardly ingrate, he is not completely evil, however. Smith, rather like Fortunato, is a boastful clown who deserves pity. Even though the Robinsons' situation would improve if they left Smith in a cave to die, they never do so. Their tolerance might stem from the hope that he will change. Regardless of Smith's self-centeredness, he shares the Robinsons' agenda. He wants to go home.

If Smith and the Robinsons ever achieve their objective, like Rosenquist's space capsule, their ship will act as a reentry vehicle. Having nothing in common with Ahab's ship, the Robinsons' vessel is a potential sister ship to the one Rosenquist depicts. The pilot for "Lost in Space," produced by Irwin Allen and written by Shimon Wincelberg, is mothered and supported by Jewish men—men who are alien to the WASP patriarchal hegemony of the United States. Like female feminist fabulators, Allen and Wincelberg use metaphorical green pencils. The antipatriarchal fabulation they create is feminist fabulation's ally.

SPLENDOR IN THE GRASS

Sheri S. Tepper also seems to write with Rosenquist's green pencils. She creates a female protagonist who becomes a hero due to, as I will explain, an alliance between feminist fabulation and antipatriarchal fabulation. Tepper's *Grass* portrays a world otherwise to a watery world, a conventional world densely covered with vegetation that is not our own. *Grass* descends from Ursula Le Guin's

The Left Hand of Darkness and Mary Gentle's *Golden Witchbreed*. Moving from Le Guin to Gentle to Tepper involves progressing from an unmarried male interplanetary emissary to an unmarried female interplanetary emissary to a female interplanetary emissary who is a wife and mother. Tepper's Marjorie Westriding Yrarier acts in terms of Stowe's notion that understanding maternal principles solves problems. While all the members of the Grassian aristocratic community are obsessed by the Hunt, a sign of manhood that blinds people to other concerns (such as the Hunt's adverse impact on children), Marjorie refuses to hunt, refuses to stop thinking and taking risks. Unlike all the Grassian parents who ignore the loss of daughters, Marjorie searches for her daughter, Stella, who disappears while hunting. During her search, she learns the true relationship between the aliens (called peepers, hippae, and foxen) the hunt involves. This information enables her to discover the origin of the plague that decimates human populations. She triumphs because she rejects manhood and acts according to motherhood.

In addition to its ties to *The Left Hand of Darkness* and *Golden Witchbreed*, *Grass* shares much in common with James Tiptree's "Your Haploid Heart." Both works describe species metamorphosis. Ian, the protagonist of "Heart," discovers that the aliens he encounters, the Esthaans and the Flenni, "are one. . . . [Esthaans] bud out Flenni, alternately and forever" (Tiptree, "Heart," 26). Marjorie learns that the peepers, hippae, and foxen are one, that peepers become hippae and "hippae metamorphose into foxen" (Tepper, 317). I hope adherents to American entrepreneurial manhood will behave in the manner of Tiptree's Esthaans, Tepper's nonhumanoid aliens, and Spielberg's Peter Banning. I hope manly entrepreneurs will metamorphose into something else and, like Marjorie, they will experience a startling behavioral change. Marjorie, who arrives on Grass as an obedient wife, realizes that she no longer wants to engage with human men—or with humans of any gender. Marjorie's metamorphosis indicates that *Grass* is feminist science fiction's version of Marilyn French's *The Women's Room*.

Both Marjorie and Mira, French's protagonist, change into women who no longer act according to the patriarchal definition of "good wife." Marjorie achieves this change by, when facing a situation in which manhood versus motherhood, choosing to emphasize motherhood. Her husband Rigo proves his manhood to the Grassian men by participating in the Hunt, an activity that, like American corporate careerism, obsesses a particular class of people. Marjorie will have no part of the addicting quest for foxen in "the grass that looked like water" (Tepper, 17). She rejects this analogue to Ahab's quest for the whale in the ocean. Unlike Rigo and the aristocratic Grassians, Marjorie does not hunt and become blind to the existence of lost daughters and maimed sons. Instead, she imagines that Rigo would make the following comment after Stella disappears: "I allowed her to be mentally and sexually crippled on Grass in order to show off my manliness to people who meant nothing to me" (Tepper, 423). The Hunt, the pursuit of manhood, means more to both the aristocratic Grassians and Rigo than children's well-being. Grassian women and children undertake, rather than question, hunting. Aristocratic Grassians are addicted to manhood and ignore motherhood. Marjorie, the charitable nurturing mother, is the antipatriarchal fabulator who reveals that Grassian master narratives about the importance of hunting (or manhood) are destructive myths.

After discarding her role as obedient wife, Marjorie undergoes a second metamorphosis. She is a new antipatriarchal fabulator who changes into a feminist fabulator—a feminist separatist. After tolerating Rigo's mistress and refusing to have an affair with an attractive Grassian, she leaves Rigo and runs off with a male foxen. Her letter to Rigo explains that "one of the foxen and I are going on a journey. No one knows whether we will arrive anywhere or be able to return. If we do not, someone else will eventually" (Tepper, 448). The metaphorical wall she builds between herself and manhood—and mankind—is much more effective than Montresor's wall that seals Fortunato in the vault. When Marjorie journeys to an environment that does not include human men and patriarchal constructions, she, from her perspective, entombs all aspects of manhood. She ventures outside the symbolic order. "*He* [the foxen] did not know her as Marjorie. This might be the last time she heard her name" (Tepper, 449). Her refusal to act in terms of manhood enables her to name him, to define foxen as "important creatures[,] . . . an intelligent race" (Tepper, 372). This discovery leads to a situation in which—echoing Le Guin's "She Unnames Them" (an alternative creation myth about Eve deviating from patriarchal language and unnaming animals)—he unnames her.

Grass hints that Marjorie may be a new Eve. Her relationship with the male foxen seems to be sexual: "His claw touched her again, teasingly" (Tepper, 449). Another form of metamorphosis is integral to *Grass* (a novel that metamorphoses from antipatriarchal fabulation to feminist fabulation): the transformation of the entire human species. *Grass* is a sister text to novels that portray this transformation: Octavia Butler's Xenogenesis series, Arthur Clarke's *Childhood's End*, and Tiptree's *Up the Walls of the World*. After Marjorie joins the male foxen, the "someone else" who eventually returns might be their child. It/she/he will not behave according to the tenets of manhood.

Whether or not this child appears, Marjorie learns that her ultimate emotional experience involves loving foxen while she is located outside patriarchy, not hunting them to prove manhood. She chooses to love a male Other to manhood whose species is persecuted in the name of proving manhood. She experiences splendor in the grass with an alien who is a counterpart to Melville's hunted white whale. *Grass*, is certainly "not one of the 'boys' books' " that "proffers a chaste male love as the ultimate emotional experience" (Fiedler, 144).

NEMESES

Males who inhabit this real, conventional world of ours can, in the manner of Marjorie, experience metamorphosis. Isaac Asimov, for example, did so. *Nemesis*, his last novel, shows that he was not one of "the daring revolutionaries . . . [who] become old fossils after a few decades. Their imaginations harden with encrusted self-love and that's their end" (Asimov, 305). *Nemesis*, an example of antipatriarchal fabulation that gestures toward feminist science fiction, shows that, at the end of his life, Asimov wrote for girls— began anew. *Nemesis* is Asimov's power fantasy for girls, his story about what Joanna Russ calls the "rescue of the female child" (Russ, "Utopias," 80, 82; I discuss this theme in chapter 13).

This child is Marlene Fisher, the teenaged daughter of Eugenia Insigna and Crile Fisher, a man who leaves his family. Although Crile succeeds in his efforts to find Marlene, she does not view him as a hero. Eugenia and Marlene do not welcome the man who deserted them:

> "Marlene, would you go anywhere with this man?" [Insigna asks.]

"I'm not going anywhere with anyone, Mother," said Marlene quietly.

Insigna said, "There's your answer, Crile. You can't leave me with my child of a year, and come back fifteen years later with a 'By the way, I'll take her over now.' . . . She's your daughter biologically but nothing more. She's mine by the right of fifteen years of loving and caring." (Asimov, 368)

The father who does not nurture is not to be trusted. Marlene and Eugenia, females who together form a family unit, are the heroes of Asimov's novel. The former is an extraordinarily intuitive adolescent who enjoys a special relationship with the planet Erythro; the latter is the astronomer who finds and names Nemesis, the veiled star that threatens to collide with earth.

Erythro, the planet that is a better parent to Marlene than Crile, finds her. This planet is "an art connoisseur, a collector of beautiful [human] minds" (Asimov, 384), a critic who determines that Marlene possesses the most beautiful mind it encounters. "It must have found Marlene's mind to be the most beautiful of all. *That* was why it seized upon her. Wouldn't you—if you had the chance to acquire a Rembrandt or a Van Gough. That was why it protected her so avidly" (Asimov, 383). Counter to the discourse of manhood, Erythro chooses to value a girl. The planet's decision points to the number of beautiful female minds that are not chosen, not nurtured—wasted.

Nemesis makes an additional statement about women's talent. Nemesis, the veiled star a woman discovers and names, "stays behind the cloud, scarcely budging from its position" (Asimov, 52). Because their achievements are shrouded, many working women do not budge from (or move beyond) marginal professional positions. Despite the potential impact of their talent, like Nemesis, many professional women are unseen. Asimov emphasizes this point when one of his female protagonists, a brilliant physicist, becomes as invisible as Nemesis:

" 'The physicist I have my eye on [says Crile Fisher's director] is one T. A. Wendel, who, I'm told, is the best hyperspatialist in the Solar System. . . . And I want Wendel.'

" 'And do you wish me to get him for you?' [answers Crile.]

" 'Her. She's a woman. Tessa Anita Wendel of Adelia.'

" 'Oh?' " (Asimov, 132).

Wendel's future world is no less conventional in regard to manhood than our own. Both worlds adhere to the same master narratives: discourses of manhood. Crile Fisher, even though he has been married to a female scientist, does not recognize that the best hyperspatialist in the solar system is female. *Nemesis* proclaims that female minds are important, that female professionals should be respected and seen, that young girls' mental acuity should be nurtured.

Like women's minds and professional roles, Nemesis is itself falsely categorized according to a fixed definition. Nemesis is not necessarily a nemesis. Wu, a member of Wendel's scientific team, "was full of plans for making use of gravitational repulsion to nudge the movement of the neighbor star. (He called it Nemesis now, but if he could formulate a plan to move it ever so slightly, it might not be Earth's nemesis at all" (Asimov, 380). Asimov's earth sans the threatening death star resembles the post–cold war United States sans the threatening Soviet Union. Both have lost their nemesis.

Both might face the same new nemesis: the retribution of professional women whose achievements are veiled. Feminist minds have the potential to collide explosively with patriarchy.[7] Nemesis, "the Goddess of Retribution, of Justified Revenge, of Punishment" (Asimov, 24), might be ready to seek vengeance for the marginalization of female professionals as well as for the lack of attention directed toward young female minds.[8] Like Mink Snopes who slowly, yet progressively, returns to Jefferson, the alien feminist green pencils are slowly, yet progressively, returning to earth. Their impact can be effective. Despite all the efforts to hide it, feminist science fiction is a nemesis of patriarchal thought. Yet, regardless of its threatening potential, feminist science fiction does not have to function as a nemesis. Wu discovers an alternative for Nemesis. I propose an alternative for feminist science fiction that involves neither retribution, revenge, nor punishment: critics who view feminist science fiction as a nemesis might change their minds and support my plan (which I outline in *Feminist Fabulation*) to move postmodern fiction toward including more women writers. This plan entails defining feminist science fiction as an integral part of literary postmodernism, a replenisher of contemporary fiction. "Nemesis *is* there" (Asimov, 51).

Feminist science fiction, like Nemesis the death star, is a powerful entity that is lost in space. Many feminist critics have ignored the fact that feminist science fiction *is* there. I decided not to be one of them. I answered when feminist science fiction, using the words Crile addresses to his employer, says to feminist critics, "I would be lost in space and you might never find me" (Asimov, 70). Hearing the words spoken by Crile, a male subaltern, as the "child cry" (Tillie Olsen's term) of feminist science fiction, I respond by saying "not to worry." Just as Eugenia found Nemesis, I am one of the pioneering critics who found feminist science fiction.

Upon ensuring that Nemesis will no longer be lost in space, Eugenia insists, "One thing, though. I must be able to name the star. If I give it a name, then it's my star. . . .Nemesis is mine. I have a say in it" (Asimov, 24, 54). Although I have argued that feminist science fiction should be renamed as a part of feminist fabulation, I do not share Eugenia's attitude. Her demand, for my taste, adheres too closely to manhood. Perhaps because I am not a female character created by Isaac Asimov (I am no "three syl-lables—Mar-LAY-nuh—with a little trill to the 'r'" [Asimov, 5]), perhaps because I am free to express myself in a manner alien to patriarchal pens, I would never claim that feminist science fiction criticism is "mine." I cast aside entrepreneurial manhood's owner-ship models in regard to my relationship with feminist science fiction criticism.

I turn to mothers—to Stowe's Mrs. Shelby and Barrie's Mrs. Dar-ling. Mrs. Shelby says, "'Feel too much! Am not I a woman,—a mother?'" (Stowe, 84). I choose motherhood, not manhood. I consider myself to be one of the nurturers of feminist science fic-tion. Adhering to the spirit of feminist science fiction's portrayals of daughters mentored by female communities, I consider myself to be one of this academic field's mothers. I am proud of the "daughter" books.[9]

When Mrs. Darling tells her husband about seeing Peter Pan and finding Peter's shadow, she asks, "'George, what can it mean?'" (*Peter Pan*, televised version). Mothers who are protagonists of feminist utopian science fiction novels never ask fathers to deter-mine meaning. Feminist science fiction, the literature in which mothers' words are law, should not be treated as a hidden, de-tached shadow. Many critics who define what we think of as canons of postmodern fiction are just beginning to agree with this state-ment. Perhaps when Peter seeks his shadow and explains that he wants a mother to tell him stories, he speaks for canonical male postmodern writers who wish to find and hear the feminist science fiction stories presently positioned as lost shadows.[10] Peter Pan could be expected to enjoy examples of antipatriarchal fabulation and to prefer Stowe's daughters' maternal stories to Melville's sons' stories of entrepreneurial manhood. Powerful American men will grow up when they act in kind.

NOTES

1. Throughout this chapter I use the word *manhood* to refer to the ideology of entrepreneurial manhood Leverenz describes.

2. Lang utilized Hermann Oberth and Willy Ley as space flight consultants. Willy Fritsch, Gerda Mauris, Klaus Pohl, and Fritz Rasp are the actors who appeared in the film.

3. The *New York Times* reports that the "United States ended World War II the globe's unquestioned leader, the only nation to enter the postwar era at full industrial capacity and in possession of nuclear weapons. As a result [according to Marc Tucker, president of the National Association on Education and the Economy], from 1945 into the late 1950's, 'we were enormously confident in our economic institutions, and in our social structure,' Mr. Tucker observed, while the Germans and the Japanese, and to some extent other Europeans, had to rebuild. . . . The Germans, Japanese and others restructured their societies . . . to suit" (Brinkley, 10).

4. On the contrary, the Pentagon is authoring myths about new threats. The *New York Times* reports that "the Pentagon envisions seven scenarios for potential foreign conflicts that could draw United States forces into combat over the next ten years. . . . Maintaining forces capable of fighting and winning one or more of these scenarios . . . would require a robust level of military spending into the next century. The [Pentagon] documents suggest levels of manpower and weapons that would appear to stall, if not reverse, the downward trend in military spending by the mid-1990's. . . . The planning described in the documents does not mean that any of the conflicts described are inevitable or imminent, and the Pentagon itself calls the scenarios 'illustrative' and 'not predictive.' . . . The seven scenarios will serve as the foundation for long range budget planning. . . . The 70 pages of planning documents were made available to the *New York Times* by an official who wished to call attention to what he considered vigorous attempts within the military establishment to invent a menu of alarming war scenarios that can be used by the Pentagon to prevent further reductions in forces or cancellations of new weapon systems from defense contractors. . . . The new documents, which could

well shape military forces for years to come, indicate that while the Pentagon has abandoned planning for a super-power military confrontation, after the collapse of the Soviet Union and the end of the cold war, it is not yet prepared to consider drastically reduced force levels" (Tyler, 1, 8). These are the seven scenarios (or myths) the article describes: Iraq invades Kuwait and Saudi Arabia; North Korea attacks South Korea; the Iraqi and North Korean invasions occur at the same time; Russia attacks Lithuania and Poland with help from Belarus; a coup in the Philippines threatens 5,000 Americans there; a coup in Panama threatens access to the Panama Canal; a new expansionist superpower emerges.

5. In early January 1992 ABC television's "Prime Time Live" featured reports on the resurgence of Nazism in Germany and Austria. At the same time, *New York Magazine* featured Peter Hellman's article "Stalking the Last Nazi."

6. Perhaps the most startling shift from manhood to the female occurred in the sports world. From an American perspective, the most important aspects of the 1980 Winter Olympics involved men: Eric Heiden's speed skating and the victory of the American hockey team over the Soviet team. In contrast, as *New York Times* sportswriter Dave Anderson announces in "The Women of Winter Save U.S.," the most exciting aspects of the 1992 Winter Olympics involved women such as figure skaters Kristi Yamaguchi and Nancy Kerrigan and speed skater Bonnie Blair. Furthermore, a nationalistic showdown was enacted by women figure skaters, America's Yamaguchi and Japan's Midori Ito, not male hockey players. (To further critique master narratives about "us" and "them," I call attention to the fact that the American skater who vanquished her Japanese rivals is related to Americans who were placed in interment camps during World War II.)

7. Robin Morgan describes this potential collision: "And they wonder why women seem so *angry* these days. . . . They will go on wondering why and how we recommit ourselves to grasp hands and hold fast, across gulfs of ethnicity and age, ability, class, sexuality. They will go on wondering as their own wives and daughters, colleagues and secretaries, turn against them. They will still be wondering when, if *Roe v. Wade* is destroyed, the most massive civil disobedience this country has ever seen will clog their streets, their communications lines, their hallowed rotundas. We have worked for a quarter of a century to name our pain and rage aloud—and now it is spoken. It should come as no surprise that what is at last heard will at first be disbelieved. . . . They can call it anything they wish, but they can never again ignore it. . . . It is the surfacing of the depths onto the shore, of the private into the public, of the hidden and despised into light. It is momentum against inertia. It is the energy of action. It is the earth erupting. It is the people speaking. *It is us*" (Morgan, 1).

8. Asimov's *Nemesis* has a real counterpart. The *New York Times* reports that "a NASA team is now suggesting that all nations get together to watch out for One Big Dumb Rock—the one with Earth's name on it. The theoretical danger is that somewhere in space is an asteroid a half-mile or so wide that's on a track to collide with Earth some day. The collision, like a boulder flung into a bathtub, would send tidal waves around the world and throw enough dust into the atmosphere to block the sun's light. Plants would wither and die, and if the intergalactic version of a nuclear winter lasted long enough, humanity would starve. Just such a collision is suspected by some of wiping out the dinosaurs 65 million years ago. . . . A half-mile-wide asteroid flew through the planet's [Earth's] path in 1989. 'The Earth had been at that point only six hours earlier,' a House report noted. 'Had it struck the Earth, it would have caused a disaster unprecedented in human history" ("Heading," 5).

9. At the conclusion of *The Female Man*, Russ calls her novel a "daughter book."

10. In chapter 10 I explain that Salman Rushdie is one such male author.

WORKS CITED

Anderson, Dave. "The Women of Winter Save U.S." *New York Times*, 23 Feb. 1992.

Andrews, Suzanna. "The Man Who Would Be Walt." *New York Times*, 6 Jan. 1992.

Asimov, Isaac. *Nemesis*. New York: Bantam, 1990.

Barr, Marleen S. *Feminist Fabulation: Space/Postmodern Fiction*. Iowa City: University of Iowa Press, 1992.

Barrie, J. M. *Peter Pan*. 1911. Reprint. New York: Scribners, 1980.

Brinkley, Joel. "U.S. Looking for a New Path as Superpower Conflict Ends." *New York Times*, 2 Feb. 1992.

Butler, Octavia. Xenogenesis Trilogy: *Dawn*; *Adulthood Rites*; *Imago*. New York: Warner, 1987–89.

Clarke, Arthur C. *Childhood's End*. New York: Harcourt, Brace and World, 1953.

Clinton, Bill. Inaugural address. 20 Jan. 1993.

"Dallas." Lorimar Productions. CBS. Produced by Philip Capice and Leonard Katzman. Created by David Jacobs. 1978–91.

The Doctor. Touchstone. Produced by Edward S. Feldman. Written by Robert Caswell (from the novel *A Taste of My Own Medicine* by Edward E. Rosenbaum). Directed by Randa Haines. 1992.

Fiedler, Leslie. "Come Back to the Raft Ag'in, Huck Honey." In *The*

Collected Essays of Leslie Fiedler, 142–51. New York: Stein and
Day, 1971.

French, Marilyn. *The Women's Room*. New York: Ballantine, 1977.

Gentle, Mary. *Golden Witchbreed*. New York: New American
Library, 1985.

Haraway, Donna. "A Manifesto for Cyborgs." In *Coming to Terms:
Feminism, Theory, Politics*, edited by Elizabeth Weed, 173–204. New
York and London: Routledge, 1989.

"Heading off the Big One." *New York Times*, 5 Apr. 1992.

Hellman, Peter. "Stalking the Last Nazi." *New York Magazine*, 13 Jan.
1992, 28–33.

Hook. Amblin Entertainment–Tristar. Produced by Jim V. Hart and Dodi
Fayed. Written by Jim V. Hart and Malia Scotch Marmo (from the
story by Jim V. Hart and Nick Castle, adapted from the book by Sir
J. M. Barrie). Directed by Steven Spielberg. 1992.

Le Guin, Ursula K. *The Left Hand of Darkness*. 1969. Reprint. New
York: Ace, 1976.

——— . "She Unnames Them." In *Buffalo Gals*, by Ursula K. Le Guin,
194–96. Santa Barbara: Capra Press, 1987.

Lessing, Doris. *The Marriages between Zones Three, Four, and Five*. New
York: Random House, 1980.

Leverenz, David. *Manhood and the American Renaissance*. Ithaca and
London: Cornell University Press, 1989.

Lewis, Anthony. "Metaphor for Failure." *New York Times*, 5 Jan. 1992.

"Lost in Space." Twentieth Century–Fox. CBS. Created and produced by
Irwin Allen. 1965–68.

Morgan, Robin. "Bearing Witness." *Ms.*, Jan./Feb. 1992.

Oberth, Hermann. *Die Rakete zu den Planetenräumen*. Munich:
R. Oldenbourg, 1923.

——— . *Wege zur Raumschiffahrt*. Munich: R. Oldenbourg, 1929.

Olsen, Tillie. *Silences*. New York: Delacorte/Seymour Lawrence, 1978.

Ordway, Frederick J., and Randy Liebermann. *Blueprint for Space
Science Fiction to Science Fact*. Washington and London: Smithsonian
Institution Press, 1992.

Peter Pan. NBC. Produced by Richard Halliday. Directed by Vincent J.
Donehue. Choreographed by Jerome Robbins. (Based on *Peter Pan* by
J. M. Barrie.) Composed by Moose Charlap, Carolyn Leigh, and Betty
Comden. Lyrics by Jules Styne and Adolph Green. Music by Elmer
Bernstein and Trude Rittman. December 8, 1960.

Petersen, Donald E., and John Hillkirk. *A Better Idea: Redefining the
Way Americans Work*. Boston: Houghton Mifflin, 1992.

Piercy, Marge. *He, She and It*. New York: Knopf, 1991.

Poe, Edgar Allan. "The Black Cat." In *The Norton Anthology of American Literature*, edited by Nina Baym et al., 1418–25. New York: Norton, 1989.

———. "The Cask of Amontillado." In *The Norton Anthology of American Literature*, edited by Nina Baym et al., 1442–46. New York: Norton, 1989.

Regarding Henry. Scott Rudin Productions–Paramount. Produced by Robert Greenhut. Written by Jeffrey Abrams. Directed by Mike Nichols. 1992.

Russ, Joanna. *The Female Man*. 1975. Reprint. New York: Gregg Press, 1977.

———. "Recent Feminist Utopias." In *Future Females: A Critical Anthology*, edited by Marleen S. Barr, 71–85. Bowling Green, Ohio: Bowling Green State University Popular Press, 1981.

Simmons, Adele. "After the Thaw 'A Moral Component.'" Interview with Felicity Barringer. *New York Times*, 2 Feb. 1992.

Star Trek. NBC. Created by Gene Roddenberry. Produced by Gene Roddenberry, John Meredith Lucas, Gene L. Coon, and Fred Freiberger. 1966–69.

Star Trek: The Next Generation. Syndicated. Created by Robert Lewin. Produced by Gene Roddenberry and Rick Berman. 1987– .

Star Trek IV: The Voyage Home. Paramount. Produced by Harve Bennett. Written by Harve Bennett, Steve Meerson, Peter Krikes, and Nicholas Meyer (based on a story by Leonard Nimoy and Harve Bennett and the television series created by Gene Roddenberry). Directed by Leonard Nimoy. 1986.

Stowe, Harriet Beecher. *Uncle Tom's Cabin*. 1852. Reprint. New York: Signet, 1966.

Strom, Stephanie. "Playing as a Team." Review of *A Better Idea: Redefining the Way Americans Work*, by Donald E. Petersen and John Hillkirk. *New York Times Book Review*, 5 Jan. 1992.

Tepper, Sheri S. *Grass*. 1989. Reprint. New York: Bantam, 1990.

Tiptree, James, Jr. "Houston, Houston, Do You Read?" In *Aurora: Beyond Equality*, edited by Vonda N. McIntyre and Susan Janice Anderson, 36–98. Greenwich, Conn.: Fawcett, 1976.

———. *Up the Walls of the World*. New York: Berkley, 1978.

———. "Your Haploid Heart." In *Star Songs of an Old Primate*, by James Tiptree, 1–38. New York: Ballantine, 1978.

Tyler, Patrick E. "Pentagon Imagines New Enemies to Fight in Post–Cold-War Era." *New York Times*, 17 Feb. 1992.

Woman in the Moon (*Frau im Mond*). Deutsche Universum Film AG. Produced by Fritz Lang. Written by Thea von Harbou. Directed by Fritz Lang. 1929.

10

HAROUN

AND

SEEING

WOMEN'S

STORIES

SALMAN
RUSHDIE
AND
MARIANNE
WIGGINS

"Do I still keep women as the subject?"

—*Philippe Sollers,* Women

Haroun and the Sea of Stories very obviously reflects recent events in Salman Rushdie's life. What is not so obvious, however, is that this work answers Sollers's question affirmatively. I want to argue that women are a subject of *Haroun*. To do so, I will act like Padma, a character in *Midnight's Children*. Linda Hutcheon explains that Padma "pushes the narration in directions its male narrator had no intention of taking, so the ex-centric have not only overlapped in some of their concerns with postmodernism, but also pushed it in new directions" (Hutcheon, 69). I push *Haroun's* narration in a direction he had no intention of taking when I explain that *Haroun* overlaps with the concern that feminist novels—especially feminist science fiction novels—have been excluded from canons of postmodern fiction.

My reading of *Haroun*, in addition to conforming to Padma's actions, resembles how the narrator of *Shame* describes the text in which he appears. This narrator explains that "the women seem to have taken over; they marched in from the peripheries of the story to demand the inclusion of their own tragedies, histories, and comedies, obliging me to couch my narrative in all manner of sinuous complexities, to see my 'male' plot refracted, so to speak, through the prisms of its reverse and 'female' side" (Rushdie, *Shame*, 173). Women take over when I read *Haroun*. I refract *Haroun's*—and Rushdie's—male plot through its reverse, female side. This tale's emphasis on the importance of stories includes seeing the importance of women's postmodern stories. Rushdie, a male postmodernist who has been threatened for saying things some people do not want to hear, alludes to postmodernism's exiled—and silenced—female science fiction writers. Although Rushdie's situation is, without question, more extreme than that of his female colleagues who write science fiction, *Haroun* easily lends itself to a female side: feminist science fiction that, instead of being recognized as a means to link feminism with postmodern fiction, has been shrouded in a veil.

At first, in contrast with postmodern canons, Haroun's family is characterized by a balanced presence of a woman's and a man's voice. He hears "his father's ready laughter and his mother's sweet voice raised in song" (Rushdie, *Haroun*, 15; all subsequent Rushdie citations refer to *Haroun*). This balance becomes upset when Haroun's father (Rashid Khalifa), because he is so concerned with his own stories, does not notice that "Soraya [his wife] no longer sang" (Rushdie, 16). Refusing to abide this situation, Soraya runs off with a man who hates stories (Rushdie, 21). Rashid is expected to be comforted by a cliché: "She may have left you *but there are plenty more fish in the sea*" (Rushdie, 43). Haroun challenges this cliché's implication that Soraya lacks individual value. He says, "Was his mother a promfret? Must she now be compared to a glumfish or a shark?" (Rushdie, 43). *Haroun* mirrors this question through "Plentimaw Fishes" who mate for life and speak in rhymes, in a different voice (Rushdie, 84–85). The Plentimaw Fish reverse and rewrite, in positive terms, a cliché about animosity between women and men. They also exemplify a corrective to the dearth of women writers within postmodern canons. Plentimaw Fish are story factories who "create new stories in their digestive systems" (Rushdie, 86). Instead of seeing individual women as an interchangeable sea of women, or instead of seeing women and men casting each other aside because they are buoyed by fishing in a sea of interchangeable people, Plentimaw Fish represent a new story about women and men freely speaking together. Plentimaw Fish address the possibility that women's and men's new stories— male postmodern fiction and feminist science fiction—can swim in tandem in the sea of canonical stories.

This objective, however, is easily accomplished neither in the real world (which contains ayatollahs and other patriarchal critics) nor in Haroun's worlds. (In addition to his own world, Haroun experiences Kahani, earth's invisible second moon, a world—from his world's perspective—that is fantastic.) The world in *Haroun* encompasses Gup City's army/Library of Pages, Chapters, and Volumes (Rushdie, 88), an army of words poised to fight a war of words. The army/Library challenges those who wish to "stitch up" the lips of the "Guppee Princess" Batcheat (Rushdie, 104) and pollute the "Ocean" of stories (Rushdie, 105). Rushdie's words become weapons aimed at those who silence him—and those who silence his female colleagues. He rewrites an "eye for an eye" as a "story for a story." His counterattack involves telling new stories, seeing nonrepressive constructions of reality.

The Plentimaw Fish insist that saving Princess Batcheat is a wasted effort to resuscitate exhausted stories about rescuing princesses (Rushdie, 118). This effort is a polluting *"anti-story"* dumped into the ocean of stories to "murder new tales" (Rushdie, 160)—such as liberating stories about women. Patriarchal critics want to marginalize these liberating stories because, in the words of Cultmaster Khattam-Shud, " 'The world is for Controlling. . . . And inside every single story, inside every Stream in the Ocean, there lies a world, a story-world, that I cannot Rule at all' " (Rushdie, 161). Khattam-Shud and his ilk try to control women by fostering sexist stories and nullifying emancipatory stories. Princess-in-distress stories—stories of helpless women who wait to be rescued by men—no longer have a relevant place in the contemporary ocean of stories. This type of story is exhausted; no one, for example, can stand to hear Batcheat's story about her lover, Prince Bolo (Rushdie, 186–87). Batcheat and her real counterparts (of both genders) who tell exhausted, sexist tales are rightfully silenced. "Batcheat kept her mouth shut, and everyone was as happy as could be" (Rushdie, 193).

Cultmaster Khattam-Shud is a member of this happy group. Rashid Khalifa explains that "you can almost understand why the Cultmaster wants to shut her [Batcheat] up for good" (Rushdie, 186). Stories of repression have become so tiresome, many adherents to ideologies that say that "the world is for Controlling" no longer want to hear them. Soviet Communism, for instance, has been undone by Soviet Communists. Journalist Serge Schmemann, writing in the *New York Times*, emphasizes that Boris Yeltsin's old association with Communism is crucial to his new role:

> This [the Soviet Union] is a nation in many ways undoing its own work. For all the rhetoric of captivity, the people at the barricades around Mr. Yeltsin's headquarters were fighting a faith in which three generations had been reared and on which they themselves had been nurtured. They were reviving the symbols their own forefathers had rejected, searching for roots their nation had tried to sever.
>
> It was central to Mr. Yeltsin's role that he arrived as a pillar of the old order, a classic party boss with a Communist lineage. The commissars he now confronts are men very much like him, and there are few among his supporters who could claim no linkage to the old order. (Schmemann, 1)

Soviet Communism is an exhausted story that some former Communist cultmasters no longer want to hear. In the United States, exhausted white male stories are beginning to be relegated to a similar fate. Within the film industry, for example, white men who control the studios are allowing younger black men to tell their stories. (I am thinking of films such as John Singleton's *Boyz 'n the Hood*.)[1] Repressive and racist stories are in the process of being drowned in the real world's ocean of stories. *Haroun* announces that (1) patriarchal stories are antistories that nullify women's postmodern stories and (2) it is necessary to see and locate women's stories in the sea of canonical postmodern stories.

Blabbermouth the Page, not Princess Batcheat, is the female character in *Haroun* who makes this declaration. In the manner of female science fiction writers who use male pseudonyms, Blabbermouth functions in the patriarchal world by concealing her sex. When Haroun discovers her deception, Blabbermouth articulates a female viewpoint about the war of the words, the problems faced by women who wish to become (or to create) pages: " 'You think it's *easy* for a girl to get a job [working as a Page] like this? Don't you know girls have to *fool people* every *day* of their *lives* if they want to get *anywhere*? You probably had your whole *life* handed to you on a *plate*, probably got a whole *mouth* full of *silver spoons*, but some of us have to *fight*' " (Rushdie, 107). What Haroun got is a whole mouth full of patriarchal language. The words are not always analogous to silver spoons, however. Although Haroun, son of Rashid the Shah of Blah, inherits the male narrative tradition, his father is silenced. Rashid regains his voice only after women are allowed to speak and to be heard. Haroun is the canonized male metafictionist who automatically inherits the father's literary stature; Blabbermouth is the ostracized feminist fabulator who wishes, when speaking in her own voice, also to be accorded high stature. Rushdie, who is himself threatened by those who wish to silence him, fights for Blabbermouth—for feminist fabulators.

Despite Blabbermouth's effectiveness as a Page, the male ruler Prince Bolo refuses to allow her to participate in the patriarchal language army. She risks her life to diffuse a bomb; Bolo, after discovering that Blabbermouth is a girl, says, " 'You're fired.' " Blabbermouth reacts by adhering to her identity and speaking in her own voice: " 'Mister, *I quit*' " (Rushdie, 183). She quits the patriarchal language army and finds an unexpected new employer. In a move that is as surprising in Blabbermouth's world as Yeltsin's new real-world role, Rashid offers to employ her (Rushdie, 184).

This fixture of the patriarchal literary establishment offers a helping hand to a defiant daughter. Rushdie, a male metafictionist, extends a similar cooperative gesture to his feminist colleagues.

Haroun optimistically proposes that female and male postmodernists can work together to create a new, inclusive order within the contemporary literary world. After Blabbermouth acts as a go-between for Chup and Gup, these cities establish a peace in which "Speech and Silence, would no longer be separated into Zones by Twilight Strips and Walls of Force." The young defiant feminist acts as an emissary for peace when speaking the "Gesture Language Abhinaya" (Rushdie, 191), a language that functions outside patriarchal definitions. For example, the word *blabbermouth* no longer demeans articulate girls: "Blabbermouth" is "a popular name in Gup for girls as well as boys" (Rushdie, 98).

Rushdie comments on the patriarchal worlds constructed by patriarchal words. Haroun and Iff the Water Genie travel to Kahani on the back of Butt the Hoopoe, a mechanical bird who flies via "P2C2E"—"A Process Too Complicated To Explain" (Rushdie, 66). This process, and Kahani itself—a moon that patriarchal science fails to detect—critiques science's agenda in regard to explaining all processes. "The Moon, Kahani, travels so fast—wonder of wonders!—that no Earth instruments can detect it" (Rushdie, 67). Kahani evades patriarchal stories, and its presence challenges these stories. *Haroun*, in the manner of the science fiction component within feminist fabulation, situates alternatives to patriarchal stories on a world that is not Earth.

Living conditions on Kahani trivialize flying saucers, science fiction's stereotypical technological trope. Kahani residents must go to Earth to secure nonbasic food items: " 'So this is where the Unidentified Flying Objects come from,' Haroun marvelled. 'And that's what they've been after: snacks' " (Rushdie, 92).[2] *Haroun* criticizes deriving power from myths about machines, science, and theories that are presented as truth; when the impossible occurs (from the perspective of the definition of possibility in *Haroun*'s fantastic world), Haroun, to end animosities between Chup and Gup and to negate Cultmaster Khattam-Shud's black magic, wishes that Kahani's orbit would turn so that the moon would no longer be half dark and half light (Rushdie, 170). Haroun's wish comes true (Rushdie, 171). He moves a world. He nullifies the "immense super-computers and gigantic gyroscopes that had controlled the behaviour of the Moon." He shows that individual "will-power" can thwart repressive master narratives and technologies (Rushdie, 172). Haroun defies his world's science and changes his world. In addition, *Haroun* suggests that aspects of the fantastic can become real. Blabbermouth's story and Kahani's science, which are fantastic from Haroun's perspective, exist in Haroun's world. Upon leaving Kahani and returning to his world, Haroun finds a text that proves that Kahani is real: Blabbermouth's invitation to return to Kahani (Rushdie, 204).

Haroun, in the manner of feminist fabulation, emphasizes women's stories and suggests that alternative stories are an important means to reconstruct the world. (Kahani, the name for Haroun's home city as well as Earth's second moon, means "story.") *Haroun* asserts that when repressive individuals and systems wield power, stories and the reality based on the systems they control become polluted. Hence, Khattam-Shud (and real-world despots) try to plug the source of stories in the ocean of stories, try to stop stories' free flow. Khattam-Shud constructs mechanisms (such as "darkbulbs" and the "Dark Ship" [Rushdie, 150]) to ensure that "all the good stories in the world will go wrong for ever and ever, or just die" (Rushdie, 137). Freely flowing stories thwart Controllers. Haroun is a hero who liberates the "many Streams of Story, of so many different colours, all pouring out of the Source at once" (Rushdie, 167). This outpouring counters the possibility that only single, fixed interpretations rise to the surface of the ocean of stories. When his Gift of Gab is restored, Rashid tells the story of Khattam-Shud (Rushdie, 206) and, by doing so, inhibits the ability of Controllers to control.

Rushdie suggests that women's stories must become an integral component of the many currents in the ocean of stories. Haroun, after all, is the inheritor of his family's temporarily silenced patriarchal storytelling tradition who seeks his voluntarily departed, lost mother. He recognizes that stealing the mother's voice, removing her from the literary mainstream, is yet another mechanism of control. He demands that Khattam-Shud "hand her [his mother] over" (Rushdie, 155). Soraya returns to her family; *Haroun* reinstates the voice of the mother as well as the voice of the father (Rushdie, 210). In *Haroun*, Blabbermouth's position as the disconcerted postmodern female storyteller—the silenced Other positioned outside the canon—is *khattam-shud*, "completely finished, over and done with" (Rushdie, 216). *Haroun* includes stories about how a young male hero functions as a feminist fabulator and how his father acts as a benevolent patriarch who assists an assertive woman. *Haroun* concludes when the female voice is restored, when Haroun's "mother had begun to sing" (Rushdie, 211). Like his father, Haroun has the potential to author stories in conjunction with a female member of his generation: he can return to Kahani and generate stories with Blabbermouth.

For the moment, though, Haroun decides that "I honestly don't need to go anywhere at all" (Rushdie, 211). Feminist critics do not have this luxury. They need to continue to go to the Source of stories and unplug this Source and release stories about mothers and daughters. The goal of this feminist journey to the story Source should be to enable women's and men's tales to resemble the discourse of Plentimaw Fish, a couple who speak intelligently, equally, and in tandem. Yes, *"there are plenty more fish in the sea"* (Rushdie, 43). *Haroun* redefines this cliché in terms of the need for changed patriarchal stories and language. Rushdie asks readers to see the Plentimaw Fish in the sea of stories, to see women's stories and men's stories as connected equals.

Rushdie's recent real story, retold in *Haroun*, also exists in a second retold version authored by his estranged wife, Marianne Wiggins. Wiggins and Rushdie, a couple who speak in tandem, act as Plentimaw Fish in relation to the life story they both experience. Wiggins's "Croeso I Gymru" and "Zelf-Portret," stories included in *Bet They'll Miss Us When We're Gone* (a collection dedicated to her father), ensure that the story of how efforts to silence Rushdie affect a woman is not lost. The woman who can call Rushdie's story her own story has not been silenced.

"Zelf-Portret" answers its own question, "Where does the past exist?": "It lies submerged, it lies in lies, a land that's disappearing even as it happens, lost to reclamation" (Wiggins, "Portret," 74–75). In terms of women's stories, the very existence of "Zelf-Portret" provides a more optimistic answer. Wiggins's version of the story she shares with Rushdie has not disappeared, does not need reclamation, has not been written as a patriarchal lie, and does not lie submerged in the sea of stories.

In both "Portret" and "Croeso," Wiggins positions herself as a stranger in a strange land who uses language to orient herself. She speaks directly to the power of language, in "Croeso," when she describes her efforts to learn Welsh while hiding in Wales:

> To learn to write was an ancient Celtic fear, an accomplishment charged with retribution and danger. Caesar, encountering the Celts, judged their belief to be that knowledge, rite, wisdom, rune—those who could write of those things held power, those who could write of the arcane, of rite and of worship, were people who deserved to be, who must be feared. Hiding one's name, never writing it down, never committing one's name into symbol, is still a recurring motif in Welsh legends and stories. It's still dangerous to put one's name on paper. *Mae'r dial drosodd* speaks the legendary Welsh voice, rising from the bottom of the river: *vengeance is over* the words mean. (Wiggins, "Croeso," 56)

Women who claim their part in stories once articulated only by men are now less feared. Wiggins can publish her version of the story she experienced while living with Rushdie. The patriarchal story about silencing women does not cause Wiggins to hide her name. It is not dangerous for her female story to rise from the river, to be part of the story water flowing from the sea of stories. Currently, when a female writer publishes her view of the story she shares with a male writer, vengeance is over, or *mae'r dial drosodd*. Vengeance is *khattam-shud*, completely finished, over and done with, in the past.

Wiggins's story of hiding is "*yn eich elfen* which means 'in your element'" (ibid., 52). Her story is within its element in the sea of stories. Rushdie is free to cast Haroun as the teller of his tale; Wiggins is free to cast a woman—Anne Frank—as the teller of hers. Wiggins defines Hitler as a version of Khattam-Shud, another dictator/Controller concerned with "plugging up" stories. She writes: "They [Nazis] were going to inundate the land [Holland]. . . . Anne Frank says so in her diary, they were going to pull the plug on Holland, *glug*, consign it to infernal depths, as unreclaimable as History, last defense" (Wiggins, "Portret," 67). Linking herself with Frank enables Wiggins to position Holland as a place of unsubmerged women's stories. When she rereads Frank and when she comments on the number of "*zee* words" (ibid., 72) in Dutch, Wiggins enables readers to "*zee*" her particular zelf-portret, women's alternative story articulated by women's alternative words.

Wiggins's reality is not appropriately expressed by her narrator's zelf-portret, however. The narrator concludes the story by commenting, "I'm invisible. Jou tell me how we end. Jou're the artist. I'm just the artist's friend" (ibid., 76). Wiggins, who is not invisible, can articulate the end of her own story of invisibility. She is the artist, not just the artist's wife. She is the singing Soraya Khalifa, a visible female writer. Wiggins has been married to an almost literally invisible man: Rushdie, a man positioned as Woman, is the male feminist fabulator who, because of politics and circumstance, shares much in common with marginalized, colonized, silenced Woman.

Before their estrangement, like Plentimaw Fish, Wiggins and Rushdie were a couple who contributed to the sea of stories together. Their relationship illustrates that since, for example, Zelda Fitzgerald's day, the plug that retards the flow of women's stories has been loosened. Now, soon after the publication of Zelda Fitzgerald's collected writings, is an appropriate time to read the Wiggins/Rushdie literary relationship as a retold, improved version of the Sayre/Fitzgerald literary relationship. (Wiggins, after all, is not in a situation analogous to the one Sollers describes when discussing Zelda Fitzgerald: "His own wife[,] . . . Zelda[,] . . . she wanted to write . . . to outdo him. . . . She went mad[,] . . . was put away" [Sollers, 324]). The story of the Fitzgeralds is also currently recast in a third version that improves on the Wiggins/Rushdie relationship. Another literary couple, Louise Erdrich and Michael Dorris, continue to act as Plentimaw Fish in the sea of stories. In *The Crown of Columbus*, a novel resulting from their collaboration, unlike Wiggins's and Rushdie's separate texts, Erdrich and Dorris speak together. *The Crown of Columbus* provides an opportunity for readers to see a new world for the equal presentation of women's and men's stories.

Crown, a story about anthropologist Virginia Twostar and her lover Roger Williams, demands to be read as a story of female/male equality. Twostar acts according to new gender roles that allow a woman and a man to costar when presenting their stories. She evokes Rupert Birkin's notion of a woman and a man acting as "two single equal stars balanced in conjunction" (Lawrence, 139). Roger Williams, of course, evokes the founder of Rhode Island who defended democracy, religious toleration, and Native American rights. The historical Williams constructed seventeenth-century Rhode Island as a landmark of freedom. Williams, like Rushdie, was banished for stating his beliefs. Rushdie and Williams (both the historical figure and the fictional character) are "good guys" who counter repressive master narratives. They are feminist fabulators who author alternatives to stories of domination. (In regard to parenting, Williams agrees to act according to Twostar's rules.)

Once upon a time (during the 1970s), female feminist fabulators wrote about separatist feminist utopias and told vengeance tales rightfully directed against patriarchal imperatives. Sollers parodies one such tale. This is how he describes a story written by the British novelist he calls Angela Lobster:

> There he [Evelyn, a young male British professor] meets the women of Beulah, an underground city run by Amazons who themselves are ruled by the Mother (The Earth-Mother, the Castrating Mother, every possible item in the litany of Woman-as-Mother). . . . The Mother is enormous, embryonic, with several breasts; she is also a surgeon. . . . Evelyn's sperm is collected and, after a remarkable operation that changes him into a woman, he is inseminated with it, in order to produce the first child created in this manner. . . . Eve then meets a one-eyed, one-legged phallocrat by the name of Zero, who has a bust of Nietzsche on his desk and a harem of seven (one for each day of the week). . . . Eve is brutally deflowered and becomes a real woman, spending her time either servicing Zero or performing household tasks. . . .
>
> And this is put out as publicity! At last a real novel! *The Hormones of the New Eve!* (Sollers, 285)

Within the worlds of separatist feminist utopias, female characters sometimes feel justified about their decisions to kill men. Now, more than a decade after separatist feminist utopias proliferated, it is time to remember men such as the real and imagined Roger Williams. It is time to emphasize that men themselves can act as both feminist fabulators and allies to female feminist fabulators. Reading *Haroun* as a male postmodernist's effort to argue for the visibility of women's stories is one reason to declare an end to literary gender war. Men can be on women's side. Women, when reading some men's stories, can declare *mae'r dial drosodd, khattam-shud*—vengeance is over, completely finished, over and done with. This declaration can be derived from juxtaposing Wiggins's female voice and Rushdie's male voice speaking about the end of vengeance. Woman's voice, "rising from the bottom of the river" (Wiggins, "Croeso," 56), is poised to join the male currents that serve as tributaries to the sea of postmodern stories. As for the people who continue to author patriarchal stories, well, there are now Plentimaw Fish in the sea.

Sollers's postmodern novel provides one such alternative. *Women*, which exhaustively depicts a male narrator's sexual exploits with intelligent women cursorily introduced to the novel's readers, is as much a parody as *The Hormones of the New Eve*. Sollers imagines that his readers demand, "WE WANT A PROPER NOVEL! . . . And what about the screwing?" (Sollers, 434). He parodies male-authored novels that cast women as sex objects. He criticizes men who silence women's stories and prevent readers from seeing women's stories. Cyd, one of the narrator's intelligent female sex partners, rightfully defends Sollers:

" 'No—you're sweet! I love you!'

" 'You love a male chauvinist pig?'

" 'Of course not! You're an angel! . . . You only pretend!' "
(Sollers, 439–40).

Sollers and his narrator only pretend to be pigs. In the manner of feminist science fiction, *Women* exaggerates patriarchy in order to unmask patriarchal repression. Cyd's death, the result of a terrorist attack (Sollers, 483–84), reflects the behavior of male authors who, when they snuff out female characters' stories, act as terrorist attackers. *Women* announces that the "male chauvinist pig" tale and the female revenge tale are exhausted literary forms.

What next? Sollers suggests that "in the glorious world of tomorrow," mothers will rejoice about their daughters' first periods and they will join hands to dance around the corpse of the dead dragon of patriarchy. In addition, boys' "first spurt of sperm" will be celebrated (Sollers, 345). Fair enough. Male authors can speak in tandem with female feminists. Male authors can facilitate readers' ability to see women's stories; feminist science fiction can include men's stories. The sea of stories is large enough to encompass female and male stories that flow together.

NOTES

1. Films created by black women include Julie Dash's *Daughters of the Dust* and Leslie Harris's *Just Another Girl on the IRT*.

2. Kurt Vonnegut trivializes technology in a similar manner when, in *The Sirens of Titan*, Salo receives trite replies from the planet Tralfamadore in regard to his malfunctioning spaceship part. Salo carries, for a million Earthling years, a message that is a "single dot" meaning *"Greetings"* (Vonnegut, 300–301).

WORKS CITED

Boyz 'n the Hood. Columbia Pictures. Produced by Steve Nicolaides. Written by John Singleton. Directed by John Singleton. 1991.

Daughters of the Dust. Kino International. Produced by Julie Dash and Arthur Jafa. Written and directed by Julie Dash. 1992.

Erdrich, Louise, and Michael Dorris. *The Crown of Columbus.* New York: Harper Collins, 1991.

Fitzgerald, Zelda. *Zelda Fitzgerald: The Collected Writings.* Edited by Matthew J. Bruccoli. New York: Scribners, 1991.

Hutcheon, Linda. *A Poetics of Postmodernism: History, Theory, Fiction.* New York and London: Routledge, 1988.

Just Another Girl on the IRT. Miramax. Produced by Leslie Harris and Erwin Wilson. Written and directed by Leslie Harris. 1993.

Lawrence, D. H. *Women in Love.* 1920. Reprint. New York: Penguin Books, 1985.

Rushdie, Salman. *Haroun and the Sea of Stories.* London: Granta Books, 1990.

——— . *Midnight's Children.* London: Picador, 1981.

——— . *Shame.* London: Picador, 1983.

Schmemann, Serge. "Across East Europe to Moscow, the Trail of Freedom Reaches Tyranny's Epicenter." *New York Times,* 25 Aug. 1991.

Sollers, Philippe. *Women.* 1983. Reprint. New York: Columbia University Press, 1990.

Vonnegut, Kurt. *The Sirens of Titan.* New York: Dell, 1959.

Wiggins, Marianne. "Croeso I Gymru." In *Bet They'll Miss Us When We're Gone,* by Marianne Wiggins, 45–57. New York: Harper Collins, 1991.

——— . "Zelf-Portret." In *Bet They'll Miss Us When We're Gone,* by Marianne Wiggins, 59–76. New York: Harper Collins, 1991.

Ursula Le Guin's "Sur" as Exemplary Humanist and Antihumanist Text

*The as yet unperceived interaction,
rather than antipathy, between
humanist and antihumanist theories
will become more important.*
—Christopher Butler,
  "The Future of Theory:
  Saving the Reader"

When Christopher Butler, in "The Future of Theory: Saving the Reader," outlines the debate about the nature of the subject, he turns to John Berger's *G* and Donald Barthelme's "Alice." Butler explains why Berger's novel is an exemplary text for the humanist position (which stresses human rational consciousness) and why Barthelme's story is an exemplary text for the antihumanist position (which stresses that human subjects make neither history nor narrative). Butler, who does not wish to dismiss the humanist position, asks, "If we play no part as individuals in the formation of the structures that constitute us, what point is there in our engaging ourselves in the attempt to alter them?" (Butler, 232). Ursula Le Guin creates characters who try to alter the structures that constitute them and who reflect Butler's question. In addition, examples of her work emphasize that structures result from impersonal processes. Reading Le Guin, then, sometimes involves encountering an alliance between humanism and antihumanism that resembles the contradiction Butler attributes to the Lacanian position. According to Butler, "Lacan thus produces an antihumanist notion of the subject, which still wishes to use the humanist rhetoric of struggle, victimization and loss" (Butler, 233). So does Le Guin.

Le Guin's "The Ones Who Walk Away from Omelas" and "She Unnames Them," for example, reflect an alliance between humanism and antihumanism. "Omelas," a reader response story, asks readers for their opinion: "Do you believe? Do you accept the festival, the city, the joy? No? Then let me describe one more thing" (Le Guin, "Omelas," 280). The narrator wishes to influence readers' choice regarding whether to believe or not to believe. No matter which choice readers make, they can never know where the ones who walk away from Omelas go: "The place they go towards is a place even less imaginable to most of us than the city of happiness. I cannot describe it at all. It is possible that it does not exist. But they seem to know where they are going, the ones who walk away from Omelas" (ibid., 284). Readers, who at once exercise control and lack of control in relation to this story, encounter a title that makes language meaningless and also clarifies this meaninglessness. Le Guin states that "Omelas," a word signifying nothing, refers to a road sign: Salem, Oregon, spelled backward (ibid., 276).

In the same vein, "She Unnames Them" at once discusses efforts to control narrative and the futility of making such efforts. At the start of the story, animals undertake the humanist/antihumanist debate. While "whales and dolphins, seals and sea otters" are happy to rescind their names, the same cannot be said for yaks (Le Guin, "Unnames," 27). The story's unnamer, an unnamed "she," chooses to attempt to alter linguistic structures when she returns patriarchal language to Adam and his father. While the unnamer's action might be successful, readers will never know her name. (Within this story's ambiguous narrative world, "she" is not necessarily Eve; the story does not indicate that its protagonists ["she" and Adam] and setting [a garden] coincide with one of the creation myths humans generate. The story might be set on an extraterrestrial world where animals talk and Adam resides in a garden with a female being who is not named Eve. The unnamer's humanist action, then, might not be undertaken by a human.) "She Unnames Them" is at once humanist and antihumanist: while the ultimate success of the female protagonist's action is not clear, she tries to change a narrative/historical system she did not make. Readers are told that "she" walks away from the garden, returns the "gift" of patriarchal language, and haltingly speaks her own new words. They cannot know, however, if her action will result in descendants (human or extraterrestrial) whose companions (probably male) are constituted by master narratives that encourage them to say, "without looking around . . . 'O.K., fine, dear. When's dinner?'" (ibid.).

"She Unnames Them" and "The Ones Who Walk Away from Omelas" exemplify Butler's point that I cite in this chapter's epigraph. The science fiction component within feminist fabulation perceives the as yet unperceived; Le Guin is a fabulator who writes stories involving interaction between humanist and antihumanist theories. This interaction forges a second alliance between disparate camps—the division in contemporary experimental fiction Butler describes as "the liberal, which includes John Fowler, Mosley, Muriel Spark, and others, and the postmodern, which includes Walter Abish, Robert Coover, John Hawkes, and Leonard Michaels" (Butler, 234). Butler is concerned with the future of theory and saving the reader; I am concerned with the future of feminist fabulation and saving from oblivion the texts constituting feminist science fiction (or fantastic feminist fabulation). I read Le Guin with an eye toward preventing feminist science fiction from being excluded from the categories "contemporary experimental fiction" and "postmodernism." As my cursory attention to

"Omelas" and "She Unnames Them" indicates, Le Guin's work is both humanist and antihumanist, liberal and postmodern. I support this statement by discussing the humanist and antihumanist characteristics of "Sur." I argue that "Sur" is an exemplary liberal and postmodern text.

The alliance "Sur" establishes between the liberal and the postmodern can be understood according to the story's connection to Robert Scholes's "structural fabulation" and my "feminist fabulation."[1] In terms of structural fabulation, members of the all-female *Yelcho* expedition to the South Pole, like men who mount expeditions of this sort, confront the system of the universe that does not care about them. In terms of feminist fabulation, female explorers, unlike their male counterparts, confront the system of patriarchy that does not care about women. Female and male explorers employ different methods to deal with structural fabulation's relationship to their expeditions. Le Guin's South American female explorers, like garden-variety male explorers, encounter a harsh, indifferent universe. While men usually try to alter nature, Le Guin's women make no such attempt.

Male explorers can be expected to leave some sign of arriving at their destination; Le Guin's narrator, in contrast, comments, " 'I was glad even then that we left no sign there [at the South Pole]' " (Le Guin, "Sur," 2020). Planting a flag does not form the crux of the women's agenda. Unlike men, they must struggle against patriarchal as well as natural impediments. It is, for example, necessary for these women to assert their subjectivity to themselves. They must understand that people named "Juana, Dolores . . . Carlota, Pepita, and Zoe" (ibid., 2017) are just as able to be explorers as people named Robert, Ernest, and Roald.[2] Thinking and acting counter to patriarchal stories regarding sex roles, the female explorers must believe that it is appropriate for them to travel to the South Pole. Opposing patriarchal stories about the importance of broadcasting achievements, they have "no intention of publishing . . . a report" (ibid., 2008) about their journey. The actions of the *Yelcho* expedition members are at once humanist and antihumanist, liberal and postmodern.

Like the protagonist of Berger's *G*, they take action as human subjects (they strive to reach the South Pole). In terms of Barthelme's "Alice," not marking the pole or publicizing their achievement is "symptomatic of that deconstruction of personal identity which is part of the postmodern aesthetic" (Butler, 234). The female explorers, then, act in accordance with the aforementioned contradiction Butler attributes to Lacan. Although both patriarchy and the universe do not care whether or not these women reach the South Pole, adhering to humanist rhetoric, they still struggle to do so. In addition, adhering to antihumanist rhetoric, they make no effort to alter the systems of the universe or patriarchy by marking the pole or publishing a report. Their liberal/postmodernist, humanist/antihumanist stance announces that, instead of trying to alter the universe and mirror patriarchy, it is more sensible for women to conduct themselves in a woman-centered manner. Antihumanist, postmodern authors declare that "men do not make history (or narrative)" (Butler, 229); Le Guin—an antihumanist, humanist, liberal, postmodern author—declares that, both under patriarchy and in the universe, women do not make history (or narrative). Her characters under discussion here act as women, not women-as-men (what Jean Bethke Elshtain calls the "new woman as the old man" [Elshtain, 128]). Her texts do not conform to the accepted masculinist definitions of the liberal and postmodern components of contemporary experimental fiction. She answers, in specifically female terms, Butler's aforementioned question about the point of attempting to alter the formation of structures that constitute us if we play no part as individuals in their formation (Butler, 232). The protagonists of "Sur," for example, imply that even though women play no part as individuals in the formation of the patriarchal and universal structures that constitute them, women can, in their own particular way, engage in the attempt to alter these structures. A new understanding of contemporary fiction should accompany this women-centered agenda that differs from the patriarchal agenda.

In "Sur" the need for new, nonmasculinist paradigms is reflected by language changed to communicate appropriately the characters' woman-centered, humanist/antihumanist behavior. The title "Sur" exemplifies strange language that reflects the protagonists' strange actions. Brian McHale, in *Postmodernist Fiction*, discusses words and worlds placed under erasure (McHale, 99–111). The title "Sur" places *sir* and all of this word's patriarchal connotations under erasure. "Sur" rewrites *sir*; the former word superimposes the ethnic (*sur* is Spanish for south) and the female (*sur* is the surname of Rosa del Sur, the daughter born at the South Pole in Le Guin's story) upon the latter word's usual implications regarding white male power. The word *sur* articulates the existence of non-WASP, nonmale people and emphasizes that individuals called "sir" are not the only viable people in the world. The word *sur* underscores that women of color can accomplish objectives reserved for white men called "sir."

Like the title "Sur," according to an alliance between humanism and antihumanism, "The Map in the Attic" (a map showing the women's names for the pole's topographical features) pictured in the story (Le Guin, "Sur," 2009) communicates the need for a new understanding of contemporary fiction and for establishing nonmasculinist paradigms. The map is a specific woman's space that represents a woman's story; women name the landscape drawn on this map that charts postmodern metafictional women's writing. While men name places in terms of themselves, the system of the universe is indifferent to these names. Pike's Peak, for example, is oblivious to Pike; his claim on the peak is a mere patriarchal story, a fiction about signifying man's control of the peak. "The Map in the Attic" is also fiction about such patriarchal fictions; it is feminist metafiction that superimposes female fiction on male fiction, rewrites male fiction. The map points out that, in terms of structural fabulation, man names the system of the universe and the system does not care. In terms of feminist fabulation, when women name the system of the universe, both patriarchy and the universe do not care. Conforming to humanist rhetoric, the female explorers struggle to map the South Pole, to create a narrative (a history) for the South Pole. Conforming to antihumanist rhetoric, by making no effort to communicate their narrative (their history) to others, they deconstruct their subjectivity. They do not wish to use their map to redirect patriarchy.

"Sur" begins by announcing this contradiction between the humanist rhetoric of struggle and the antihumanist notion of the subject. The story refers to both the private female essence of a woman's voice and the erasing of a woman's voice from public contexts. Although the narrator does not want to publish the expedition report, she will, for the benefit of grandchildren, keep it in an attic trunk with her wedding attire and her baby's possessions. She explains: "Although I have no intention of publishing this report, I think it would be nice if a grandchild of mine, or somebody's grandchild, happened to find it someday; so I shall keep it in the leather trunk in the attic, along with Rosita's christening dress and Juanito's silver rattle and my wedding shoes and finneskos" (ibid., 2008). Her comment, the opening sentence of "Sur," indicates that readers encounter a marginalized, unpublished ethnic woman's voice. The narrator's concerns about funding the expedition (ibid.) signal that she inhabits a world that shares some characteristics of our world. Like the women Virginia Woolf's "A Room of One's Own" addresses, these women require a salary and their own space. Armed with money from an unnamed "benefactor" (ibid., 2010), the women are positioned to create a specifically female history and narrative of the South Pole. The fact that they derive the idea for their expedition from male texts further adheres to our reality. Because the female expedition members have no women's story to motivate them, Juana provides inspiration by referring to a man's story: " 'Well, if Captain Scott can do it, why can't we?' " (ibid.). They write their experience over a man's experience, live a woman's story in response to a rewritten (or in McHale's terms, "recalled or rescinded," "un-narrated" [McHale 101, 103]) male story. The title "She Unnames Them" articulates the relationship between "The Map in the Attic" and male explorers' South Pole mappings. The map the *Yelcho* expedition creates is a picture that mirrors McHale's pictures of crossed-out words (McHale 101, 103).

The *Yelcho* expedition does not mirror male expeditions, however. Le Guin's explorers travel to the South Pole in a particularly female manner that reflects the fact that women and men do different things in the world. Some women are prevented from joining the expedition because of particularly female responsibilities: "an ailing parent; an anxious husband beset by business cares; a child at home with only ignorant or incompetent servants to look after it: these are not responsibilities lightly to be set aside. And those who wished to evade such claims were not the companions we wanted in hard work, risk, and privation" (Le Guin, "Sur," 2011). Unlike patriarchal society, these women respect what women do. Although most men would not employ such criteria, it is, in fact, prudent to avoid traveling to the South Pole with someone who would ignore ailing parents or children. These women privately question and change the expected characteristics of explorers.

Their changes, like the question regarding believability in "Omelas," invite readers' participation. "Sur" challenges readers to consider whether or not they respect and accept these changed characteristics; the story asks if readers really believe that a group of Third World women can reach the South Pole. The question is stated indirectly: "On the seventeenth of August, 1909, in Punta Arenas, Chile, all the members of the Expedition met for the first time: Juana and I, the two Peruvians; from Argentina, Zoe, Berta, and Teresa; and our Chileans, Carlota and her friends Eva, Pepita, and Dolores" (ibid.). According to patriarchal stories, women named Eva, Pepita, and Dolores—doubly marginalized Third World women—do not have the wherewithal to mount a successful expedition. I expect that when readers first learn that Eva, Pepita, and Dolores will attempt to reach the South Pole, they expect the women to fail. The image of women of color journeying to the South Pole without men is almost as jarring as this sentence from *The Left Hand of Darkness*: "The king was pregnant" (Le Guin, *Left Hand*, 100). The female explorers at once do not control and act in opposition to patriarchal narratives that define as ludicrous the notion that Third World women can be heroic explorers.

Their opposition involves both countering the stereotypical conception of what kind of people are explorers and rewriting narratives about how explorers behave. Casting patriarchal stories aside, the *Yelcho* expedition members author their own behavioral codes. They realize, for example, that women do not need to act in terms of masculinist hierarchical systems. The narrator's role as leader is never tested: "The nine of us worked things out amongst us from beginning to end without any orders being given by anybody, and only two or three times with recourse to a vote by voice or show of hands" (Le Guin, "Sur," 2012). These women who are "all crew" (ibid.) understand that people do not need to try to vanquish nature. They respect penguins' viewpoints: "Eight Adelie penguins immediately came to greet us with many exclamations of interest not unmixed with disapproval" (ibid., 2013). The penguins who act as a receiving party have their own language and own Antarctica. Le Guin emphasizes that male explorers treat the penguins differently. When the women encounter Hut Point, the "large structure" (ibid.) built by Captain Scott's party, they enter male space and view the implications of large patriarchal structures. The area surrounding Hut Point "was disgusting—a kind of graveyard of seal skins, seal bones, penguin bones, and rubbish" (ibid.). While men rape the environment and fail to clean the mess, the women respect nature—and they value housework.

Hut Point's inside space is not more pleasant than its outside space. The narrator observes that "it was dirty, and had about it a mean disorder. . . . Empty meat tins lay about; biscuits were spilled on the floor; a lot of dog turds were underfoot—frozen, of course, but not a great deal improved by that" (ibid., 2014). Her observation calls for exploring new paradigms regarding the characteristics necessary for explorers. She points out that housekeeping, women's work, is not trivial. Housekeeping requires expertise: "Housekeeping, the art of the infinite, is no game for amateurs" (ibid.). Following a female game plan, the women literally and figuratively close the door on a patriarchal structure without destroying that structure: "Zoe counterproposed that we set fire to it [Captain Scott's hut]. We finally shut the door and left it as we had found it. The penguins appeared to approve" (ibid.). The members of the *Yelcho* expedition celebrate the difference between female efficiency and male efficiency and deconstruct patriarchal stories that justify men's domination of women. They coin a new definition of heroism. These women who are more concerned about penguin's approval than men's approval do not waste energy destroying patriarchal structures. When positioned outside patriarchal society, the *Yelcho* expedition members become a "significant [group] of people [who] find themselves talking about human identity in one way rather than another" (Butler, 246). According to the women's conversation, male explorers are subjects who act like slobs, not heroes.

Le Guin's female explorers, in the manner of the protagonist of Berger's *G*, adhere to the humanist notion of intentionality. In addition, they are protagonists of a story that functions like Barthelme's "Alice." "Sur" is "an attempt at systematic [redescription] that engage[s] us with a certain kind of decentered irrationality, and thus leads us to look at new aspects of behavior" (Butler, 246). "Sur" leads us to look at new aspects of the definition of heroism, emphasizes that some components of the definition are irrational. Male explorers automatically conform to this definition that resists including women. In truth, however, Robert Falcon Scott, Sir Ernest Henry Shackleton, and Roald Amundsen are—like Zoe, Pepita, and Delores—protagonists of fictions. These men are a part of patriarchal history and narrative that exalts male heroes. Despite this exaltation, however, the details of Scott's, Shackleton's, and Amundsen's specific achievements have been erased from the public mind. (It was necessary for me to refer to footnotes to learn exactly what Scott, Shackleton, and Amundsen accomplished.) Hence, the women's decision not to publish their report—not to seek notoriety—is both counter to patriarchal stories and extremely rational. Their humanist decision-making process reflects the anti-humanist situation male heroes downplay: natural structures and human discourse structures erase human achievement.

"Sur" redescribes men's stories and calls for respecting narratives that do not conform to patriarchal conceptions of importance. In "Sur," for example, the usual attributes explorers possess—as well as the ability to undertake housework efficiently—position women as authors and architects who write nonpatriarchal stories and build nonpatriarchal structures. The women's base is superior to Scott's hut: "They [Berta and Eva] were its chief architect-designers, its most ingenious builder-excavators, and its most diligent and contented occupants, forever inventing an improvement in ventilation, or learning how to make skylights. . . . It was thanks to them that our stores were stowed so handily, that our stove drew and heated so efficiently" (Le Guin, "Sur," 2016). The women are successful. At this point in the story, the notion of competent South American female explorers no longer strikes readers as ludicrous. Because readers encounter evidence that women can construct viable alternative systems, readers do, finally, believe in Pepita, Zoe, and Dolores.

"Sur" emphasizes that women who do not adhere to male behavior patterns are, nonetheless, effective. Although the *Yelcho* expedition members "could not have expected to pull as much or as fast as his [Scott's] men" (ibid., 2017), they reach their goal in their own way. They deconstruct the myth that women should defer to men's greater physical strength. This myth, in fact, deconstructs itself in technological society: women's ability to push buttons equals men's ability to push buttons. The same holds true for driving sledges. "The Southern Party consisted of two sledge teams: Juana, Dolores, and myself; Carlota, Pepita, and Zoe" (ibid.). This litany of female names now denotes efficiency. "Sur" rewrites patriarchal stories and presents intrepid Third World female explorers.

Feminist fabulation superimposes female stories on male terrain and trains readers to rethink gender stereotypes. The *Yelcho* expedition members name topographical features according to women's experiences; they deviate from the usual practice of men naming the environment in terms of themselves. While Shackleton calls a glacier the Beardmore, "Zoe and Juana had called the vast ice river that flowed through that gateway the Florence Nightingale Glacier" (ibid., 2018). Giving Nightingale's name to the glacier is humanist and liberal: the characters take action. This action is also antihumanist and postmodern: even though renaming a glacier in terms of women asserts the importance of female achievement, "on maps, of course, this glacier bears the name Mr. Shackleton gave it" (ibid.). The female explorers' decision to rename the glacier, which is important to them, affects neither natural nor manmade structures. In terms of an alliance between humanism and anti-humanism, the explorers acknowledge that the names they give to terrain will be ignored by the geographical community: "We gave names to these peaks, not very seriously, since we did not expect our discoveries to come to the attention of geographers" (ibid., 2019). Patriarchal stories require men to be less quick to admit that their discoveries do not affect the system of the uni-verse. The name *Beardmore* underscores that, even though the system of the universe does not care, more of the people who have beards will continue to name things after themselves. Beardmore is synonymous with patriarchy.

The universe is equally inhospitable to women and men. When the *Yelcho* expedition reaches twelve thousand feet, the narrator explains "that is not a place where people have any business to be. We should have turned back; but since we had worked so hard to get there, it seemed that we should go on, at least for a while" (ibid.). Her comment applies to women's place in the system of patriarchy as well as to people's place in the system of the uni-verse. (It often seems as if women's efforts to establish footholds within patriarchal professional systems are as difficult as journey-ing to the South Pole.) In the business world, powerful positions are high places where, according to patriarchal stories, women have no business to be. Should women who try to attain these positions turn back? Some do. Those who persevere, those who had worked so hard to get there, want to go on—at least for a while. Women, after all, are still unable to change patriarchal professional master narratives into feminist professional master narratives—to make all-female heroic expeditions real. Women do not inhabit a world that considers *sur* to be as important as *sir*. Professional women still must find a space for themselves within a story called "Sir." I echo

Joanna Russ's term "female man," to underscore that, because all institutions are patriarchal, a professional woman is a female sir. I hope this situation will not be permanent. (Although Russ's title "When It Changed" can never describe the universe's domination of people, this title can apply to men's domination of women.) It is not impossible to coin *sur* as a term to represent respect for nonpatriarchal difference. It is not impossible for feminists to leave a permanent mark on patriarchy. Attempting to mark the system of the universe, however, is futile. The female explorers recognize this futility.

The members of the *Yelcho* expedition deviate from patriarchal imperatives when they reach the South Pole and pitch a tent. Instead of leaving a mark to communicate the glory and durability of human achievement, these women merely wish to enjoy tea in a sheltered environment: "Nothing of any kind marked the dreary whiteness [at the South Pole]. We discussed leaving some kind of mark or monument . . . but there seemed no particular reason to do so. Anything we could do, anything we were, was insignificant, in that awful place. We put up the tent for shelter for an hour and made a cup of tea" (Le Guin, "Sur," 2020). The dreary whiteness always erases all human marks. While male explorers engage in futile undertakings such as planting flags, Le Guin's women acknowledge their insignificance within the system of the universe. Like the South Pole, patriarchy is an awful place controlled by a dreary whiteness (white men). Despite this awfulness, women who confront patriarchy differ from men who confront the universe: the former confrontation is not hopeless. "Sur" describes people's relationship to the universe in terms of antihumanism; people cannot act as effective subjects in relation to the universe's impersonal structures. Importantly for feminists, the story positions women's relationship to patriarchy in terms of humanism; women can act as effective subjects in relation to patriarchy's impersonal structures. According to "Sur," women are most effective when they deviate from, rather than mirror, these structures.

Domination—one-upmanship of any kind—plays no part in the *Yelcho* expedition. The narrator explains that "I was glad even then that we had left no sign there, for some man longing to be first might come some day, and find it, and know then what a fool he had been, and break his heart" (ibid.). It is rather foolish for people to venture to the South Pole; markers have no logical purpose there. Leaving behind no flag, preparing no published report, these women will record their presence at the pole by passing on their story to members of their family: "My Rosita and my Juanito heard many stories when they were little, about . . . the transparent cattle of the invisible gauchos, and a river of ice eight thousand feet high called Nightingale, and how Cousin Juana drank a cup of tea standing on the bottom of the world under seven suns, and other fairy tales" (ibid., 2021). The narrator's comment calls the fixed definitions of "fiction" and "fact" into question.

On one level, the women's expedition to the South Pole is a fairy tale. Yet, the possibility that South American women were the first people to reach the South Pole exists. "Sur" might be true. There is another possibility: like "She Unnames Them," "Sur" might be the story of extraterrestrials who inhabit a parallel world that both resembles and differs from our own world. When the *Yelcho* expedition members reach twelve thousand feet, they see "three or four suns" (ibid., 2019). Although this sighting can be attributed to exhaustion-induced mirage, the same cannot be said of the narrator's retrospective memory of Juana standing on the bottom of the world under seven suns. This ambiguity in relation to reality connotes hopefulness. Like "Sur," patriarchy (or "sir") can be understood as a fairy tale, a fictional historical narrative about reality that is open to feminist revision.

The Left Hand of Darkness, when it announces "the king was pregnant," revises biology. "Sur," when it announces "Teresa was pregnant" (ibid., 2021), revises and chastises patriarchy. Because patriarchal stories "had concealed from her" (ibid.) the nature of her physical condition, when Teresa joins the expedition, she is unaware of her pregnancy. Her condition counters the patriarchal story about how pregnant women cannot be effective South Pole expedition members. Patriarchal stories are rewritten in the face of such truths.[3]

The birth of Teresa's daughter coincides with the birth of a narrative about women's success defined in terms of female difference: a female explorer who becomes a mother at the South Pole proves that female difference does not breed female ineptitude. The child born into a female community that resembles a science fiction separatist feminist utopia is named "Rosa—Rosa del Sur . . . Rose of the South" (ibid., 2022). Here, readers discover why Le Guin calls her story about exploration "Sur." "Rosa del Sur" names geographical space as a Latin American woman's south and critiques using northern European male names to designate locations. Within the story, the word *sur* names a woman who is not a WASP. Although the patriarchal world does not recognize this particular meaning of *sur*, the women of the *Yelcho* expedition do. They define achievement according to their own terms. Men who explore the South Pole make no enduring mark on the system of the universe; Le Guin's female South Pole explorers make no enduring mark on the system of patriarchy—and they are not concerned about doing so. Instead of contributing to patriarchal narratives, feminist science fiction authors write their own stories. Although the universe always triumphs over people, patriarchy does not always triumph over women.

Despite the patriarchal stories that would proclaim otherwise, nonpublic female histories and narratives are most important to the *Yelcho* expedition members. These women have "left no footprints" (ibid.) at the South Pole. Male explorers' footprints are equally unenduring. The universe counters the bravura about human male importance in patriarchal narratives. So can women. Although the female explorers return and appear to live in a patriarchally sanctioned manner, their expedition does alter their lives. Having left no footprints at the South Pole and refusing to use their presence there to affect patriarchy, these women walk through life in a manner that differs from the manner in which men walk through life. "Sur" is about respecting this difference and obliterating impediments that block women's paths.

"Sur" presents "a contest between entrenched vocabularies" (Butler, 246), a contest between patriarchy's *sir* and a female community's *sur*. Cultural change occurs when "significant groups of people find themselves talking about human identity in one way rather than another" (Butler, 246); "Sur" is about making the particular way women talk about human identity, their language, significant. "Sur" is about accepting "new vocabulary as liberating us to do more things than the old, to which we can always recur" (Butler, 247). *Sire*, a word meaning person of authority (i.e., a man of high rank) is antiquated and exhausted and has been replaced by a clone: *sir*, an example of new vocabulary that is no more liberating than the old. It is time to retire *sire* and *sir*, to accept the new instead of allowing the old to recur. We might extend white male power to those who are not white and male. The word *sur* liberates us to do more things than the old *sire* and *sir* allowed. The word *sur*, for example, encompasses such newness as redesignating the presently marginal mommy track as the right track; or, to paraphrase the title of Suzanne Gordon's book, *Prisoners of Men's Dreams: Striking out for a New Feminine Future*, "Sur" allows female prisoners of men's dreams to create new feminine futures. Margaret Thatcher is a female sir; Madeleine Kunin is a sur. Instead of trying to retain power by seeking a fourth term as Vermont's governor, Kunin wishes to write, to improve the environment, and to inspire women.[4]

A female sir misrepresents the same as being different. (Again, in Elshtain's terms, the new woman is cast as the old man.) Language reflects this charade. "The king was pregnant" currently conveys a meaning that is as impossible as the meaning of "The president of the United States was pregnant." The latter sentence may not always communicate a fantastic circumstance. (We have, at least, reached a point where this sentence could represent reality: "The publicly acknowledged most trusted advisor of the president of the United States was pregnant.") Retiring *sire* and *sir* simply entails recognizing that *person of authority* is not synonymous with *male*. Such recognition is congruent with realizing that, instead of marginalizing women because they do not conform to men's systems, it is necessary to change those systems to suit women.

Butler's conclusion does not consider this point. He surmises that feminists would "see more to work from in the Berger/Kantian position than the Barthelme/Barthes one" (Butler, 249). Instead of saying that women have nothing in common with a major contemporary theoretical and artistic mode, it is necessary to expand our understanding of that mode to include women. "Sur" is an exemplary text in regard to this expansion. Le Guin's story establishes an alliance between humanism and antihumanism, between the feminine and the postmodern.

Despite the female explorers' individual thoughts and actions regarding the relationship of the word *sur* to new woman-centered methods and meanings, "little Rosa del Sur died of the scarlet fever when she was five years old" (Le Guin, "Sur," 2022). Those who wish to marginalize feminist science fiction by severing it from postmodern canons should take note of her demise. "Sur," according to its own criteria that differ from the established definition of masculinist postmodernism, concerns the death of the subject. In addition, "Sur" applauds individual women who attempt to alter patriarchal structures.

NOTES

1. For a discussion of feminist fabulation and structural fabulation, see this volume's introduction.

2. "Sur" refers to three explorers: Robert Falcon Scott (1868–1912), who explored the Ross Sea region; Sir Ernest Henry Shackleton (1874–1922), who was a member of Scott's expedition; and Roald Amundsen (1872–1928), a Norwegian, who was the first man to reach the South Pole.

3. For example, because of women's active role during the Gulf War, the law that states that women cannot be combat pilots is being changed.

4. Kunin explains: "I think our democratic political system is kept alive and vital when people like me understand that public service in the form of holding political office is not a lifelong occupation. Power is difficult to release. What enabled me to arrive at this decision with a new sense of purpose was the realization that there are other ways to create change. I want to write a book. I want to develop new ideas and strategies on global environmental issues, and I want to continue to inspire women to reach their full capacity" ("New Politician," 59).

WORKS CITED

Barthelme, Donald. "Alice." In *Sixty Stories*, by Donald Barthelme, 68–75. New York: Putnam, 1981.

Berger, John. *G.* 1970. Reprint. London: Weidenfeld and Nicolson, 1972.

Butler, Christopher. "The Future of Theory: Saving the Reader." In *The Future of Literary Theory*, edited by Ralph Cohen, 229–49. New York and London: Routledge, 1989.

Elshtain, Jean Bethke. "Cultural Conundrums and Gender: America's Present Past." In *Cultural Politics in Contemporary America*, edited by Ian Angus and Sut Jhally, 123–34. New York and London: Routledge, 1989.

Gordon, Suzanne. *Prisoners of Men's Dreams: Striking out for a New Feminine Future*. Boston: Little, Brown, 1991.

Le Guin, Ursula K. *The Left Hand of Darkness*. 1969. Reprint. New York: Berkley, 1976.

———. "The Ones Who Walk away from Omelas." In *The Wind's Twelve Quarters*, by Ursula K. Le Guin, 275–84. New York: Harper and Row, 1975.

———. "She Unnames Them." *New Yorker*, 21 Jan. 1985.

———. "Sur." In *The Norton Anthology of Literature by Women*, edited by Sandra M. Gilbert and Susan Gubar, 2008–22. New York: Norton, 1985.

McHale, Brian. *Postmodernist Fiction*. New York and London: Methuen, 1987.

"The New Politician." *Ms.*, July/Aug. 1990.

Russ, Joanna. "When It Changed." In *The Norton Anthology of Literature by Women*, edited by Sandra M. Gilbert and Susan Gubar, 2262–69. New York: Norton, 1985.

12

ALIENS,

AIRPLANES,

AND

CULTURAL

CROSS-DRESSING

"Society," Faulkner said and I don't remember where, "should rest on generosity, that is to say, on the disposition to consider itself as being of a noble race, of a race heroic and even divine."

—*Kathy Acker,* In Memoriam to Identity

In difference is the irretrievable loss of the illusion of one.

—*Donna Haraway,* "Reading Buchi Emecheta"

Buchi Emecheta's *The Rape of Shavi*, Haruki Murakami's "TV People," and Paul Theroux's *O-Zone* explore how "generosity" is extended to a particular social group designated as more noble and heroic than other groups. Emecheta, Murakami, and Theroux, by portraying characters who grapple with the definition of *human*, try to imagine societies that are more noble and heroic than the ones we know.

These authors present imaginative visions by anchoring science fiction tropes to reality. In their texts, airplanes replace spaceships, humans of various races and classes replace extraterrestrial aliens, and foreign countries replace differing planets. Alien encounters between humans provide opportunities for protagonists to undertake cultural cross-dressing. Airplanes—in *O-Zone*, *Shavi*, and "TV People"—enable people to enter foreign cultures, to "try on" difference, to wear difference as newly acquired components of themselves. Emecheta's, Murakami's, and Theroux's realistic fiction presents itself in the guise of science fiction. The authors' textual costuming pertains to reconsidering fixed definitions of literary margins and centers. In this chapter I show how three authors of differing genders and races—a black African woman, a Japanese man (a member of the world's new power elite), and a white North American man—speak to Faulkner's vision of social generosity. I attribute a unified approach to these authors, and I explain why my illusion regarding the potential oneness that reading *Shavi* might enable me to share with Emecheta is irretrievably lost.

Kathy Acker's *In Memoriam to Identity* depicts aliens and airplanes in a manner that both addresses and differs from Emecheta's, Murakami's, and Theroux's presentational modes. In the world of Acker's novel, where lack of generosity prevails as a fixed meaning, human aliens do not use airplanes to engage in cross-cultural encounters. Airplane, Acker's protagonist, a sex-show worker who has been raped, is alienated from patriarchy. Forever remaining outside society's mainstream, she will never array herself in terms of the privilege powerful men can secure for her. Acker portrays unceasing cultural stagnation; Emecheta, Murakami, and Theroux portray cross-cultural interchange accomplished in terms of realistic science fiction tropes. I will briefly focus on Acker's description of two separate cultural groups—marginalized female Others and influential men—before turning to Emecheta's, Murakami's, and Theroux's portrayals of aliens, airplanes, and cultural cross-dressing.

THE RAPE OF AIRPLANE

Memoriam mirrors the structure of Faulkner's blend tale, *The Wild Palms*. Acker's re-creation emphasizes that, according to patriarchal master narratives, women do not blend with society's power structures. Airplane is imprisoned within a patriarchal story about women's subordination. She cannot fly above this story that, as she informs us, demands that if girls do not become whores, at least for a while, they die (Acker, 99). Airplane rightly insists that "males have the power" (Acker, 114) and "women don't have history" (Acker, 219). While Emecheta, Murakami, and Theroux use airplanes to speak about removing the social barriers that have an adverse impact on people designated as Other, Acker's Airplane cannot transcend these barriers.

Airplane does not have the power at once to play a role in mainstream society and counter fixed definitions of female roles. Patriarchy provides no appropriate space for her identity to develop. Acker evokes Faulkner when she indicates that women are prevented from dressing in the guise of power and forging identities that influence the world:

> In Faulkner's novels, men who are patriarchs either kill or maim
> by subverting their daughters. . . . One result, a critic who per-
> haps does not like women has said, is that women have shifting
> identities (perhaps it is that men don't recognize the shifting
> nature of identity), are sluts (is a whore a slut? . . .). Air-
> plane had decided, after considering the facts of herself, that
> women don't have shifting identities today, but rather they roam.
> She was talking, not exactly about Faulkner, but about her own
> self-destructiveness and strength. We are not dead pilots, she
> would say, because we don't roam for the purpose of dying. . . .
> Because she had not made any public thing, history, because
> she wasn't a man, Airplane lived in her imagination. (Acker,
> 220, 221)

According to Acker, patriarchy does not recognize women's shift-ing identities and permits them either to become sluts or whores or to die. Patriarchy casts women as Airplane, individuals who roam from one version of the slut role to another. Contrary to Airplane's statement, society in fact turns female Others into "dead pilots," people who cannot fly from limiting roles. Emecheta, Murakami, and Theroux, in contrast, portray airplanes as mechanisms to enliven the dead pilots who do not contribute to human history. They position airplanes as correctives to the social restrictions Airplane experiences. Their planes are celebrations of rather than memorials to the differing identities of the Other. Airplanes, both symbolic and real, provide a means for Emecheta, Murakami, and Theroux to reflect on Faulkner's notion of a utopian society relying on generosity.

By calling forth a literary patriarch, Acker unmasks patriarchy's lack of generosity toward those who are not powerful. She uses Faulkner's words and structures to speak against narratives that conceptualize white male privilege. Acker, then, discusses difference in terms of sameness. I use a similar tactic. When Emecheta, Murakami, and Theroux write about the same subject, authors who represent different races, genders, and nations cancel distinctions used to categorize literary voices as either marginal or central. Marginality disappears as these three authors—who differ in relation to one another—say the same thing.[1]

This disappearance is accomplished by reevaluating the distinctions between marginalized science fiction and canonical realistic literature. Acker seems to allude to this reevaluation when she describes white people who dress as science fiction characters. She imagines a performance of staged sex involving race and gender in which women and men—and science fiction and reality—merge: "While fucking, two more women at each end of stage walked onto stage. Wearing science-fiction clothes and holding tremendous white plastic dildos. Airplane thought, perhaps it's the white race" (Acker, 247). Emecheta, Murakami, and Theroux also discuss race and gender by dressing reality in science fiction tropes. They present airplanes in the guise of fantastic machines, and humans in the guise of aliens. *O-Zone*, *Shavi*, and "TV People"— realistic fiction that becomes science fiction—cross genres; the protagonists within these works, humans who become marginal aliens, cross cultures.

Like Margaret Atwood's *The Handmaid's Tale*, *O-Zone* is a science fiction future vision derived from plausible extensions of present American reality. In the world of *O-Zone*, America is divided into demarcated spaces: walled cities and a postnuclear no-man's-land. O-Zone, the no-man's-land in what was Missouri, is a space that functions as outer space: "It was the only part of America that was genuinely empty—empty by law, feared by everyone, and heavily guarded. People dreamed about it and used it as a backdrop for their fantasies. Its very name was a word for wilderness and waste, and all its associations made it a complicated and ambiguous metaphor, as if it were not merely a closed-off area in the state of Missouri, but a remote place, with the features of another planet" (Theroux, 326). This description is unreliable; O-Zone is not empty. O-Zone is inhabited by humans (called aliens) who meet wealthy New Yorkers resembling Acker's members of the white race attired in science fiction clothes.

When these white "Owners" fly to O-Zone in rotors (planes), they function as astronauts encountering extraterrestrial aliens. (The Owners/astronauts eat "space food . . . designed for the space program" [Theroux, 46].) The O-Zone aliens (designated by such names as Roaches, Starkies, Skells, and Diggers) experience a cross-cultural encounter with New Yorkers who are cross-dressed as space travelers. "In his suit and helmet and mask and businesslike boots" one of the Owners "looked like an astronaut prepared for free-flight—just swimming in space" (Theroux, 88). *O-Zone* depicts people as analogous to the zones comprising a newly demarcated America, characters relegated to constructed social classification systems.

These classifications, the differences between New York Owners and O-Zone aliens, are subjective and are not based on race. At the start of *O-Zone*, readers cannot discern Owners' reasons for justifying prejudice. Readers simply do not understand the meaning of the words *Roaches*, *Skells*, *Starkies*, and *Diggers*. In addition, the differences between Owners and aliens are further blurred as it becomes apparent that Owners are aliens in O-Zone, the space beyond their system. Theroux, then, explores what makes human aliens alien. Answers emerge after readers observe characters who board planes and approach reciprocal cultural exchange by cross-dressing.

For example, Hooper Allbright, one of the Owners who first flies to O-Zone, returns there and acts according to the classic science fiction trope of an alien kidnapping an earthling. He captures a young O-Zone dweller named Bligh, ensconces her in his rotor, and takes her to New York. Bligh immediately adapts to Owners' privileges. In turn, Hooper's nephew Fisher, a boy who is hermetically sealed in a New York high-rise apartment building called Coldharbor, quickly adjusts to the wilderness after O-Zone aliens kidnap him. Bligh becomes an Owner; Fisher becomes an alien. This reciprocal cross-cultural exchange challenges those who wrongfully define racial behavioral traits as negative, fixed characteristics and unmasks these definitions as mere constructed social designations that place some people outside the category *human*.

In the real world, those who seek a better life emigrate to a different country; in science fiction, such people emigrate to a different planet. *O-Zone* fuses real and science fiction versions of emigration when it presents the idea that real-world humans can improve their lives in outer space. One proponent of this idea tells Hooper that "you don't have to accept this planet. . . . Millions are rejecting it for a better life in space" (Theroux, 339). Theroux's protagonists are emigrants who travel to different real earth locations (countries) presented in the guise of different planets. They flee a social classification system that damages the rich as well as the poor. This system constructs false classifications: male Owners, not the residents of O-Zone, conform to one type of behavior. Hooper Allbright, who, before he meets Bligh, has a personality aptly described as a zero, is almost indistinguishable from his brother Hardy. Hooper's love for Bligh makes it possible for him to broaden himself. Hardy, in contrast, continues to function as a stereotypical powerful white male. (Fisher is spared from becoming another, more extreme, version of his uncles.)

A plane flight serves as a coda to *O-Zone* and addresses the problematical nature of men, such as Hardy, who do not deviate from macho stereotypes. Moura, Hardy's wife, embarks on a return flight to O-Zone to locate the person she perceives to be a nonstereotypical male: the unidentified donor to an artificial insemination clinic who became Fisher's father. Moura, alienated by Hardy's predictability, is an explorer trying to discover a man who is a well-rounded person. Although Moura does not find Fisher's biological father, she encounters a man who is more satisfactory than Hardy. Unlike Hooper, who must have a specific woman (Bligh), Moura does not require a specific man. Any virile, nonpowerful male O-Zone resident—any alternative to the stereotypical Hardy—will suit her. Her plane is her vehicle to discover an alternative to the male stereotypes she has known, the patriarchs who are the true aliens in *O-Zone*.

Theroux imagines correctives to patriarchy and its prejudices. Fisher, the boy who never meets his father, will never function as an Owner/patriarch. He realizes that " 'I don't have a father. . . . That's part of my strength' " (Theroux, 475). Fisher becomes a diversified person who "had the wealth of an Owner and the strength of an alien" (Theroux, 470). He becomes the new man. When Theroux posits this new man, he admits that there is something wrong with the old version. In addition, he creates Moura, a smart, effective woman of initiative who is certainly no dead pilot. As *O-Zone* transcends classifications that separate realistic literature from science fiction, Theroux transcends classifications that separate male authors from female feminist authors.

Moura observes that words "like *alien* or *Owner* or *perimeter* or *clinic* or *O-Zone* . . . had all acquired different meanings this year" (Theroux, 485). This alteration of supposed fixed meanings applies to what feminist critics can now expect from someone designated as "male author." Theroux himself exemplifies the possibility that these critics will encounter male authors who depict interesting female characters and nonsexist scenarios. Theroux, after all, announces that "O-Zone was the world" (Theroux, 510). So does Erica Jong. Her poem "Another Language" echoes Moura's point about words acquiring different meanings. Jong, in a specifically female manner, also announces that O-Zone was the world:

> The whole world is flat
> & I am round. . . .
> The sound of O,
> not the sound of I
> embarrasses the world.
> . . . My world is round
> & bounded by the mountain of my fear;

while all the great geographers agree
the world is flat
& roundness cannot be. (Jong, 343–44)

"Another Language" asserts that the round O, the pregnant female Other, is the world; the pregnant female is a powerful O-Zone. Jong's female poem and Theroux's novel both see the world as a wild zone (Elaine Showalter's term),[2] not a demarcated space ruled by patriarchal definitions.

Jong points out that people do not wish to associate themselves with "the sound of O"; Owners use a plane to separate themselves from space occupied by starving African aliens:

> The party looked around and saw the others [Africans]—fifty, sixty, probably more—it was impossible to count them. They were a mass of dusty rags and death's-heads, big and small, moving slowly, close to the ground. Their faces were sunken and hollow, and their frail skeletons showed through their skin. . . . The starved people shrieked, but they were so weakened their voices were like the cries of small birds. . . . Hardy led the travelers back to the rotor. . . . And then the travelers were safely in the air, and underneath them was the mass of scavenging people that had swarmed out of the crack in the hillside. (Theroux, 369)

Emecheta's Prince Asogba encounters a similar situation when, as a result of his interaction with whites, most of the Shavian men die. Emecheta and Theroux seem to speak in terms of a question Alice Walker poses in "The Right to Life: What Can the White Man Say to the Black Woman?," one of her collected "earthling poems." Walker presents her answer in terms of the fantastic and the real. She imagines the white man saying that he will "call back from the dead" (Walker, 447) black children who died as a result of racism. In terms of reality, she imagines the white man saying, "I will remove myself as an obstacle in the path that your children, against all odds, are making toward the light. I will not assassinate them for dreaming dreams and offering new visions of how to live" (Walker, 448). Theroux is a white man who says what Walker wants to hear. In addition, when he speaks against white people who act as obstacles to the Other, when he himself creates a new vision of how white men might live, Theroux echoes Emecheta. Both Emecheta and Theroux portray white men who might say, "I will cease trying to lead your children, for I can see I have never understood where I was going" (Walker, 448).

Ista, one of the white women who flies to Shavi, articulates the crux of *Shavi* and *O-Zone*: "The fact that their [the Shavian] culture's different doesn't make us more human than they are" (Emecheta, 86). The two novels use the same plot structure to approach the question of how to define *human*. In *Shavi*, the cross-cultural interchange involving O-Zone and New York occurs between Shavi and England, and in both *O-Zone* and *Shavi*, individual protagonists cross-dress as and eventually become "the alien." Fisher becomes an alien after spending time in O-Zone; Asogba behaves like a white British man after spending time in England. However, despite Asogba's behavior, he is relegated to a status resembling that of an O-Zone alien: "He's black, he has no papers and he won't be well treated" (Emecheta, 129).

Again, as in *O-Zone*, genres as well as characters cross-dress. When white aliens from England land their plane in Shavi, reality presents itself in the guise of science fiction. According to the bird-worshiping Shavians, the British plane is as fantastic as a flying saucer. In turn, the white people visiting Shavi become analogous to astronauts journeying to a strange planet. Emecheta and Theroux describe Africa in terms of birds, planes, and aliens. Theroux answers Walker's question by concluding that—although he is unable to harness the fantastic to make right the wrongs white men inflict on black women—he can write a combination of reality and science fiction; he can write the same story as Emecheta.

Theroux is critical of the Allbright brothers; Emecheta points an accusing finger at Ista Kidea, one of her female characters. Ista, a gynecologist, believes that Western medical childbirth methods are superior to their Shavian counterparts (Emecheta, 130–33). Her "western arrogance" (Emecheta, 132) becomes ridiculous when she observes how effectively Shavian women approach childbirth. Like her male counterparts, Ista needs to revise her attitude toward nonwhite culture—and she does. She rewrites her ideas—just as the Shavians rewrite themselves in light of their past role as dominated Other and their present role as would-be dominators of another African culture. More specifically, the Shavians change themselves after they escape from enslavement in the land of the Kukumas.

Shavians must change again after their attack on another tribe results in catastrophe for Shavi. In the face of his community's devastation, Asogba must "find a place for the New Shavi" (Emecheta, 177). The white people, in turn, also attempt to inhabit a new society. They enter a plane to seek an alternative to nuclear weapon proliferation. Ista explains: "We ran away from our over-civilised [*sic*] society because we were about to destroy ourselves" (Emecheta, 64). In Emecheta's novel, both black and white cultures remake themselves (the whites' efforts to do so, however, are temporary). *O-Zone* envisions a remade male; *Shavi* envisions revised cultures. *O-Zone* is a retold version of Emecheta's story about aliens, airplanes, and cultural cross-dressing.

Shavi tells a tale readers already know: the story of how men and whites cause trouble for women and blacks. The "rape" in Emecheta's novel is individual as well as cultural. Ronje, a white man, rapes Asogba's future wife, Ayoko. Despite the Shavians' confusion about whether or not whites can be defined as "human," Ronje's inhumanity is clear to them. As Ayoko's mother, Siegbo, explains, "The creature, Ronje, is an animal, for what human would destroy a beautiful person like you?" (Emecheta, 98). The rape of Ayoko causes Shavian women to deviate from female culture, to become warriors. War becomes the business of mothers; Ayoko "saw her mother transformed into a warrior" (Emecheta, 98). Ayoko, enacting another role reversal, rescues her attacker. Unlike his white fellows, Ronje remains in Africa. His fate is unknown. For once, a white man's story remains untold. Ayoko's story indicates that, counter to racist myths about black women's subhuman status, she is human. She disproves the dehumanizing myth "that most women were created simply to cause men trouble" (Emecheta, 12). Through its discussion of racial interchange, *Shavi* proclaims that "all women, whether the first or ninth wife, were people, just like men" (Emecheta, 78).

"TV People" makes a similar point. Murakami depicts an electronic cross-cultural encounter to emphasize that wives are people. His story's unnamed wife and husband speak in an estranged discourse analogous to the lack of communication between TV people and viewers. The couple's alienation from each other is reflected by TV PEOPLE who step through the TV and build a machine that is at once a plane, a flying saucer, and a domestic image. The husband explains that it "is unlike anything I've ever seen: an upright cylinder except that it narrows toward the top, with streamlined protrusions along its surface. Looks more like some kind of gigantic orange juicer than an airplane. No wings, no seats" (Murakami, 23). Here, as in *O-Zone* and *Shavi*, a cross-cultural encounter between estranged aliens (the TV PEOPLE and the TV viewer) involves airplanes, reality, and science fiction. This encounter is not completely fantastic. TV people can enter realities beyond TV screens; all people can treat each other in the manner of the estrangement existing between viewers and TV people. Murakami emphasizes that wives and husbands routinely seem to be separated by TV screens. The "flying orange juicer" (Murakami, 23) addresses the separate worlds women and men inhabit: "feminine" domesticity and "masculine" technology. When the husband and wife try to use language to bridge the gap separating their worlds, they become TV PEOPLE. According to "TV People," the TV PEOPLE routinely appearing in our homes are our spouses.

At first, the husband, doubting that the cylindrical machine is an airplane, questions how it can fly. He soon changes his mind, accepts that the machine "has to be an airplane. Even if it doesn't appear so" (Murakami, 25). His reaction to the plane resembles his reaction to his marriage. He decides that the nonplane, which does not fly effectively, is a plane; he decides that his nonmarriage, which does not include effective communication, is a marriage. The airplane is an "insane machine, all black and grimy, floating in a field of white light" (Murakami, 24); his marriage, an unsuccessful union of estranged male and female discourse, is also an insane machine. It is a mechanism for a woman and a man to live together in the manner of TV PEOPLE. Murakami's couple, who converse without satisfactory response, merely play the role of wife and husband. Unlike the interchange between the TV PEOPLE and the real world—and, later, the wife and the TV world—the couple, when trying to address each other, uses noninteractive discourse.

Murakami stresses that TV discourse is at once alien and familiar; it is analogous to female discourse and male discourse, which, in relation to each other, are also alien and familiar. Meaningful communication occurs in his story only when women speak together, when "the wife has gone out with the girls—some close friends from her high-school days—getting together to talk" (Murakami, 7). The husband is alienated from the women's meaningful talk. When he is told about his wife's conversation, he reacts in a manner appropriate to an inattentive TV viewer: "I pour myself a beer and follow along, inserting attentive uh-huhs at proper intervals. Though in fact I hardly hear a thing she says. I'm thinking about the TV PEOPLE" (Murakami, 13). He is not engaging in fruitful conversation, nor is he concerned with the printed version of women's language. He does not care about the articles in his wife's copy of *Elle* (Murakami, 14). The couple's involvement with differing language modes extends to their professional lives: "After a nearly wordless breakfast" (Murakami, 15), the wife commutes to her job as an editor of a natural food lifestyle magazine (the world of the humanistic domestic text); the husband commutes to his job in the advertising department of an electrical appliance manufacturer (the world of the mechanistic commercial text). Like their nonexistent breakfast conversation, the texts wife and husband professionally create do not address each other. The wife, unlike her husband, speaks a language that could be called *Elle*. This language is as unintelligible to the husband as the capitalized letters—such as TRPP Q SCHAOUS—that appear throughout Murakami's story. He cannot speak She.

TV PEOPLE picture the couple's alienation. The husband uses the word "reduced" (Murakami, 6) to explain that the TV PEOPLE are small. His lack of respect for his wife's discourse diminishes her. He treats her as the TV PEOPLE treat him: "The TV PEOPLE ignore me from the very outset. All three of them have this look that says the likes of me don't exist" (Murakami, 8). He ignores his wife, reduces her to an invisible woman. He even expects that her reaction to his behavior is scripted: "I can just hear it, line for line" (Murakami, 9). When he hears her words before she has a chance to articulate them, he reduces her to a stereotype. The wife, in turn, treats him similarly. She evokes the stereotypical domestically inept man when she sarcastically informs him that cooking a dinner consisting of vegetables and frozen foods is something that he "can handle" (Murakami, 7). Both the wife and the husband compromise each other's humanity. Neither engages with the other's culture.

In addition, at work the husband acts like the TV PEOPLE. He goes to "endless meetings" (Murakami, 19), endures the repetition a TV character experiences. During these meetings, like a TV news commentator, he must "keep talking." If he fails to do so, he becomes "a dead man" (Murakami, 21). Silence is death on TV.

Although the husband feels that he must generate engaging conversation while on the job (Murakami, 16), he does not feel similarly responsible about his marriage. In addition to considering "uh huh" to be a sufficient response to his wife, he sometimes forgets to phone her when he is late (Murakami, 21). When communicating with her, the husband changes from a fully engaged person to one of the TV PEOPLE. (Murakami, then, portrays cultural cross-dressing as a change of language, not a change of attire.) Originality and response are not important components of their conversations. Even when his professional "world may be crumbling" (Murakami, 17), the husband is reluctant to phone his wife. During his potential crisis, he is at a loss for words to say to her.

While the husband acts like a TV person, the wife becomes one. Although Murakami does not make this analogy, like Alice going through the looking glass, the wife goes through the TV screen, crosses over into TV culture: the TV PEOPLE enter the world of her home; she enters the world of the TV PEOPLE. She is "out there"; she fails "to materialize"; "she isn't coming home" (Murakami, 24). She is lost in space. Without engaged conversation to propel it, without the participants' willingness to enter the culture of the other gender, the couple's marriage does not fly. The marriage, instead, becomes analogous to a canceled TV program. The husband who cannot access his wife faces the possibility that his marriage will never become a rerun.

The story's conclusion is not devoid of hope, though. One of the TV PEOPLE informs the husband that the phone will ring in five minutes. Yet, despite this hope, if his wife is on the line, the husband will have nothing to say. His words, like his wife, "slip away" (Murakami, 26). While the TV PEOPLE possess the paint to add "a touch of color to make it [the mechanistic orange juicer] an airplane" (Murakami, 26), the husband cannot articulate a touch of understanding to his wife. He cannot transform their vacuous relationship into a meaningful marriage. Ironically, though, when the husband first encounters the TV PEOPLE, he articulates what could be his wife's response to his lack of verbal engagement with her: " 'But *you* have people right in front of you denying your very presence like that, then see if you don't doubt whether you actually exist. I look at my hands half expecting to see clear through them. I'm devastated, powerless, in a trance' " (Murakami, 11). Instead of being able to apply his own words to his wife's response to him, he remains frozen in the role of obtuse male. The cross-cultural encounters in "TV People" occur between the real world and the TV world, not between the worlds of women and men. The wife and the husband remain mutually estranged aliens in relation to each other. They are dead pilots who futilely try to fly a domestic mechanism that looks more like an orange juicer than an airplane.

Murakami, however, does not behave in the manner of his male protagonist. He does not have an obtuse reaction to the silencing of women's words. Like Theroux, Murakami is a male author who can speak to women. Emecheta, Murakami, and Theroux—authors representing different races and genders—respond to racism and sexism by creating similar plots.

BUILDING OPPOSITIONS INSTEAD OF AFFINITIES

Donna Haraway discusses "the delicate construction of the just-barely-possible affinities, the just-barely-possible connections that might actually make a difference in local and global histories." She continues:

> Feminist discourse and anti-colonial discourse are engaged in this very subtle and delicate effort to build connections and affinities, and not to produce one's own or another's experience as a resource for a closed narrative. These are difficult issues, and "we" fail frequently. It is easy to find feminist, anti-racist, and anti-colonial discourses reproducing others and selves as resources for closed narratives, not knowing how to build affinities, knowing instead how to build oppositions. But "our" writing is also full of hope that we will learn how to structure affinities instead of identification. (Haraway, 113)

I have so far approached *Shavi* as an open narrative that shares connections and affinities with narratives written by men who are not black. My personal response to *Shavi*, however, involves building oppositions. Even after tracing the affinities between authors who are products of different global histories, when reading Buchi Emecheta, I find myself confronting "the irretrievable loss of the illusion of one." Despite my observations about Emecheta's, Murakami's, and Theroux's shared insights and plot modes, I cannot consider myself to be "one" with Emecheta. My own response privileges the need to structure identification over the need to structure affinities. More directly, although white men and women (including Jews) have, of course, perpetuated negative images of blacks, I am a Jew who is troubled by Emecheta's portrayals of Jews.

I want to shift voices before turning to *Shavi* to explain this statement. I move from a scholarly tone to a personal tone to share some of my experiences during the two separate years I spent as a Fulbright scholar in Germany. I approach these years as a juxtaposition of science fiction and reality, a cross-cultural encounter involving aliens, airplanes, and cultural cross-dressing. The acknowledgment I included in *Alien to Femininity: Speculative Fiction and Feminist Theory*, a book I completed while living in Düsseldorf, coincides with this observation. I wrote:

> I remember receiving the Fulbright grant application and thinking about the section that asks candidates to list preferences for potential host countries. Exciting possibilities came to my mind: Whileaway, Mattapoisett, Gethen. I imagined having the grant pay for my starship fare. I would beam up and spend the flight preparing for a conversation with [James Tiptree's] Tivonel on Tyree. Instead, I boarded a Lufthansa jet and chatted with Ulrich Littmann, the head of the West German Fulbright Commission, at Commission headquarters in Bonn. The chance to live abroad was quite marvelous. I was able to think about extraterrestrial alien societies from the standpoint of a culture which differs from my own. (Barr, xxiii)

Although, at the time, I intended my comments about cultural difference to refer to contemporary Americans and Germans, I now read them as applicable to the fact that I completed *Alien to Femininity* in the country that tried to arrive at the final solution to the problem of alien Jews.

Even though I grew up in a New York City apartment building inhabited by many concentration camp survivors, details about the Holocaust were, throughout my childhood, unknown—alien—to me. I remember asking my mother to explain the meaning of the word *refugee*. Her answer: "Refugees come from the other side." I enjoyed close friendships with survivors' children; the Holocaust was never discussed. I accidentally learned about the Holocaust at the age of ten while reading in the local public library. Because this subject was silenced, Germany became, from my perspective, an O-Zone, a forbidden unknown territory. German was the language of TV people, the TV and movie Nazis who incessantly screamed "achtung" and "schnell." Although I had never met a German until I was a young adult—or even heard the German language spoken calmly by a female—I learned to regard Germans as the monstrous rapists of my people.

It was not until I was an assistant professor engaged with reading feminist science fiction's relationship to the silencing of feminist narratives that I ended the silence regarding my knowledge of Germany. I wished to replace the non-information of my childhood with firsthand experience. My family and my American Jewish friends still remain uncomfortable with my decision. They become argumentative when I describe the many close relationships with Germans I enjoy. They cannot understand why I have a very positive opinion of contemporary Germany. (This opinion is strong enough to motivate me to participate in the cross-cultural exchanges that occur at Manhattan's Goethe House.) The fact that I encountered German culture by living in the manner of a German professional—not as an American tourist—might account for my feelings of connection and affinity toward present-day Germany.

My strongest link to German society, however, involves neither language, literature, nor any other form of high culture. This link, instead, concerns the enjoyment I derive from wearing German clothing. My cross-cultural encounter with Germany centered upon cultural cross-dressing. Julian Dibbell's observations about Carmen Miranda's relationship to camp applies to my relationship to German culture. He says:

> Funny: camp declares itself to be utterly apolitical and so did Carmen Miranda. But if a camp approach to sexual politics is possible, then why not a camp approach to identity politics in general? Surely that is the message coded up in Miranda's story, a message full of warning and encouragement to anyone seeking to shoot the rapids of a true multiculturalism and come out alive. . . . The uses that have been made of Miranda's memory in Brazil and throughout the world remind us never to give up on the liberating promise of her dress-up life. And that's a crucial reminder, because though all of us know by now that biology is not destiny, it's a little harder to remember that neither is

identity. Camp says we can make identity our plaything and get away with it—if we're lucky. (Dibbell, 45)

Although I never walked around Düsseldorf and Tübingen with bananas piled on my head, when I dressed in German clothing whose style, cut, and color differs from American clothing, I acted out a camp approach to identity politics. I was lucky enough to be a Jew in Germany who could make identity a plaything, a Jew who could get away with it, a Jew who could come out alive. I structured affinity by restructuring identity. I looked to a dress-up life—dressing in German fashions—to function as a liberating tool for coping with a past I could do nothing about. I replaced pain and alienation with play and assimilation.[3] While residing in Germany, I behaved like the stereotypical Jewish American princess who shops until she drops. I lived the title of this chapter; I used cultural cross-dressing as a means to merge with an alien society.

While dressed like a German, I flew to cities throughout Europe to lecture about feminist science fiction. The masquerade was effective enough to cause American tourists who looked at my German clothes and my German features (the ones I inherited from my German great-grandparents) to inquire about whether or not I spoke English. One plane trip caused me to drop my guise, however. When flying from Frankfurt to Tel Aviv, I noted the irony of the German airport police, armed with machine guns and tanks, protecting Jews. Upon arriving in Israel on a Lufthansa plane, I changed my deutsche marks for shekels and immediately told the money exchange clerk, "I am an American Jew." My statement to the exchanger indicated that, while in Israel, I wanted no part of the cultural exchange I had previously undertaken.

Reading Buchi Emecheta's *The Rape of Shavi* presents another occasion for me to find it necessary to say I am a Jew. Relationships between Jews and blacks are, as we are all aware, often strained; we fail frequently when trying to resolve our differences. I include my anecdotes about being a Jew who likes contemporary Germany—about being a Jew who enjoys cross-dressing as a German—because I am troubled, in regard to this chapter that I hoped would focus on affinities, about building oppositions between myself and a black female author. I am troubled because, when I read *Shavi*, I encounter negative depictions of Jews.

Haraway states that she sought a utopian moment when she

analyzed Barbara Christian's and Chikwenye Okonjo Ogunyemi's response to Emecheta:

> As for Ogunyemi and Christian, there was a utopian moment nestled in my reading, one that hoped for a space for political accountability and for cherishing ambiguities, multiplicities, and affinities without freezing identities. These risk being the pleasures of the eternal tourist of experience in devastated postmodern terrains. But I wanted to stay with affinities that refused to resolve into identities or searches for a true self. . . . Contradiction held in tension with the crafting of accountability was my image of the hoped-for unity of women across the holocaust of imperialism, racism, and masculinist supremacy. (Haraway, 121)

When I first thought of tracing the affinities between Emecheta, Murakami, and Theroux, I too hoped for a utopian moment. I wanted to show that Alice Walker's question regarding what a white man can say to a black woman could be answered when men (including Murakami, who—of course—is not white) and a black woman share the same literary subject matter and agenda. I surmised that Emecheta would espouse a liberating, antiracist ideal in *Shavi*. I planned to write a noncontentious chapter about how two particular male authors share her viewpoints. My hoped-for utopian moment was quashed after I observed that Emecheta freezes Jewish identity in terms of uncomplimentary stereotypes. Although my own search for a true self—an identity masquerade enacted while being a tourist of experience in Germany—involved not blaming the present for past devastation, I cannot look across the Holocaust incited by some of the very images Emecheta places in *Shavi*. I feel no sense of unity with this female author whom I unite with two male authors.

Hence, my reading of Buchi Emecheta involves a crafting of accountability regarding her depiction of Jews. Judaism immediately announces itself when Emecheta introduces the members of the British Newark flying club. "Newark" brings an obvious biblical allusion to mind. (And Newark is, of course, also a presently predominantly black New Jersey city that was once the home of Leslie Fiedler and Philip Roth.) The flying club member who dies when the plane crashes in Shavi is named Moshem. Other club members are linked to Judaism. *Shavi* mentions boyhood Sunday school experiences to emphasize that the Yiddish-speaking

Dr. Philip Wagner (called Flip) is gentile (Emecheta, 28, 129). The novel also directly states that Mendoza is Jewish. Flip says, "You're [Mendoza] much more English than any of us. Your mother was a lady, your father, whose ancestors were both Jewish and Spanish, was a product of Eton" (Emecheta, 145). Flip is a good guy who marries Andria and does not want to derive economic gain from Shavian minerals; Mendoza is a bad guy who deserts Ista and wishes to profit from the minerals. Innocence and guilt regarding the destruction of Shavi are respectively conveyed by Flip's and Mendoza's comments. Flip hopes that "the stones are worthless" (Emecheta, 145). Mendoza, in contrast, would "like to see how much [money] we make from those stones" (Emecheta, 144).

Mendoza is obsessed with Flip's discovery of the minerals: " 'What minerals have you two discovered, eh?' asked Mendoza, leaning toward Andria with an ugly sardonic leer" (Emecheta, 74). Mendoza's ugly sardonic leer appears on the faces of the Jews portrayed in the Nazi propaganda film Goebbels produced, *The Eternal Jew*, and Flip's observation that Mendoza is much more English than "any of us" echoes the film's point that Jews are aliens. According to *The Eternal Jew*, Jews masquerade as humans by changing to look like their hosts and assuming characteristics of the cultures they invade. (My own cross-dressing, by the way, disproves the thesis of *The Eternal Jew*. I wear German clothes in America as well as in Germany—an action that causes me to appear alien in America.) Mendoza, in addition to being obsessed with money, "could be so obscenely loud and showy, it made something inside one recoil" (Emecheta, 167). Mendoza seems to be called from central casting for *The Eternal Jew*.

While Flip declines to undertake a second flight to Shavi, Mendoza returns with the guns responsible for ruining the Shavian utopia. He places profit above responsibility: "He wanted to make his pile and get out quickly. . . . He wanted to consolidate his profits quickly, and pull out, then if the stones proved industrially useful in the future, he would invest in them again. . . . With that, Mendoza felt he had acquitted himself of his Shavian responsibility" (Emecheta, 156). Ronje rapes one Shavian woman; Mendoza rapes the entire Shavian society. Ista indicates that Mendoza's monopoly on importing Shavian minerals, his ability to make the Shavians rich, " 'would be no better than a rape!' " (Emecheta, 169). The rapist of Shavi is a money-hungry, loudmouthed, leering Jew.

Is Emecheta accountable for creating Mendoza? Is it fair for me to point out that *Shavi* makes an accusation that conforms to the charge that Jews are responsible for the exploitation of black Africans? Ista's description of her childhood addresses these questions. She explains that her efforts to make Shavi a comfortable home stem from her upbringing: " 'My father was a doctor too, remember? But he didn't practice in Germany. He went to the Sudan, then to Nepal.' " Mendoza responds: " 'He probably didn't like the orderly life,' Mendoza said with a forced smile" (Emecheta, 110). The implication that Ista is Jewish can account for her father's decision to leave Germany and for Mendoza's forced smile when he mentions the orderly life (a stereotypical aspect of German society). This implication, however, is absent when Ista repeats her story. According to Ista's second version of her childhood, "she and her parents had lived in the smartest part of London's Kentish Town. She had gone to Camden School for Girls, but had to change when her father, a doctor like herself, decided to go to Yemen for a few years" (Emecheta, 165). The possibility that Ista might be Jewish is not found in this second version. Readers cannot know if her father is a Jew who was forced to flee Germany and settle in Sudan or a gentile interested in Yemen. His protean identity bears upon Emecheta's accountability for creating Mendoza.

Is Emecheta an anti-Semite, or is she merely masquerading as one to speak against racism? Is accusing her of anti-Semitism because she creates an uncomplimentary depiction of a Jew as unfounded as accusing Kathy Acker of sexism because she describes a marginalized woman? These questions can only be addressed in terms of diverse interpretations—not fixed meanings. It is necessary to read the text that is absent. Haraway explains: " 'We' are accountable for the inclusions and exclusions, identifications and separations, produced in the highly political practices called reading fiction. *To whom* we are accountable is part of what is produced in the readings themselves. All readings are also mis-readings, re-readings, partial readings, imposed readings, and imagined readings of a text that is originally and finally never simply there. Just as the world is *originally* fallen apart, the text is always already enmeshed in contending practices and hopes" (Haraway, 123–24). I have produced a reading of *Shavi* that links Emecheta to Murakami and Theroux. I have also produced a reading of *Shavi* that makes Emecheta accountable to her Jewish readers. In *Shavi*, anti-Semitism is there, but it is not simply there.

OTHER RACES AND THE ILLUSION OF ONE

I am one of the "other races" in regard to my discussion of the affinities between texts authored by a black African woman and a Japanese man. I am also one of the "other races" in regard to Mr. Berman's comment about Saratoga horse races: " 'They'll be other races,' Mr. Berman said" (Doctorow, 365). During Mr. Berman's day, the elite audience who watched Saratoga races probably consisted of WASPs, not Jews. "Other races" makes me think of posing Alice Walker's question in terms of the "other gender." I ask: What can a female feminist black author whose work includes anti-Semitic stereotypes and a female feminist Jewish critic say to each other? My question reflects the irretrievable loss of the illusion of one (an affinity between Emecheta and myself), the utopian hoped-for moment that inspired this chapter.

Murakami does not say that his TV PEOPLE are Jewish media moguls. Theroux does not say that the Allbrights, New Yorkers who are heirs to a department store fortune, are Jewish. I read no anti-Semitism in these texts. I can build affinities with Murakami and Theroux. In light of the racist stereotypes *Shavi* contains, I cannot say the same for my attitude toward Emecheta. How would Emecheta respond? Perhaps she would speak in the manner of Ista's conversation with Andria. While these women are singing and dancing with Shavian women, Ista says, "Take that look of fear and mistrust off your face. . . . We're being taught the universal lingo—laughter, happiness, and food" (Emecheta, 65). This idea of resolving differences in terms of fixed meaning—of resolving differences in terms of one universal lingo of utopian happiness—belongs to the realm of utopian literature.

More specifically, the idea belongs to African science fiction. In "Jazz and Palm Wine," a story by the Congolese poet and short-story writer Emmanuel Boundzeki Dongala, one of Africa's leading satirists, vehicles that appear over Africa—the "two luminous spheres in the sky" (Dongala, 194)—are flying saucers, not airplanes. The aliens who emerge from the flying spheres "are blue, blue like tempered steel. . . . They have green hair" (Dongala,

194), not white. Individual countries depend on national "business as usual" to cope with the extraterrestrials' presence. The United States wants to employ the saturation bombing used in Viet Nam; the former USSR wants to rely upon the tanks they resorted to in Hungary and Czechoslovakia; China wants to use millions of men; Cuba advocates guerrilla warfare (Dongala, 196). Counter to these suggestions, the world agrees to proceed in terms of African culture. This decision results in building affinities between the aliens and the earth people that make a difference in local and global histories:

> The Kenyan delegate finally got up and moved that in keeping with African tradition one should attempt to find the chieftains of the invaders and the elders among them; they should then be invited to sit around a big tree in the centre of a village square, and it would be possible to palaver with them over some calabashes of palm-wine. . . . You can say that again! Jazz and palm wine. The palm wine put them [the alien invaders] into a very receptive frame of mind . . . and they just loved drinking it. They were no longer sensitive to wounding, piercing or burning . . . nothing but jazz and palm wine. . . . The best palm wine drinker of the year is regularly appointed Secretary-General of the United Nations, and jazz has conquered the world. (Dongala, 199, 201)

The aliens dance to the rhythm of jazz; a jazz musician becomes president of the United States (Dongala, 201). Peace is achieved when the dominant cultures of terrestrials and extraterrestrials alike become one culture: black culture. This utopian moment is nestled in African science fiction.

I want to conclude by returning to the real world, the world that lacks flying saucers and includes "planes . . . parked liked cars" (Doctorow, 363). Doctorow's *Billy Bathgate*, a fantasy about escaping the Bronx (written by a Jewish author who himself escaped an outer borough), centers on real-world cultural cross-dressing. Billy dresses as (and becomes) a gangster to flee poverty; Drew Preston dresses as (and becomes) a gun moll to flee boredom. She is analogous to a Coldharbor resident journeying to O-Zone. She enters the world of her future's TV people, our present's fascination with gangster films.

The film *Billy Bathgate* is advertised as being "about power, ambition, seduction, portrayal." This advertisement neglects to say that Doctorow's story is about class. Italian and Jewish gangsters kill each other; rich WASPs who view the Saratoga races remain unaffected. Mrs. Preston—unlike the Italians and Jews—can, at any time, leave the gangsters' world.

She can always rely on her husband to rescue her. Mr. Preston swoops her up in his airplane, a flying machine that represents upper-class WASP economic power. Despite the fact that Mrs. Preston experiences a cross-cultural encounter and cross-dresses, she literally hovers above lower-class Italians and Jews. She survives because America dances to a WASP rhythm. Her experience shows that, contrary to Faulkner's comment, society does not rely on generosity. Mr. Preston—a flying WASP, a member of a class that considers itself as being of a noble race, of a race heroic or even divine—does not belong to a group that is routinely generous to Other races. According to the story Mr. Preston and his counterparts tell, Other races lack the proper social license to fly. The fact that members of Other races often become dead pilots is of no consequence to the Mr. and Mrs. Prestons of the world.

In the literary world, feminist science fiction is the Other race ostracized from mainstream texts. Feminist fabulation, a corrective to the trivialization of important feminist literature, enables feminist science fiction to cross-dress, to present itself as respected literature. The plain truth is that racism and cultural elitism still fly high. Cross-dressing, superficially eradicating difference, results in the illusion of one.

NOTES

1. Haraway states that canceled distinctions and disappearing marginality are a part of Emecheta's biography: "Emecheta found herself a single mother in London, black, immigrant, on welfare, living in council housing. . . . Emecheta also became a writer. . . . My reading valorized her heterogeneous states as exile, Nigerian, Ibo, Irish-British feminist, black woman, writer canonized in the African Writers Series, popular writer published in cheap paperback books and children's literature, librarian, mother on welfare, sociologist, single woman, reinventor of African tradition, deconstructor of African tradition, member of the Advisory Council to the British Home Secretary on race and equality, subject of contention among committed multi-racial womanist and feminist theorists, and international figure" (Haraway, 115, 121).

2. Showalter explains that the wild zone, the space of women's cul-

ture, is outside the dominant boundary of mainstream patriarchal culture (Showalter, 262).

3. Naomi Wolf states that approaching appearance in terms of play and masquerade is a positive feminist undertaking: "But we can imagine, to save ourselves, a life in the body that is not value-laden; a masquerade, a voluntary theatricality that emerges from abundant self-love. A pro-woman redefinition of beauty reflects our redefinitions of what power is. . . . A woman-loving definition of beauty supplants desperation with play" (Wolf, 290–91).

WORKS CITED

Acker, Kathy. *In Memoriam to Identity*. New York: Grove Weidenfeld, 1990.

Atwood, Margaret. *The Handmaid's Tale*. Boston: Houghton Mifflin, 1986.

Barr, Marleen S. *Alien to Femininity: Speculative Fiction and Feminist Theory*. Westport, Conn.: Greenwood Press, 1987.

Christian, Barbara. *Black Feminist Criticism: Perspectives on Black Women Writers*. New York: Pergamon Press, 1985.

Dibbell, Julian. "Notes on Carmen." *Village Voice*, 29 Oct. 1991.

Doctorow, E. L. *Billy Bathgate*. New York: Harper, 1990.

Dongala, Emmanuel Boundzeki. "Jazz and Palm Wine." In *Jazz and Palm Wine and Other Stories*, edited by Willfried F. Feuser, 194–202. Essex, U.K.: Longman, 1981.

Emecheta, Buchi. *The Rape of Shavi*. 1983. Reprint. New York: George Braziller, 1985.

The Eternal Jew (Der ewige Jude). National Socialist German Workers Party. Produced by Paul Joseph Goebbels. Written by Eberhard Taubert. Directed by Fritz Hippler. 1940.

Faulkner, William. *The Wild Palms*. New York: Random House, 1939.

Haraway, Donna. "Reading Buchi Emecheta: Contests for 'Women's Experience' in Women's Studies." In *Simians, Cyborgs, and Women: The Reinvention of Nature*, by Donna Haraway, 109–24. London: Free Association Books, 1991.

Jong, Erica. "Another Language." In *Becoming Light*, by Erica Jong, 343–44. New York: Harper Collins, 1991.

Murakami, Haruki. "TV People." In *Monkey Brain Sushi: New Tastes in Japanese Fiction*, edited by Alfred Birnbaum, 5–27. New York and Tokyo: Kodansha International, 1991.

Ogunyemi, Chikwenye Okonjo. "Womanism: The Dynamics of the Contemporary Black Female Novel in English." *Signs* 11 (1985): 63–80.

Showalter, Elaine. "Feminist Criticism in the Wilderness." In *The New Feminist Criticism: Essays on Women, Literature, and Theory*, edited by Elaine Showalter, 243–70. New York: Pantheon Books, 1985.

Theroux, Paul. *O-Zone*. New York: Putnam, 1986.

Walker, Alice. "The Right to Life: What Can the White Man Say to the Black Woman?" In *Her Blue Body Everything We Know: Earthling Poems, 1965–1990 Complete*, by Alice Walker. San Diego: Harcourt Brace Jovanovich, 1991.

Wolf, Naomi. *The Beauty Myth: How Images of Beauty Are Used against Women*. New York: William Morrow, 1991.

13

Ms.

Sammler's

Planet

MARGARET ATWOOD,
SAUL BELLOW,
AND JOANNA RUSS
RESCUE THE
FEMALE CHILD'S
STORY

Puberty is an awakening into sexual adulthood for both sexes. According to Simone de Beauvoir in The Second Sex, *it is also the time when the prison bars of "femininity," enforced by law and custom, shut the girl in for good. . . . Feminist utopias offer an alternative model of female puberty, one which allows the girl to move into a full and free adulthood. . . . The last thing (say the tales) that matters for the adolescent girl is that she be awakened by a kiss; what is crucial is that she be free. . . . The rescue of the female child speaks to an adolescence that is still the rule rather than the exception for women, one made painful by the closing in of sexist restrictions, sexual objectification, or even outright persecution.*
—Joanna Russ, "Recent Feminist Utopias"

Paradise, the film written and directed by Mary Agnes Donoghue, portrays a female child's power. Nine-year-old Billie Pike is more feisty than her new friend, Willard Young, who is one year her senior. Unlike Willard, Billie is not afraid to walk atop the railing of an extremely high observation tower. Her self-confident approach to the world towers over his. Willard does take the initiative to save a marriage, however. The second rescue in *Paradise* (a female artist helps Billie when she teaches the girl to respect herself and her talent) was almost edited out.[1] If the girl realizes her creative potential, unlike her powerless mother, the adult Billie might not be forced to attain security by marrying a man she does not love. The artist informs Billie that women do not have to sacrifice the power, creativity, and independent spirit that often characterize girlhood.

Paradise shares something with feminist utopian literature. The film depicts Billie in terms of the science fiction trope Joanna Russ calls "the rescue of the female child" (Russ, 82). In this chapter I argue that Margaret Atwood and Saul Bellow rescue the female child's story. Atwood's *Cat's Eye* and Bellow's *Mr. Sammler's Planet* and *A Theft*, texts that note the absence of girls' stories from most fictional narratives, adhere to feminist science fiction's rescue of the female child trope.[2] *Cat's Eye* concerns a woman's retelling of her childhood tale. *A Theft* and its predecessor *Mr. Sammler's Planet* assert that the female child's story has been stolen.

Julia Kristeva's *Strangers to Ourselves* can link these three works to each other as well as to the feminist science fiction texts Russ discusses. Kristeva's discussion of Freud's definition of the uncanny provides a means to situate *Cat's Eye*, *Sammler*, and *A Theft* within the fantastic. She discusses placing the strange within the familiar, the *unheimlich* within the *heimlich*:

> Thus, in the very word *heimlich*, the familiar and intimate are reversed into their opposites, brought together with the contrary meaning of "uncanny strangeness" harbored in *unheimlich*. Such an immanence of the strange within the familiar is considered as an etymological proof of the psychoanalytic hypothesis according to which "the uncanny is that class of the frightening which leads back to what is known of old and long familiar." . . . Consequently therefore, that which *is* strangely uncanny would be that which *was* (the past tense is important)

familiar and, under certain conditions (which ones?), emerges. (Kristeva, 182–83; Freud, 17:220)

A woman's suppressed, untold childhood story is at once *heimlich* and *unheimlich*—simultaneously familiar, intimate, and uncannily strange. This story, a tale of the strange within the familiar, includes that which *is* as well as that which *was*. It also involves a frightening narrative journey back to the long familiar past that, under conditions of patriarchal repression, emerges in the present as an uncanny strangeness.

Hence, like some feminist science fiction authors, Atwood and Bellow unite feminism with the fantastic and call attention to stories patriarchy does not want to hear. While feminist science fiction authors envision alternatives to patriarchal social constructions, Atwood implies that the courage to articulate these alternatives emerges from the sense of self women form during childhood. She defies impediments that mitigate against women who wish to tell their childhood stories. Bellow is in sympathy with her defiance. *Cat's Eye*, *Sammler*, and *A Theft*, like most feminist science fiction texts, are examples of feminist fabulation that critique patriarchal master narratives. Feminist science fiction writers discuss "that which *is*" in terms of what might be; Atwood and Bellow discuss "that which *was*" in terms of adult women who reclaim their strong childhood selves. These writers echo Emily Hancock's notion that "rediscovering the girl within appears to be the key to women's identity. . . . The real fertilization of the female is held in coming back to the girl she is in the first place—rather than in the penetration of the male" (Hancock, 16, 181). Feminist science fiction writers rescue the female child; Atwood and Bellow rescue the female child's stolen story.

In the manner of writers of feminist science fiction, Atwood and Bellow, by linking women with the alien, communicate their concern about the nullification of female power. Feminist science fiction writers rescue daughters who reside on different planets; Atwood and Bellow define daughters' stories as Other in relation to patriarchal master narratives. Their definition implies that the adult woman functions as an alien in relation to her society. Separated from her childhood, she suffers from being a stranger who lacks a background known to her community. She is the powerless foreigner Kristeva describes: "Your speech has no past and will have no power over the future of the group: why should one listen to it? You do not have enough status—'no social standing'—to make your speech useful. . . . One will forget you in order to go on with serious matters" (Kristeva, 20–21). The adult woman's silenced childhood story makes it impossible for her to wield sufficient power to construct feminist futures. Atwood and Bellow create textual correctives to the silencing that functions as a means for patriarchy to perpetuate itself.

It is not surprising that Atwood and Bellow create works that share the feminist science fiction writer's agenda. These mainstream writers, after all, are outside the culture of the United States, which dominates North America. Atwood, a Canadian woman, and Bellow, a Canadian Jew, are respectively excluded from hegemonic patriarchal and Protestant culture. Atwood and Bellow, who position women as foreigners, are themselves the Other.[3] Their experiences regarding juxtaposing the *heimlich* and the *unheimlich* allow them to emphasize a version of the uncanny involving the theft of women's childhood story and the effort to return it. I read *Cat's Eye* as an uncanny text that appropriately follows Atwood's *The Handmaid's Tale*, a feminist dystopia. I interpret *Sammler* and *A Theft* as advocating the need to tell the female child's story. In other words, I position two novels written by Bellow as handmaids to *Cat's Eye*. When connecting these mainstream texts to feminist science fiction, I unite women's and men's stories in terms of a feminist agenda—and I retard efforts to marginalize feminist science fiction.

PICTURING A FEMALE CHILD'S STORY

Kristeva states that "uncanniness occurs when the boundaries between *imagination* and *reality* are erased" (Kristeva, 188). In *Cat's Eye*, Atwood erases these boundaries by evoking the uncanny female childhood story. *Cat's Eye*, instead of signaling Atwood's turn from the fantastic to the real, is an appropriate speculative follower to *The Handmaid's Tale*. *Cat's Eye* contains an equivalent to the image of Atwood's handmaid attired in a red dress and white head covering: a painting of a woman clad in a black garment who mourns her lost childhood story. In this self-portrait (called "Unified Field Theory"), created by protagonist Elaine Risley, a woman named the "Virgin of Lost Things" is "dressed in black, with a black hood or veil covering her hair" (Atwood, *Cat's Eye*, 430). She holds a large cat's eye marble with a blue center. The background of the painting includes the lower half of the moon seen underneath a bridge. Its night sky is described in this way: "Star upon star, red, blue, yellow, and white, swirling nebulae, galaxy upon galaxy: the universe, in its incandescence and darkness" (ibid.). The simultaneous presence of light and dark characterizes the painted female figure as well as the universe: pinpoints of light shine on her black dress, and her face is partly in shadow. The Virgin of Lost Things represents an adult woman's initiation into her lost childhood story, a story illuminated when a "strange light then shines on that obscurity that was in you" (Kristeva, 21). The marble the Virgin holds, an object derived from her childhood, pictures a woman's whole life story (or world) and addresses the darkness the painting includes. Because a cat sees more efficiently in the dark than a human, the cat's eye marble might bring to mind seeing differently.

Cat's Eye enables readers to see more efficiently in the dark of women's lost childhood story. This novel and "Unified Field Theory" concern women defining their lives as round, marblelike, spatial dimensions instead of straight lines. When regarding her experiences from this different perspective, a woman better admits the light that can illuminate her entire life. She removes the shadow on her face that represents her eclipsed, attenuated life story. She can resee her life as a complete rounded entity rather than as a partly illuminated moon. Instead of remaining totally dark and untold, women's uncanny childhood stories can function as incandescent bridges to the universe of powerful female adulthood. In Hancock's words, "the task of a woman's lifetime boils down to reclaiming the authentic identity she'd embodied as a girl" (Hancock, 2).

It is necessary to connect Elaine's paintings to her childhood experience in order to understand why the word "eminence" (Atwood, *Cat's Eye*, 434) appropriately describes her artistic achievement. Two of Elaine's well-known paintings depict Mrs. Smeath, the mother of a childhood friend, and depend on an exact memory of this woman. Elaine explains: "I know that in real life the bloomers on Mrs. Smeath are an intense indigo blue that took me weeks to get right, a blue that appears to radiate a dark and stifling light. I scan the first paragraph [of the Toronto newspaper]: 'Eminent artist

Elaine Risley returns to hometown Toronto this week for a long overdue retrospective.' *Eminent*, the mausoleum word. I might as well climb into the marble slab right now and pull the bedsheet over my head" (ibid. 242). Here, again, a new way of seeing women's dark and uncanny childhood story emphasizes that story. Dark childhood memory illuminates both Elaine's art and adulthood, causes her adult story to resemble a round blue marble—not a linear marble slab that marks an adult woman's living death within patriarchal myths.

Cat's Eye begins with the information about lines and time Elaine's brother Stephen provides: "Time is not a line but a dimension, like the dimensions of space" (ibid., 3). Elaine's return to her hometown, Toronto, involves entering a new dimension, a science fiction landscape. When reentering the space she inhabited as a child, Elaine re-sees her childhood—thwarts time's linear components. She describes the present form of this space as a science fiction panorama: "Outside, the skyline has changed. . . . This is the sort of architecture you used to see only in science fiction comic books, and seeing it pasted flat against the monotone lake-sky I feel I've stepped not forward in time but sideways, into a universe of two dimensions" (ibid., 388). Against this background of science fiction architecture, a two-dimensional universe accessed via stepping sideways in time consists of Elaine's adult present and childhood past. From this dual perspective, she rewrites her brother's words, causes them to refer to the childhood story she articulates as an adult.

Cat's Eye recasts Stephen's professional discourse; "Unified Field Theory" redraws the night sky Stephen describes. The painting sheds different light upon Stephen's notion that when

"we gaze at the night sky . . . we are looking at fragments of the past. Not only in the sense that the stars as we see them are echoes of events that occurred light-years distant in time and space: everything up there and indeed everything down here is a fossil, a leftover from the first picoseconds of creation, when the universe crystallized out from the primal homogeneous plasma. In the first picosecond, conditions were scarcely imaginable. If we could travel in a time machine back toward this explosive moment, we would find ourselves in a universe replete with energies we do not understand and strangely behaving forces distorted beyond recognition. The farther back we probe, the more extreme these conditions become. Current experimental facilities can take us only a short way along this path. Beyond that point, theory is our only guide." After this he continues, in a language that sounds like English but is not, because I don't understand one word of it. (ibid., 352)

Atwood and Elaine redirect, according to science fiction imagery, the male gaze toward the night sky Stephen describes. Elaine looks back at fragments of her past, her childhood. Like the stars, her adulthood and her art echo past events. Like a time machine, she travels back to childhood moments and locates the energies and strange forces of an uncanny, distorted childhood universe. In Hancock's words, "The women in my study came fully into their own and became fully themselves only when they recaptured the girl they'd been in the first place" (Hancock, 1). Feminist theorizing about women's childhood provides a guide for women who embark on this path backward.

Elaine reconceives Stephen's pictures as well as his language. When he shows slides to illuminate his lecture, the "room darkens and the screen lights up, and there is the universe, or parts of it: the black void punctuated by galaxies and stars, white-hot, blue-hot, red" (Atwood, *Cat's Eye*, 352). "Unified Field Theory," with its aforementioned "star upon star, red, blue, yellow, and white, swirling nebulae, galaxy upon galaxy . . . the universe in its incandescence and darkness" (ibid., 430), re-represents the universe Stephen's slides portray. Elaine's own simultaneous psychological light and dark, drawn according to understanding the present in terms of the uncanny past, illuminates another part of the universe projected on the darkened room's lit screen. Her effort to locate her childhood friend Cordelia does not form the crux of this newly highlighted portion of the universe. It does not matter that Elaine never finds Cordelia in the present. Her own identity is most important.

Unlike Shakespeare's Cordelia, Elaine has neither sisters nor a need to rebel against her father. He is a forest-insect field researcher and professor who ensconces her within the natural world. (In the manner of Benn Crader, the botanist protagonist of Bellow's *More Die of Heartbreak*, Elaine's father is a good guy who eschews patriarchal science.) It is Elaine's brother who functions as the nemesis located within her early childhood universe. Stephen, who has "the ears of the green-tinged, oval-headed aliens from outer space he draws with his colored pencils" (ibid., 22–23), is the male whose discourse alienates her. Elaine responds by appropriating her brother's spoken and pictorial texts and using them to articulate her own childhood story. Elaine, within her family, is most threatened by the brother, not the father. Stephen's death liberates Elaine from what Juliet Flower MacCannell describes as "what we have in the place of the patriarchy[,] . . . the Regime of the Brother" (MacCannell, 30).[4] Elaine assumes her brother's place in terms of her own artistic regime.

Plane hijackers kill Stephen precisely because he is male: "Women and the children have all been allowed off [the plane], but he [Stephen] is not a woman or a child. Everyone left on the plane is a man" (Atwood, *Cat's Eye*, 411). Backgrounded by the scene outside the plane—the "dun landscape alien as the moon" (ibid.)—the hijackers kill the alien story Elaine's brother tells. They murder his discourse, articulated in words Elaine does not understand, about a universe that, in relation to female childhood, appears as an alien landscape. The brother's story is silenced; the sister's story will continue. In Elaine's words, "What I thought about then [while identifying Stephen's body] was the space twin, the one who went on an interplanetary journey and returned in a week to find his brother ten years older. Now I will get older, I thought. And he will not" (ibid., 414). Elaine's story, a space twin of her brother's story, will progress on its own. Ending Stephen's male story makes space for women's art about women's whole self, a product of reclaiming women's childhood story. As a child, Stephen used "red and yellow and orange" pencils to draw men's stories. These stories are about wars involving explosions and tanks and spaceships. Young Elaine used these same colors to "draw girls" (ibid., 30). *Cat's Eye* reveals the picture young Elaine draws. This novel enables readers to peer behind the "GIRLS door" (ibid., 85) Elaine and her female friends use during school recess, a portal to the separate world girls inhabit. The vision behind the GIRLS door has nothing to do with writing the universe in the manner of young Stephen. He uses "pee" to form the words MARS and JUPITER in beach sand (ibid., 72).

Elaine, who shares part of her childhood story with Stephen, can tell her own version in terms of herself. In other words, despite her memories of Stephen's numerous marbles, she focuses on her own marble: "'Remember all those marbles Stephen used to collect?'. . . But this one was mine. I look into it, and see my life entire" (ibid., 420). Stephen and his childhood are not indelible. His urine-created youthful text quickly becomes blank sand. He buries his marbles and the treasure map that describes their location (ibid., 67). Dirt prematurely covers his grave. Elaine's painting called "Cat's Eye" is "a self-portrait" (ibid., 430) depicting adult and young versions of Elaine surrounded by three childhood friends. Their "faces [are] shadowed, against a field of snow" (ibid., 43). The picture, unlike Stephen, endures. It portrays shadowed uncanny female childhood's ability to empower female adulthood according to woman-centered terms.

Stephen teaches Elaine to see in the dark in terms of men's stories, in terms of war: "Stephen is teaching me to see in the dark, as commandos do. . . . You can't use a flashlight; you have to stay still in the darkness, waiting until your eyes become accustomed to no light. . . . Now I can see in the dark" (ibid., 27). Elaine, however, chooses to see in the dark in her own way: "Now it's full night, clear, moonless and filled with stars[,] . . . echoes of light, shining out of the midst of nothing. It's old light, and there's not much of it. But it's enough to see by" (ibid., 445). The eclipsed moon that pictures her shadowy childhood story disappears. It is erased by the light shining from her retold childhood story that was once defined as "nothing." Although this light is old, it is enough for her to see how her childhood applies to her adulthood. Elaine is not overshadowed by young Stephen's story. In the manner of a cat's eye, she has enough light to see into the uncanny childhood dark—differently.

QUESTIONING THE QUESTIONS

Kristeva's questions—"Who is the Nephew? The philosopher's opponent or his hidden self?" (Kristeva, 134)[5]—apply to what seems to be the sole important aspect of *Mr. Sammler's Planet*: men's stories, the story of Artur Sammler's relationship with Elya Gruner, his nephew who financially supports him in America. *Sammler* is, of course, a precursor to the uncle/nephew tale related in *More Die of Heartbreak*. What is not so apparent is that *Sammler* anticipates the loss of the female child's story depicted in *A Theft*. The importance of the female child's story becomes clear, in regard to *Sammler*, after readers question Kristeva's question. Who is Sammler's nephew? This question should not be asked at the expense of another, more important, question: Who is Sammler's daughter? Is she Sammler's opponent or his hidden self? Who is this literally hidden self, this hidden daughter named Shula?

Although *Sammler* provides details about how Sammler emerges from a mass grave filled with Jewish victims of Nazism, the novel contains no such details about Shula's experience as a hidden child housed in a convent. Shula is "the opposite other," Sammler's "nocturnal double" who also "comes to the surface" (Kristeva, 134). Even though readers see none of Shula's childhood in the nunnery, Bellow does not have "nunavit" (the name of a conference location in *The Handmaid's Tale*) in regard to recognizing the importance of her buried story. *Sammler*—which begins by describing a theft perpetrated by a black pickpocket and concerns a stolen manuscript called *The Future of the Moon*—like *Cat's Eye* and feminist science fiction, concerns the rescue of the female child.

Sammler, who, in Shula's opinion, would benefit from reading *The Future of the Moon*, is an alien. He is advised to "speak like a prophet, like from another world" (Bellow, *Sammler*, 122). Sammler emerges from a mass grave in Poland and arrives in Manhattan as a refugee from the world of the foreign living dead. He has "been inside death" (ibid., 273). Kristeva explains that the "fantasy of being buried alive induces the feeling of uncanny strangeness, accompanied by 'a certain lasciviousness'— the phantasy, I mean, of intra-uterine existence" (Kristeva, 185; Freud, 17:244). Being buried alive is exceedingly strange and uncanny for Sammler—and his burial is no fantasy. His adult intrauterine experience involves an inside relation to death. The previously buried Sammler shares the experience of his daughter, who, as a woman denied opportunities to articulate her hidden childhood story about being a hidden child, suffers from a buried childhood. Sammler is no patriarch: "*He* never bestrode the world like a Colossus with armies and navies. . . . He was only an old Jew whom they had hacked at, shot at, but missed killing somehow" (Bellow, *Sammler*, 197). He survives the attempts to kill him and his story, a situation that does not apply to the narrative silencing Shula experiences.

Sammler states that he and Shula are "written-off": "And I know now that humankind marks certain people for death. Against them there shuts a door. Shula and I have been in this written-off category" (ibid., 230). Bellow is an open-minded male author who, like Atwood and the feminist science fiction writers who focus on the rescue of the female child, brings Montaigne's ideas about individual self-worth to women's childhood stories. Kristeva points out that "Montaigne expressed for the first time this major fact that we each have our own self, worthy of interest—deficient and amusing, blurred and nevertheless substantial, to the extent of transcending contingencies through the mere desire to know ourselves: 'If I study, I seek only the learning that treats the knowledge of myself'" (Kristeva, 118–19; Montaigne, 297). While Sammler's community stands ready to respect his wartime stories, Shula's story of being a hidden child is itself hidden. *Sammler* describes her efforts to transcend the contingency of being part of a human category called female, a group whose childhood story is routinely erased. While both Shula and Sammler have been in a position where their "speech has no past and will have no power over the future of the group" (Kristeva, 20), unlike her father, Shula continues to suffer from this silencing.

Although *Sammler* does not focus on Shula's childhood—the story of "puberty in a Polish convent or what terror could do to the psyche of a young girl" (Bellow, *Sammler*, 132)—the novel does convey the hope that women's childhood stories can survive. Women can follow Sammler's example. If Sammler can dig himself out of a grave—transform a grave into a womb from which he emerges reborn—then women can pull their childhood stories out of the mass narrative grave in which patriarchy buries them. Women can regain their childhood stories by imitating the black pickpocket Sammler witnesses in the act of stealing. Women can take back their stories (and men's false stories about females), give birth to their stories anew. The silenced Shula twice behaves in this fashion: (1) she steals a manuscript about a man's story of the moon, and (2) she solves the mystery about the location of Gruner's hidden money. These acts enable her to control narrative. She becomes a story thief, a pickpocket: "Then suddenly she too was like the Negro pickpocket" (ibid., 162). Although Shula thinks Sammler is analogous to Prospero (ibid., 115), she is Prospero herself. She is a controller of texts.

Both Shula and Sammler experience a particular instance of the uncanny involving the destruction of the self. Kristeva notes that "uncanniness . . . is a *destruction* of the self that may either *remain* as a psychotic symptom or fit in as an *opening* toward the new, as an attempt to tally with the incongruous" (Kristeva, 188). Both Shula and Sammler allow the destruction of the self to become an opening toward the new. Sammler is reborn and begins a new life in America; Shula is no longer the victim of a silenced childhood story. Further, in the manner of Atwood, Bellow uses women's silenced uncanny childhood story (a particular destruction of the female self) to venture toward a new literary opening. Reconstructing women's uncanny childhood story signals a new feminist foray into the fantastic, a move undertaken by Atwood, Bellow, and feminist science fiction writers. This joining of female and male authors, and of marginalized and respected literary modes, depicts what Kristeva calls "the strange within the familiar" (Kristeva, 183). A familiar white male canonized writer can share common ground with strange denigrated feminist science fiction writers.

Ironically, Shula, the foreign hidden child, is treated as familiar rather than strange. Both the community in *Sammler* and Sammler himself do not define her as a foreigner. Kristeva explains that foreigners attribute importance to their own biographies and resist acknowledging that those who are not foreign possess biographies: "The foreigner tends to think he is the only one to have a biography, that is, a life made up of ordeals—neither catastrophes nor adventures (although these might equally happen), but simply a life in which acts constitute events because they imply choice, surprises, breaks, adaptations, or cunning, but neither routine nor rest. In the eyes of the foreigner those who are not foreign have no life at all: barely do they exist, haughty or mediocre, but out of the running and thus almost already cadaverized" (Kristeva, 7). While Sammler's acquaintances and family respect his ordeal, Shula's wartime story is judged to be neither useful nor serious. Her status as a woman takes precedence over her status as a refugee. Silencing women's childhood story is familiar and usual—not strange and uncanny. Her wartime narrative is "out of the running"; her time in the convent is as hidden as she was when residing there.

A game of hide and seek, the only description of Shula's childhood *Sammler* provides, seems to address the hiding and silencing of her story:

He [Sammler] and she had played hide-and-go-seek in London thirty-five years ago. He had been good at it, talking aloud to himself. "Is Shula in the broom closet? Let me see. Where can she be? She is not in the broom closet. How mystifying! Is she under the bed? No. My, what a clever little girl. How well she hides herself. She's simply disappeared." While the child, just five years old, thrilling with game fever, positively white, crouched behind the brass scuttle where he pretended not to see her, her bottom near the floor, her large kinky head with the small red bow—a whole life there. Melancholy. Even if there hadn't been the war. However, theft! That was serious. (Bellow, *Sammler*, 193)

In both *Sammler* and *A Theft*, theft involves not directing attention toward women's stories, stealing the importance of women's stories. Shula responds to this theft by becoming a thief herself.

Shula's decision to steal the moon manuscript, her transformation into a pickpocket who steals back her childhood story, is childish. She commits a crime to receive attention; her theft repositions her within her childhood story. This hidden child hides as an adult. "Sammler had not seen her for several days. Now a thief, she very likely was in hiding" (ibid., 126). She compensates for her ignored childhood story by speaking childhood language, recreating childhood events, becoming a child again (ibid., 195). She transforms herself into a child before Sammler's eye. He sees the black pickpocket as he "exhibited himself" (ibid., 121); he sees Shula exhibit her childhood self.

The pickpocket and Shula display what respectively has been stolen from them: the power of black manhood and the power women derive from their childhood story. Sammler, who reconstructs himself, witnesses other victims (blacks and women) who attempt to act in kind. Buried people reveal themselves to the man who has been buried himself. These people want to share Sammler's status as a foreigner whose story is respected. They want to be respected aliens. The pickpocket dresses as if he were a prince. Sammler imagines his daughter the thief dressed "in space shoes . . . coming up like a little demon body from *Grimms' Fairy Tales*, making off with the treasure of a Hindu sage" (ibid., 114–15). According to his vision, she is shod like someone traveling to an unearthly environment. She emerges from a childhood story text as a fantastic creature. She becomes an alien—a foreigner—whose story is finally valued after she steals a manuscript written by Govinda Lal, a respected alien Other. The father's fantasy coincides with the daughter's real desire.

Shula wants to tell her story, to name the silencing she experiences. While Lal, the Indian author of the moon manuscript, refers to "the Great Calcutta Killing" (ibid., 210), the name given to the 1947 fighting between Hindus and Moslems, there is no name given to the killing of women's childhood story. Lacking the grounding telling this story could provide, Shula is "a scavenger or magpie" (ibid., 161–62), "a trash-collector, treasure hunter" (ibid., 310). She fits Kristeva's description of a "lost origin, the impossibility to take root, a rummaging memory, the present in abeyance" (Kristeva, 7). She rootlessly rummages through Manhattan while carrying diverse possessions in shopping bags. Unlike Sammler, she continues to experience a living death; her unnamed story remains buried in an unmarked grave. Elya Gruner's daughter Angela's notion that "everybody was born human" (Bellow, *Sammler*, 304) is in error. *Sammler* emphasizes that Nazis defined Jews as not being born human and hints that the same definition is often applied to blacks and women. Sammler's response involves hoping that when the human race moves "into space, away from earth," there might be "new conduct" (ibid., 284).

When she becomes a thief, Shula calls for this new conduct beyond earth's boundaries. Lacking an audience for her past story, she describes present attention to herself by stealing Lal's story about the future. The first sentences of his *The Future of the Moon* read, "How long . . . will this earth remain the only home of Man?" (ibid., 51). Shula questions this question by posing a different question: How long will this earth remain the home of only those who are defined as Man, as human? Or, more specifically, when will earth be defined as a place women and men can inhabit equally? She steals a man's version of the moon's future to articulate the hope that the silencing of women on earth will not be repeated in space.

Sammler misinterprets her reason for stealing Lal's manuscript: "Only to dig a pit and cover it with brushwood, and when a man fell into it to lie flat on the ground and converse with him amorously. For Sammler now suspected that she had run away with *The Future of the Moon* in order to create this very opportunity, this meeting. Were he and Wells really secondary, then? Was it really done to provoke interest?" (ibid., 207). No trap to seduce a man, the pit Shula metaphorically digs evokes the mass grave that covered Sammler. She claws her way out of her buried childhood story. In order for Shula to unearth herself, Sammler (the father) and Wells (the male writer) must assume a secondary position in relation to the buried daughter's story. Shula steals Lal's manuscript to signal that, despite the power of male stories, women—such as Ms. Sammler—can write the future of women and space. *The Future of the Moon* is not necessarily a man's story.

Shula's pit exemplifies that—like blacks and whites, and Jews and Nazis—"the sexes [are] like two different savage tribes" (ibid., 208). However, Shula's theft, in addition to enabling her to call attention to herself, is a gesture toward mitigating savagery. During World War II, a gentile assists Sammler. During the war between the two sexes, a woman assists Sammler. Shula sincerely wants to help Sammler "in his intellectual cultural work" (ibid., 207). Even though men routinely silence women, she does not wish to silence men. *Sammler* is no sex-role-reversal revenge tale. Sammler, the uncle who is financially assisted by his nephew, lives with his niece Margotte. Like Elaine Risley, Margotte speaks in the place of a male professor who has been killed in a plane. Sammler notices that Margotte begins "to impersonate" her deceased husband Arkin: "She had become the political theorist. She spoke in his name, as presumably he would have done, and there was no one to protect his ideas" (ibid., 16). Bellow is open to imagining women controlling men's texts. Even though readers know nothing about Margotte's childhood, even though Shula never delivers a Columbia University lecture about her life in the convent, Bellow is sympathetic toward Atwood's and feminist science fiction's attention to women's life stories.

Shula, not Elya Gruner's son Wallace, is the successful detective who locates the money Elya hides in his house. Wallace conducts his search for the money in terms of men's activities and stories. Sammler guesses that Wallace, who is "so mathematical, loved equations" and "had prepared a plumbing blueprint before taking up the wrench" (ibid., 232), damages the water pipe system in the Gruner house. Because of his adherence to male behavior, Wallace acts according to a parody of the patriarchal story: he becomes a ridiculous combination of Noah and god, the perpetrator of a flood he cannot control. Shula, on the other hand, succeeds when enacting a story involving nurturing. While serving coffee, she realizes that the money is hidden in a hassock (ibid., 308). Her generosity again becomes evident when she offers to share the money with her father (ibid., 310). Her behavior underscores that, in truth, Mr. Sammler shares the planet with his daughter and nieces. When Shula absconds with *The Future of the Moon*, she does not commit the most crucial theft *Sammler* describes: obliterating women's story and spreading the tale that earth's past, present, and future are best described by male heroes and male texts.

Shula solves the mystery about Gruner's money when she acts according to women's nurturing role. Sammler never writes the great man's story—the story of H. G. Wells—nor does Gruner achieve greatness in the usual patriarchal manner. He is a great man because he assists the Sammlers, not because he is a wealthy surgeon. Bellow, then, redefines the components of a great man's biography. He suggests a new male story about men who achieve greatness by behaving as feminine nurturers. Some of Bellow's male colleagues also write this new story. For example, the protagonist of Amos Oz's *To Know a Woman*, Yoel Ravid, shares much in common with Elya Gruner, who achieves greatness as a nurturer, not as a successful member of a male-dominated profession. Ravid becomes great as a hospital orderly, not as a master spy. Oz's title names Bellow's subtext. *Sammler* is, in part, about how to know a woman. Bellow's novel hints that, like the texts Sammler sees when readers first encounter him, patriarchal stories are "the wrong books, the wrong papers" (ibid., 3).

RECLAIMING THE INNER GIRL

Shula, the successful detective, is a hero of *Sammler*. Kristeva explains that the hero and the detective might share the same process: "The 'detective' and the 'hero' are (perhaps?) only two facets of the same process. . . . For the polyphonic mastery of writing consists in ceaselessly doing and undoing a jigsaw puzzle piece by piece" (Kristeva, 33). *A Theft* is a detective story about how women ceaselessly do and undo patriarchal stories. It centers upon women who piece together a puzzle about how to become the hero of their own childhood stories.

In Hancock's words, *A Theft* concerns "reclaiming the girl's sense of self as a subject[,] . . . countering women's position as object[,] . . . [a] feminine world that survives apart from the patriarchy's hierarchical devaluation of the female. . . . In the alliance between the girl within who possesses initiative and the woman who embodies mature generativity lies the creative force we need to become fully ourselves and shape this culture in the way it so desperately needs to be shaped" (Hancock, 192–93). *A Theft*, a mystery story, when portraying the alliance between a newly mature female (Gina Wegman) and a girl who possesses initiative (Lucy), speaks against the routine theft of women's childhood stories. Asking Lucy to act in a manner that emphasizes her sense of self as a subject allows Gina creatively and forcefully to direct the return of Clara Velde's ring.

Bellow's text, in contrast to Gina's behavior, stresses that patriarchal stories routinely do not treat young girls as subjects. Clara, in response to the lack of initiative emphasized by her husband Wilder Velde reading, throws his paperback book out of their apartment window. Bellow, in response to the silencing of women's childhood stories in literature, throws this silencing out of *A Theft*. I would like to think that *A Theft*, a mystery first published in paperback, reflects Bellow's dissatisfaction with a system that calls paperback feminist science fiction "genre fiction" and tosses it out of the canon. At the start of *A Theft*, readers are unaware that Bellow creates a new story—a mystery whose solution involves discovering that a girl acts as a subject. Clara, early in the story, unknowingly articulates the solution to the mystery: " 'There's a lot of woman in that child [Lucy]. A handsome powerful woman. Gina Wegman intuits the same about her' " (Bellow, *Theft*, 48). This solution eludes Clara and readers until the conclusion of *A Theft*. Bellow's new story contains a new symbol: a ring that represents women's potential to act in their own stories, not women's role in the story of marriage. The opinion that "Teddy Regler should have married Clara" (ibid., 51) does not form the crux of Clara's life.

When Bellow tosses out a particular patriarchal story, he imbues its replacement with humor. *A Theft* parodies stereotypes to reveal the theft of women's childhood stories. Bellow signals his departure from patriarchal stories in terms of another departure. Instead of again creating complex Jewish characters, he populates *A Theft* with metagoyim. The gentiles who exist as fusions of opposing stereotypes simplistically and humorously counter stereotypes.

Clara Velde is an ultra-sophisticated bumpkin. Wilder Velde is tame, an ineffective wealthy male WASP who, instead of wielding power, acts as Clara's "fourth child" (ibid., 91). Gina Wegman is an Italian Austrian, the personification of two incompatible extremes. Her lover, Frederic Vigneron, possesses a name that does not seem appropriately to belong to a "hood" from Harlem. Clara loves the charismatic Ithiel "Teddy" Regler, who has been married to Etta Wolfenstein. This formerly married couple evokes the image of James Bond preferring a yenta named Etta to Pussy Galore.

Why does Bellow fuse stereotypes when creating these characters? Gottschalk, the name of the private eye Clara hires to find Gina, provides a clue. *A Theft* announces that "Gottschalk was no Philip Marlowe in a Raymond Chandler story" (ibid., 86). Gottschalk does not possess the chalk; Bellow erases the story of the heroic male detective and shifts emphasis to "children's fingerpaints" (ibid., 86). He stresses that the story of female artists— Elaine Risley is one such artist—is grounded in women's lost childhood story. Gottschalk is no detective/hero. Instead, Gina and Lucy collaborate and assume this role. These young females illustrate Kristeva's aforementioned point that the detective and the hero are two facets of the same process. As the result of yet another incongruous union between two characters (Gina and Lucy), Gina, not detective Gottschalk, controls the text of the mystery.

A Theft questions patriarchal stories by forcing readers to ask questions. They must consider why a Nobel laureate creates a text whose main symbol, the emerald ring Teddy gives to Clara, baldly announces itself as "major symbol" (ibid., 93). Bellow's novella stresses that the ring's significance calls for interpretation: "Twice losing and recovering this ring is a sign, a message. It forces me [Clara] to interpret" (ibid., 89). At this point in the narrative, Clara, like Bellow's readers, does not yet know that the ring symbolizes women's potential to recognize the importance of their childhood stories. Clara engages in very "unlaureate-like" interpretation while discussing the loss of the emerald ring with a psychiatrist named Glad*stone* (italics mine). She states: "'You may be a stone, but you're not a gem'" (ibid., 76). Bellow's forced symbols and interpretations, which smack of a mediocre undergraduate paper, make fun of and subvert the patriarchal stories that routinely take precedence over women's stories. They are at once serious and humorous. *A Theft* emphasizes that instead of acting as interpreters who disregard patriarchal stories, many women construct their lives in terms of them. Because of these stories, many women toss themselves, not patriarchal texts, from windows. Women sometimes commit suicide after failing to adhere to love stories. For example, Clara twice tries to end her life because of her own unsuccessful love stories.

Bellow's mystery story, then, involves killing a story that kills women. When writing this new story, he resembles Carolyn Heilbrun, another eminent Jewish author who veers from "respectable" literary ventures to create detective fiction about Protestants. Heilbrun and Bellow, themselves members of a marginal ethnic group, turn to detective fiction to widen margins. They reinvent WASPs, and when doing so, they reinvent womanhood; they allow women to become the detective/hero. Heilbrun states that she wrote her first detective stories because she "must have wanted, with extraordinary fervor, to create a space for" herself (Heilbrun, 113). Bellow also turns to detective fiction to create a wider space for women's stories. After having articulated how men seize the day, he creates a text that mirrors Heilbrun's notion that women "seize upon their own stories, and . . . tell them with a directness that shocks as it enlightens" (Heilbrun, 64). Heilbrun, in the guise of Amanda Cross, is a literary critic who writes genre fiction. Bellow, a man who is ensconced within the American literary canon, crosses over to the concerns of women. He creates a mystery plot— a story about unmasking women's childhood stories—that is itself a hidden mystery to be solved by readers.

By erasing the male mystery story (authored by someone such as Raymond Chandler), Bellow articulates the hidden story of the relationship between the power and the childhood of adult women. He rewrites expectations associated with genre fiction, plays with mystery story codes, and envisions allowing women's private eyes to regard childhood stories as a means to find clues about adult identity. In the manner of the returned stolen ring, Bellow returns women's complete life story. *A Theft* speaks to the theft of this life story. It takes issue with considering the female child's invisibility—Lucy's sisters' (Patsy and Selma) lack of participation in *A Theft*, for example—as natural. Both Heilbrun and Bellow turn to mystery fiction and articulate similar conclusions about the importance of women's stories. Bellow, then, is currently a man in feminism. In the manner of feminist science fiction writers, he creates genre fiction (a mystery story) that is important to women's concerns.

More specifically, in the manner of James Tiptree's story, Bellow discusses the women men don't see.[6] Readers indirectly learn that young Clara exchanges her powerful girlhood story for the story of female subservience: she types Teddy's notes and prepares his manuscript "to link herself with him" (Bellow, *Theft*, 20). Significantly, she notices a book in the Columbia University library called *The Human Pair in the Novels of Thomas Hardy* (ibid., 20). Clara's attention to Teddy's manuscript illustrates how the human pair's female component is unequally treated in literature: women, who receive no credit for their efforts, labor to assist male writers who tell men's stories. Bellow does not try to correct this situation in terms of the human pair, the equal depiction of women and men in men's stories (such as Hardy's novels). Instead, he focuses on the individual woman's potential and makes her draw upon her lost childhood story to become an interpreter, not the male writer's handmaid. Clara says, " 'It's conceivable that the world-spirit gets into mere girls and makes them its demon interpreters' " (ibid., 21). Bellow advocates returning this stolen spirit and enabling women to become controlling interpreters.

The mystery in *A Theft* is solved when women act like Carolyn Heilbrun, the empowered interpreter who creates the female detective/hero. Bellow seems to imply that women such as Heilbrun and her protagonist Kate Fansler become strong and successful because they remember their childhood story. In *A Theft*, whose characters are created in terms of unlikely fusions, this story is revealed to be the combination of Gina's initiative to act as an author of life plots and Lucy's initiative to act according to the story Gina creates and makes real. Gina's and Lucy's collaboration causes them to function as a human pair. In regard to women's childhood stories, this "Human Pair was also a rescue operation" (ibid., 30).

Bellow casts this rescue operation in terms of respecting the female child's story and acknowledging that many men's stories have become exhausted. Teddy refers to one such exhausted male story: " 'When the president has to go to Walter Reed Hospital for surgery and the papers are full of sketches of his bladder and his prostate—I can remember the horrible drawings of Eisenhower's ileitis—then I'm glad there are no diagrams of my vitals in the press and the great public isn't staring at my anus' " (ibid., 54).

The story Teddy describes was repeated when Ronald Reagan contracted colon cancer. Bellow suggests that repeated attention to a male leader's anus is an exhausted story. He further suggests that a culture that at once hides the childhood story of half of its population and spotlights a male leader's intestines needs, to paraphrase Hancock, desperately to be shaped anew. Bellow critiques patriarchal stories, becomes their reviewer, and complains about a culture that simultaneously directs an inappropriate public private eye at men's private parts and publicly erases women's private childhood lives. In other words, to solve the mystery in *A Theft*, readers must recognize a specific clue: Lucy's lack of participation in the text is just as problematical as Wilder Velde's lack of participation in the text.

Many clues in *A Theft* reveal that the fact of Lucy's hidden childhood presence should be jarring rather than normal. "Tell" (ibid., 14, 79, 40, 100, 106) is one of Clara's "code words" (ibid., 14) that she often uses to elicit information. *A Theft*, however, does not tell—reveal its code and solve its mystery—until its conclusion. The ring is returned "set on a handkerchief" (ibid., 83); the maid "had never taken so much as a handkerchief" (ibid., 64). The handkerchief is certainly a clue. Bellow, in the manner of a woman flirtatiously and frequently dropping a handkerchief, provides clues about the mystery concerning the active, involved female child. Clara mentions "the unforeseen usefulness of anomalies" (ibid., 18). The story of little girls is an anomaly that does not fit within the patriarchal story. Men such as Teddy, who "think about the Atlantic Alliance[,] . . . deterrence, theater nuclear forces" (ibid., 44), do not think about little girls. Yet, although Lucy does not participate in the main action of *A Theft* until near its conclusion, according to Clara, "Lucy was the main thing" (ibid., 46). While Clara—and Bellow's text—ignores Lucy's sisters, Clara believes that "Lucy is the one with the brains. There's something *major* in Lucy" (ibid., 47). Because of Gina's intervention, Lucy is given the chance to prove her mother right, to act as an unforeseen useful anomaly.

A Theft emphasizes that this chance is stolen from many girls—such as Patsy and Selma. Clara's friend Mrs. Wong reminds her that "you're thinking of three daughters" (ibid., 66). Bellow knows that his readers are not thinking of these daughters. Clara tells Dr. Gladstone, " 'There may be more somebodies than I've been able to see'" (ibid., 74). She provides a clue to her daughters' invisibility. She provides a clue to what Bellow wants his readers to observe: "There was a lot of woman in that small girl, already visible" (ibid., 81). Like Atwood and feminist science fiction writers, Bellow is concerned about the adult woman who suffers after she loses the womanhood inscribed within her girlhood.

Clara asks, "Was there anybody who was somebody?" (ibid., 98). *A Theft* answers by insisting that Lucy is somebody. Gina creates this answer when she gives the emerald ring "to Lucy! To a young child" (ibid., 105). Gina becomes an author who positions Lucy as an active participant in the story. Clara explains: "'I see how you [Gina] brought it all together through my own child. You gave her something significant to do, and she was equal to it. . . . That level of observation and control in a girl of ten . . . how do you suppose it feels to discover that?" (ibid., 107). Readers themselves, who can be expected not to recognize Lucy's potential role in *A Theft*, are called upon to make a discovery. The story about the ring's return enacted by Gina and Lucy signals that *A Theft* is not a love story. The notion that "the ring stood for hope of Teddy Regler" (ibid., 90) is a false clue. Gina and Lucy, instead, reveal that the ring symbolizes the silenced potential of girls—and the disadvantageous impact of this silencing upon adult women. The mystery in *A Theft* is solved when readers understand that the ring's return signals hope for the return of the girl's childhood story, a stolen source of adult female power.

Gina asks, "'Which people are the lost people?'" (ibid., 108). Her question itself is the answer, the solution to the mystery in *A Theft*. The lost people are Patsy and Selma, girls who do not participate in narratives. The lost people are adult women who, due to the loss of their childhood stories, cannot function as complete, powerful entities. Clara, who is not one of these lost women, becomes a successful executive who runs "a feminine household" (ibid., 45). She uses her female power to create a multiethnic female community built on love and trust. Clara tries to make her home a female utopia (inhabited by herself, her "invisible" husband—who does not count—her daughters, and her fairly treated female employees) in which it is not necessary to safeguard her jewels. The return of the ring, then, coincides with depicting how feminist utopias might function in reality. Clara creates a woman's utopia in Manhattan; Lucy is the rescued female child who resides there.

At the conclusion of *A Theft*, Clara cries while running along Madison Avenue. She holds a handkerchief to her face with her ringed hand and acts like "one of those street people turned loose from an institution" (ibid., 109). In other words, Clara's behavior emphasizes that the male text Clara throws from the window lands on the street; patriarchal stories about erasing the female child's potential are beginning to assume the position of the marginalized, homeless street person. Clara, Gina, and Lucy—females turned loose from the institution of patriarchal stories—behave according to feminist stories. Despite Clara's statement to the contrary (ibid., 78), Gina does reenact aspects of Clara's life story. Gina has sex with a hoodlum from East Harlem; young Clara has sex with Clifford, a man who will later reside in Attica prison. Gina, like Clara, is a strong woman who leaves home—becomes a foreigner—and experiences sexual escapades with unsurly men before marrying a socially acceptable person.

Clara names the three life stages women such as herself experience: the kindly baby time, a monstrous brutish time, and the time of improved judgment derived from clues (ibid., 105). Lucy, Gina, and Clara respectively reflect these three stages. The third becomes actualized when the female reader recognizes what Clara sees in Lucy: the daughter who represents an early version of the powerful adult female self. According to Clara, "There was a lot of power under this [Lucy's childhood] clumsiness" (ibid., 47). The return of the ring symbolizes the return of this power. Clara explains that, rather than trying to act as a hot red sexual ruby, it is better to be green like the inside of mountains where gems are mined. She thinks "of the inside of her own body" and concludes that she is "an infant mine" (ibid., 43). She both mines the child within her and gives birth to three children. In addition, she realizes that the ring's symbolism pertains to her inside self, not to union with a man. She explains, " 'I do seem to have an idea who it is that's at the middle of me. There may not be more than one in a xillion, more's the pity, that do have. And my own child possibly one of these' " (ibid., 109). She solves the mystery; she knows that her childhood self is at the middle of her present adult power. She is one of the few women who manages to attain power from this realization, and Lucy has the potential to act in kind. Feminist insight rings true at the conclusion of *A Theft*.

Clara recognizes the uncanny strangeness of her childhood story and enjoys locating this story inside her present self. Kristeva seems to articulate Clara's self-observation: "By recognizing *our* uncanny strangeness we shall neither suffer from it nor enjoy it from the outside. The foreigner is within me, hence we are all foreigners. If I am a foreigner, there are no foreigners" (Kristeva, 192). Feminist science fiction is uncanny, strange, and positioned outside the canon. Reading *Cat's Eye*, *Sammler*, and *A Theft* with feminist science fiction in mind reveals that the foreigner is within canonized female and male writers as well as within feminist science fiction writers. Feminist science fiction writers should share Atwood's and Bellow's license to articulate their strangeness while positioned inside the canon.

GROWING UP INTO A WOMAN

Marshall Blonsky believes people are blind to the present and future because they are steeped in myths about a false nostalgia for a nonexistent past.[7] The imaginary and theoretical texts I discuss explain women's present according to a recast version of Blonsky's point: women are blind to the full potential of their present and future because myths of nostalgia for the power they experienced as girls have been stolen from them. These myths of nostalgia are replaced by present mythologies: media images of impossible-to-obtain beauty standards[8] and impossible-to-achieve balances between the personal and the professional. It is necessary for women to erase these present mythologies, to stalk the makers of impossible female dreams, and to embrace the nostalgia for their lost girlhood power.

I conclude by turning from fiction and theory to reality. I think of European women who spent their childhood in countries that do not adhere to Western socialization practices. Women brought up as foreigners in relation to Western culture view as uncanny and strange Western culture's imperative that women bury the story of their childhood power. Three women who exemplify this point come to my mind: Hélène Cixous, who grew up in Algeria; Doris Lessing, who grew up in Rhodesia; and Beryl Markham, who grew up in Kenya. These women might be able to attribute their successful creative adulthood to circumstances that prevented their childhood story of power from being stolen from them. A childhood spent as foreigners in relation to both African and European cultures placed them outside these cultures' destructive influence on women's ability to be empowered by their childhood story.

A world populated by women such as Cixous, Lessing, and Markham would enable people to step closer toward achieving paradise. Taking this step involves ceasing, in fiction and reality, to silence women's childhood stories. More specifically, this step involves realizing that *Paradise* ventures beyond the title of Janet Maslin's review of the film: "Reconciliation of a Grieving Couple by a Wise Boy" (Maslin, C16). In addition to the grieving couple and the wise boy, *Paradise* pictures powerful female childhood, the "inner girl" (Hancock, 2) whose story becomes uncanny and strange to female adults. *Paradise* portrays the rescue of a female child by a wise female artist. Billie Pike, who lacks a strong mother and who loses her father and male friend, has the potential to become Elaine Risley.

Billie can paint a picture of her adulthood that is based on her powerful girlhood. Her comment, "I'm sorry I have to grow up into a woman," does not have to ring true. Her powerful girlhood self-conception can affect her adult years. If Billie's future is drawn from her childhood, it will not be necessary for her to steal a man's text about the future of the moon.

NOTES

1. The film's producer Patrick Palmer provided this information when he addressed the Media Educators Association in New York City on 14 September 1991.

2. C. J. Cherryh's *Rusalka* is a more recent work about rescuing the female child. Rusalka is the ghost of a murdered girl who seeks to exist by drawing life energy from living things. Her father and a young man who loves her attempt to bring her back to life. For a critical study of women's psychology and girls' development, see Brown and Gilligan, *Meeting at the Crossroads*.

3. The biographical information provided in the Penguin edition of *Mr. Sammler's Planet* and the Bantam edition of *Cat's Eye* emphasizes that the authors spent a lot of time living as foreigners. The Bantam edition states: "Throughout her life, Ms. Atwood has traveled extensively, living for periods of time in England, Germany, France, Italy, and the United States." The Penguin edition states: "Bellow grew up and taught in the United States and has also lived in Paris and traveled extensively in Europe."

4. MacCannell believes that "the time has come to subject the hidden superego to a radical critique: the society formed by it and which it forms is not one of the fathers, not one ruled by elders, but by sons. Unfortunately they have managed to act as sovereigns . . . rather than 'well-meaning' Oedipal patriarchs" (MacCannell, 2). Her book analyzes "the occupation of the 'superegoic' position not by a neutral, third person, but by a 'He,' the Brother, who must be recognized as such and whose tendency to exercise power without responsibility must be examined critically." She also addresses "the suppression of the 'sister' who replaces the mother as the primary other woman whom the new 'man' must reject in order to become a man" (MacCannell, 5). The adult Elaine, freed from the regime of the brother, searches for Cordelia, the childhood friend who is her "sister."

5. Kristeva refers to Denis Diderot's *Rameau's Nephew*, written in 1762.

6. See James Tiptree, Jr., "The Women Men Don't See," in *Warm Worlds and Otherwise*, ed. Robert Silverberg (New York: Random House, 1975), 131–64.

7. Marshall Blonsky made this point in a lecture he presented at The New School on 19 September 1991. A more lengthy argument appears in his *American Mythologies* (Oxford University Press, 1992).

8. See Naomi Wolf, *The Beauty Myth: How Images of Beauty Are Used against Women* (New York: William Morrow, 1991).

WORKS CITED

Atwood, Margaret. *Cat's Eye*. New York, Bantam, 1989.
———. *The Handmaid's Tale*. Boston: Houghton Mifflin, 1986.
Bellow, Saul. *A Theft*. New York: Penguin, 1989.
———. *More Die of Heartbreak*. New York: William Morrow, 1987.
———. *Mr. Sammler's Planet*. 1969. Reprint. New York: Penguin, 1977.
Brown, Lyn Mikel, and Carol Gilligan. *Meeting at the Crossroads: Women's Psychology and Girls' Development*. Cambridge, Mass.: Harvard University Press, 1992.
Cherryh, C. J. *Rusalka*. New York: Ballantine, 1990.
Diderot, Denis. *Rameau's Nephew and Other Works*. Translated by Jacques Barzun and Ralph H. Bowen. Garden City, N.Y.: Doubleday, 1956.
Freud, Sigmund. "The Uncanny." In *The Standard Edition of the Complete Psychological Works of Sigmund Freud*, edited by James Strachey, vol. 17. London: Hogarth Press, 1953–74.

Hancock, Emily. *The Girl Within*. New York: E. P. Dutton, 1989.

Heilbrun, Carolyn G. *Writing a Woman's Life*. New York: Ballantine, 1988.

Kristeva, Julia. *Strangers to Ourselves*. Translated by Leon S. Roudiez. New York: Columbia University Press, 1991.

MacCannell, Juliet Flower. *The Regime of the Brother: After the Patriarchy*. London and New York: Routledge, 1991.

Maslin, Janet. "Reconciliation of a Grieving Couple by a Wise Boy." Review of *Paradise*. *New York Times*, 18 Sept. 1991.

Montaigne, Michel de. *The Complete Essays of Montaigne*. Translated by Donald M. Frame. Stanford: Stanford University Press, 1958.

Oz, Amos. *To Know a Woman*. Translated by Nicholas de Lange. San Diego: Harcourt Brace Jovanovich, 1991.

Paradise. Interscope Communications, Grand Highway Productions, Touchstone Pictures. Produced by Jean-François Lepetit, Ted Field, and Robert W. Cort. Written by Mary Agnes Donoghue (from the short story "Le Grand Chemin" by Jean-Loup Hubert). Directed by Mary Agnes Donoghue. 1991.

Russ, Joanna. "Recent Feminist Utopias." In *Future Females: A Critical Anthology*, edited by Marleen S. Barr, 71–85. Bowling Green, Ohio: Bowling Green State University Popular Press, 1981.

PERMISSIONS

An earlier version of Chapter 1 appeared in somewhat different form as "*Thelma and Louise*: Driving toward Feminist Science Fiction; or, Yes, Women Do Dream of Not Being Electric Sheep," in *Foundation*, no. 53 (1991): 80–86.

An earlier version of Chapter 2 appeared in somewhat different form as "Science Fiction and the Fact of Women's Repressed Creativity: Anne McCaffrey Portrays a Female Artist" in *Extrapolation* 23 (1982): 70–76. Reprinted with permission of Kent State University Press.

An earlier version of Chapter 3 appeared in somewhat different form as "Permissive, Unspectacular, a Little Baffling: Sex and the Single Feminist Utopian Quasi-tribesperson" in *Erotic Universe*, edited by Donald Palumbo. © 1986 by Greenwood Press, an imprint of Greenwood Publishing Group, Inc., Westport, Connecticut.

An earlier version of Chapter 4 appeared in somewhat different form as "Dame Unise, Feminist Maiden Who Fares Well with the Patriarchy: Jessica Amanda Salmonson's 'The Prodigal Daughter' and the Emerging Tradition in Feminist Speculative Fiction" in *Women's Studies International Forum* 7 (1984): 111–15. Reprinted with permission from Pergamon Press Ltd., Headington Hill Hall, Oxford OX3 OBW, UK.

An earlier version of Chapter 5 appeared in somewhat different form as "Science Fiction's Invisible Female Man: Feminism, Formula, Word, and World in 'When It Changed' and 'The Women Men Don't See' in *Restant* 11 (1985): 433–37 and (in French) in *Metaphores* 12–13 (1986): 167–73.

An earlier version of Chapter 6 appeared in somewhat different form as "Men in Feminist Science Fiction: Marge Piercy, Thomas

Berger, and the End of Masculinity" in *Science Fiction Roots and Branches*, edited by Rhys Garnett and Richard Ellis. © 1990 by Macmillan and Co. and reprinted with permission.

An earlier version of Chapter 7 appeared in somewhat different form as "Blurred Generic Conventions: Pregnancy and Power in Feminist Science Fiction" in *Reproductive and Genetic Engineering* 1 (1988): 167–74. Reprinted with permission from Pergamon Press Ltd., Headington Hill Hall, Oxford OX3 OBW, UK. The article appeared as a portion of a chapter in *Alien to Femininity: Speculative Fiction and Feminist Theory*, by Marleen S. Barr. © 1987 by Greenwood Press, an imprint of Greenwood Pubishing Group, Inc., Westport, Connecticut.

Lines from "Another Language" from *Becoming Light* by Erica Mann Jong. © 1991 by Erica Mann Jong. Reprinted by permission of HarperCollins Publishers Inc.

INDEX

ACO 9987

11/1/93

PS
374
S35
B33
1993

0 00 02 0574413 9
MIDDLEBURY COLLEGE